Your
PREGNANCY
week by week

Your PREGNANCY week by week

Third Edition

GLADE B. CURTIS, MD, OB/GYN

FISHER BOOKS™

Publishers: Bill Fisher
Helen V. Fisher
Howard W. Fisher

Editor: Judith Schuler
Managing
Editor: Sarah Trotta

Illustrations: David Fischer
Book design: Deanie Wood
Production: Randy Schultz
Cover design: FifthStreet*design*
Berkeley, CA

Library of Congress
Cataloging-in-Publication Data

Curtis, Glade B.
Your Pregnancy week by week /
Glade B. Curtis. --3rd ed.
p. cm.
Includes index.
ISBN 1-55561-143-5
1. Pregnancy.
2. Fetus--Growth. I. Title.
RG525.C92 1997
618.2--dc21   97-22933
CIP

Published by Fisher Books
4239 W. Ina Road, Suite 101
Tucson, Arizona 85741
(520) 744-6110

Printed in U.S.A.
10 9 8 7 6 5 4 3

Note: The information in this book is true and complete to the best of our knowledge. This book is intended only as an informative guide for those wishing to know more about pregnancy. In no way is this book intended to replace, countermand or conflict with the advice given to you by your own physician. The ultimate decision concerning care should be made between you and your doctor. We strongly recommend you follow his or her advice. The information in this book is general and is offered with no guarantees on the part of the author or Fisher Books. The author and publisher disclaim all liabiity in connection with the use of this book. The names and identifying details of people associated with events described in this book have been changed. Any similarity to actual persons is coincidental.

About the Third Edition

Dr. Glade Curtis may be the most beloved obstetrician in the world. Hundreds of thousands of his pregnancy books are in print in many editions, in the United States, Europe and Asia. Dr. Curtis's success is based squarely on his commitment to providing the most up-to-date information about pregnancy. Drawing on his experience as a practicing obstetrician, Dr. Curtis has met that commitment in this completely revised edition of *Your Pregnancy Week by Week*.

The unique week-by-week format helps women from the time before they conceive their baby until they give birth. Read this book straight through when you buy it, then re-read chapters as the weeks pass—one for each week throughout your entire pregnancy. Learn how your baby is developing and review changes in your own body as they happen. In a timely way, read about lab tests you may take, how your actions affect your baby and any possible complications you may be facing. These essential facts are easily absorbed at the right time.

Several attractive features were added for this edition:

- Tip of the Week: quick, helpful ideas that both new and experienced mothers-to-be can put to immediate use.
- Boxes and charts make it easy to find the information you want, when you want it.
- New illustrations show how you and your baby are growing and developing each week.

Having a baby is an exciting event in your life. There's a lot to learn and a lot to look forward to. With this new edition of *Your Pregnancy Week by Week*, you'll be prepared for all the big and little changes coming your way.

About the Author

Glade B. Curtis, MD, is board-certified by the American College of Obstetricians and Gynecologists. He is in private practice in obstetrics, gynecology and infertility in Sandy, Utah.

One of Dr. Curtis' goals as a doctor is to provide patients with many types of information about gynecological and obstetrical conditions they may have, problems they may encounter and procedures they may undergo. In pursuit of that goal, he has written several books especially for pregnant women, including *Your Pregnancy Questions & Answers* and *Your Pregnancy After 30.*

Dr. Curtis is a graduate of the University of Utah and the University of Rochester School of Medicine and Dentistry, Rochester, New York. He was an intern, resident and chief resident in Obstetrics and Gynecology at the University of Rochester Strong Memorial Hospital. He lives in Sandy with his wife and their five children.

Acknowledgments

In this, the third edition of *Your Pregnancy Week by Week*, I have continued to draw upon the many questions from discussions with my patients and their partners, and my professional colleagues. Nearly every day brings new insights and greater understanding of the joy and anticipation of impending parenthood. I rejoice in my patients' happiness and thank all of them for allowing me to be part of this miraculous process.

Credit must also be given to my understanding and generous wife, Debbie, and our family, who support me in a profession that requires much of them. Beyond that commitment, they have supported and encouraged me to pursue the challenge of this project. And my parents have always offered their love and support.

Judi Schuler continues to be a fresh source of energy and enthusiasm. I appreciate her commitment to excellence and accuracy. Special thanks to Elizabeth Warner, MD, and Marcia Vavich, RN, for reviewing the text and to Kathy Michael for her valuable help.

Contents

Preparing for Pregnancy *1*

Weeks 1 & 2 *Pregnancy Begins* *23*

Week 3 *Age of Fetus ~ 1 Week* *37*

Week 4 *Age of Fetus ~ 2 Weeks* *46*

Week 5 *Age of Fetus ~ 3 Weeks* *53*

Week 6 *Age of Fetus ~ 4 Weeks* *62*

Week 7 *Age of Fetus ~ 5 Weeks* *69*

Week 8 *Age of Fetus ~ 6 Weeks* *77*

Week 9 *Age of Fetus ~ 7 Weeks* *85*

Week 10 *Age of Fetus ~ 8 Weeks* *93*

Week 11 *Age of Fetus ~ 9 Weeks* *101*

Week 12 *Age of Fetus ~ 10 Weeks* *108*

Week 13 *Age of Fetus ~ 11 Weeks* *116*

Week 14 *Age of Fetus ~ 12 Weeks* *124*

Week 15 *Age of Fetus ~ 13 Weeks* *130*

Week 16 *Age of Fetus ~ 14 Weeks* *137*

Week 17 *Age of Fetus ~ 15 Weeks* *144*

Week 18 *Age of Fetus ~ 16 Weeks* *152*

Week 19 *Age of Fetus ~ 17 Weeks* *160*

Week 20 *Age of Fetus ~ 18 Weeks* *166*

Week 21 *Age of Fetus ~ 19 Weeks* *175*

Week 22 *Age of Fetus ~ 20 Weeks* *183*

Week 23 *Age of Fetus ~ 21 Weeks* *192*

Week 24 *Age of Fetus ~ 22 Weeks* *201*

Week 25 *Age of Fetus ~ 23 Weeks* *207*

Week 26 *Age of Fetus ~ 24 Weeks* *215*

Week 27 *Age of Fetus ~ 25 Weeks* *222*

Week 28 *Age of Fetus ~ 26 Weeks* *231*

Week 29 *Age of Fetus ~ 27 Weeks* *238*

Week 30 *Age of Fetus ~ 28 Weeks* *247*

Week 31 *Age of Fetus ~ 29 Weeks* *254*

Week 32 *Age of Fetus ~ 30 Weeks* *263*

Week 33 *Age of Fetus ~ 31 Weeks* *273*

Week 34 *Age of Fetus ~ 32 Weeks* *281*

Week 35 *Age of Fetus ~ 33 Weeks* *291*

Week 36 *Age of Fetus ~ 34 Weeks* *298*

Week 37 *Age of Fetus ~ 35 Weeks* *307*

Week 38 *Age of Fetus ~ 36 Weeks* *316*

Week 39 *Age of Fetus ~ 37 Weeks* *325*

Week 40 *Age of Fetus ~ 38 Weeks* *336*

Glossary *351*

Index *363*

Preparing for Pregnancy

Nothing compares with the miracle and magic that occur while you are pregnant. It is your chance to be involved in life's creative process. Planning ahead for this experience can improve your chances of doing well yourself and of having a healthy baby.

You can have an effect on one of the most important factors in your baby's health—*your lifestyle.* By planning ahead, you can be certain you and your baby are exposed to good things and not exposed to harmful things during your pregnancy.

By the time most women realize they are pregnant, they are 1 to 2 months into their pregnancy. By the time they see their doctor, they are 2 or 3 months along. The first 12 weeks of pregnancy are extremely important because this is when the baby forms its major organ systems. Many important things can happen before you realize you are pregnant or before you see your doctor. Getting in shape for pregnancy means physical and mental preparation.

Pregnancy is a condition, not an illness; a pregnant woman is not sick. However, you will experience major changes during the course of your pregnancy. Having good general health before pregnancy can help you deal with the physical and emotional stresses of pregnancy, labor and delivery. It can help you prepare to take care of a newborn baby.

Your General Health

There has been an explosion of technology, new medications, medical advances and medical treatments in recent years. Through these advances, we have learned that your health at the beginning of pregnancy and during pregnancy can have a major effect on you and your developing baby.

In the past, the emphasis was on being healthy while being pregnant. Some doctors suggest a new way of looking at pregnancy that includes more than just the 9 months of pregnancy. It has been suggested 12 months or more should be the "norm" for a pregnancy. This includes at least a 3-month period of preparation. Preparing your body with good general health can certainly help.

——— Preparing for Pregnancy ———

Questions to ask yourself as you prepare for pregnancy might include the following.

- Am I the weight I want to be when I get pregnant?
- Do I exercise regularly?
- Am I planning on undergoing tests, such as X-rays?
- Do I need any vaccinations, such as MMR (measles, mumps, rubella)?
- How does my pregnancy fit into my future plans (education, career, travel)?
- Should I stop smoking before getting pregnant rather than trying to stop while I am pregnant?
- Do I use drugs or alcohol?

The answers to these questions become more complicated if they have to be decided *during* a pregnancy. Deal with these issues *before* pregnancy, know you are healthy, and you won't have to worry about the risks they may pose while you're pregnant. It makes sense to continue birth control while you seek the answers to these questions.

——— ✳ ———

Seeking Medical Advice

Seeing a doctor before you get pregnant is good preparation for pregnancy. It's also helpful to pick someone to take care of you during your pregnancy. Arrange for a checkup and discuss your plans for pregnancy with your doctor before you get pregnant. Then you will know that when you do get pregnant, you are in the best possible health.

You may have a medical condition that requires attention before pregnancy. If you don't take care of it before trying to conceive, it may affect your ability to get pregnant. You may need to change medications you are taking, or you may need to make lifestyle changes before attempting a pregnancy.

✃ *Tests for You*

A general physical exam before you get pregnant helps ensure you won't have to deal with new medical problems during pregnancy. A Pap smear and a breast exam should be included in this physical. Lab tests to consider before pregnancy include tests for rubella, blood type and Rh-factor. If you are 35 or over, a mammogram is also a good idea.

If you have been exposed to AIDS or hepatitis, have your doctor conduct tests for these. If you have a family history of other medical problems, such as diabetes, ask your doctor whether you should have any tests to rule them out. If you have other chronic medical problems, such as anemia or recurrent miscarriages, your doctor may suggest other specific tests.

✃ *X-rays and Other Imaging Tests*

When you are scheduled to have any test involving radiation, you may want to ask for a pregnancy test first. Use reliable contraception before these tests so you know you are not pregnant. These tests include X-rays, CT scans and MRIs. A good time to schedule these tests is right after the end of your period, so you know you're not pregnant. If you must receive a series of these tests, continue to use contraception. (Also see Week 14.)

I've had new patients come in who are pregnant and tell me they had a series of X-rays during the first or second month of pregnancy. I saw Susan for her first prenatal visit when she was 8 weeks pregnant. She told me she'd had a series of X-rays for some bowel problems 3 weeks before, and she was worried about radiation exposure. There wasn't much I could tell her. It's difficult to determine whether a test will harm a pregnancy. It's much better to know you aren't pregnant before these tests are done.

✑ Weight

Before trying to get pregnant, it's a good idea to pay attention to your weight; you don't want to be too overweight or too underweight. Either condition can make pregnancy more difficult for you.

It's not a good idea to be on a weight-loss diet while you are trying to get pregnant. If you do get pregnant while you're dieting, you might deprive your developing baby of valuable nutrients.

Medical History

A prepregnancy visit with your doctor is the best time to discuss your medical history and any problems you may have had in other pregnancies. Ask your doctor what you can do to eliminate or to decrease chances of the same problems recurring in your next pregnancy. This includes dealing with ectopic pregnancy, miscarriage, previous C-sections (Cesarean deliveries) or other complications.

This is also a good time to talk about exposure to and problems with sexually transmitted diseases or other infections. If you have had major surgery or any female surgery in the past, discuss it now. If you are being treated for other medical problems, discuss them with your doctor. Make plans to take medications that are safe during your pregnancy before you try to get pregnant.

Discontinuing Contraception

It's important to continue using some form of contraception until you are ready to get pregnant. If you are in the middle of treatment for a medical problem or if you are undergoing tests, finish the course of treatment or tests before trying to conceive. (If you're not using some form of birth control, you're trying to get pregnant.)

Most doctors recommend you have two or three normal periods after you stop taking birth-control pills before you get pregnant. If you get pregnant immediately after stopping oral contraceptives, it may be difficult to know when you conceived. This can make it harder to determine your due date. This may not seem important now, but it will be very important to you during pregnancy and at the end of the pregnancy.

If you have an IUD (intrauterine device), you'll have to have it removed before you try to conceive. If you have any sign of infection with the IUD, take care of it before trying to get pregnant. The best time to remove an IUD is during a menstrual period.

If you use Norplant®, it should be removed and you should have at least two or three normal menstrual cycles before trying to get pregnant. It may take a few months for your periods to return to normal after Norplant is removed. If you get pregnant immediately after removing Norplant, it may be difficult to determine when you got pregnant and what your due date is.

Depo-provera®, a hormone injection used for birth control, should be discontinued for at least 3 to 6 months before trying to conceive. Wait until you have had at least two or three normal periods.

After discontinuing your regular contraceptive, use some other method until your periods become normal. You can choose from condoms, spermicides, the sponge or a diaphragm.

Current Medical Problems

Before you become pregnant, look critically at your lifestyle, diet, physical activity and any chronic medical problems you have, such as high blood pressure or diabetes. You may require extra care before and during pregnancy. Tell your doctor about any medications you currently take. Discuss any tests you may be planning to have, such as X-rays, and cover all medical problems you are being treated for. It's easier to answer questions about these problems, their treatment and their complications before you get pregnant rather than after you are pregnant.

✣ Diabetes

Diabetes is a medical problem that can have serious effects during pregnancy. If you have diabetes, it may be harder for you to become pregnant. It can also increase the chance of miscarriage, stillbirth and birth defects. These risks can be decreased by good control of blood sugar or control of your diabetes during pregnancy.

If your diabetes is not controlled, the combination of pregnancy and diabetes can be dangerous for you and your baby. Most problems or damage caused by diabetes occur during the first trimester (the first 13 weeks of pregnancy).

Pregnancy may affect diabetes by increasing your body's need for insulin. Insulin makes it possible for the body to use sugar. This can be determined by blood-sugar tests. Most doctors recommend you have diabetes under good control for at least 2 to 3 months before pregnancy begins.

Having your diabetes under control may require checking your blood sugar several times a day. Historically, women with diabetes have had problems with pregnancy. With good control, today a diabetic woman is usually able to have a healthy outcome with her pregnancy.

If you have a family history of diabetes or suspect you might have diabetes, have it checked before getting pregnant. This will help you lower your risks of miscarriage and other problems. If you haven't had diabetes before and develop it during pregnancy, it is called *gestational diabetes*. (See Week 23.)

❧ Asthma

Asthma affects about 1% of all pregnant women. Half of those women with asthma see no change in their condition during pregnancy. For about 25% of them, asthma improves and for about another 25% of them, the condition worsens.

Most asthma medications are safe to take during pregnancy, but talk to your doctor about taking any medication. Most people with asthma know what triggers attacks. While you're trying to get pregnant and during pregnancy, be especially careful to avoid things that trigger attacks. Try to get asthma under good control before trying to become pregnant.

❧ Hypertension

Hypertension, or high blood pressure, can cause problems for a pregnant woman and her unborn baby. For the woman, these problems may include kidney damage, stroke or headaches. For a developing baby, high blood pressure in a mother-to-be can cause decreased blood flow to the placenta, resulting in a smaller baby or intrauterine-growth retardation (IUGR).

If you have high blood pressure before pregnancy, you must closely monitor your blood pressure during pregnancy. Your doctor may ask you to see an internist to help in the control of your blood pressure.

Some high-blood-pressure medications are safe to take during pregnancy; others are not. Do not stop or decrease any medication on your own! This can be dangerous. If you're planning a pregnancy, ask your doctor about the medication you take for high blood pressure and its safety during conception and pregnancy.

❧ Heart Disease

During pregnancy, the workload on your heart increases by about 50%. If you have any kind of heart condition, it is important for your doctor to know about it before you get pregnant.

Some heart problems, such as mitral-valve prolapse, may be serious during pregnancy and may require antibiotics at the time of delivery. Other heart problems, such as congenital heart problems, may seriously affect your health. Your doctor may advise against pregnancy in these cases. Consult your doctor about any heart condition so it can be dealt with before you become pregnant.

✑ *Bladder and Kidney Problems*

Bladder infections, commonly called *urinary-tract infections* or *UTIs,* may occur more often during pregnancy. If a urinary-tract infection is not treated, it can cause an inflammation of the kidneys, called *pyelonephritis.*

Urinary-tract infections and pyelonephritis are associated with premature delivery. If you have a history of pyelonephritis or repeated urinary-tract infections, you should be evaluated before you begin pregnancy.

Kidney stones may also create problems during pregnancy. Because they cause pain, it may be difficult to differentiate between kidney stones and other problems that can occur during pregnancy. Kidney stones can also cause an increased chance of urinary-tract infections and pyelonephritis.

If you have had kidney or bladder surgery, major kidney problems or know your kidney function is less than normal, tell your doctor. It may be necessary to evaluate your kidney function with tests before you become pregnant.

If you have had an occasional bladder infection, don't be alarmed. Your doctor will decide whether further testing is necessary before you become pregnant.

✑ *Thyroid Problems*

Thyroid problems can appear as either too much or too little thyroid hormone. Too much thyroid hormone, *hyperthyroidism,* results in a faster metabolism; it is usually caused by Graves' disease. The problem is often treated by surgery or medication to reduce the amount of thyroid hormone in your system. If left untreated during pregnancy, there is a higher risk of premature delivery and low birth weight. If treatment is necessary during pregnancy, there are safe medications you can take.

Too little thyroid hormone, *hypothyroidism,* is usually caused by autoimmune problems; the thyroid gland is damaged by your own antibodies. Doctors treat this problem with thyroid hormones. If left untreated, you may suffer from infertility or have a miscarriage.

If you have either thyroid problem, you should be tested before pregnancy to determine the correct amount of medication for you. Pregnancy can change medication requirements, so you will also need to be checked during pregnancy.

ᔰ *Anemia*

Anemia means you do not have enough hemoglobin to carry oxygen to your body's cells. There are several types of anemia. Symptoms include weakness, fatigue, shortness of breath and pale skin.

While you are pregnant, the baby makes great demands on your body for iron and iron stores. If you have low iron levels at the beginning of pregnancy, pregnancy can tip the balance and make you anemic. Ask for a CBC (complete blood count) as a part of your prepregnancy physical.

One specific type of anemia is *sickle-cell anemia,* a genetically transmitted anemia that mainly affects people of African and Mediterranean descent. If you have sickle-cell anemia, your body may be deprived of oxygen, which can be very painful and may cause infections and other problems during pregnancy.

Women with sickle-cell anemia have a higher rate of miscarriages and urinary-tract infections. They may also have high blood pressure and painful sickle-cell crises. There is no cure for sickle-cell anemia.

Another specific anemia is *thalassemia,* a genetically inherited anemia found primarily in those of Mediterranean descent. If you have relatives with thalassemia or think you are at risk, have your doctor check for it before you become pregnant.

ᔰ *Lupus*

Systemic lupus erythematosus (SLE) is an autoimmune disease. This means you produce antibodies to your own organs, which may destroy or damage those organs and their function. Lupus can affect many parts of the body, including joints, kidneys, lungs and the heart.

This problem can be difficult to diagnose. Lupus occurs in about 1 in 700 women between 15 and 64 years of age. In black women, it occurs once in 254 women. Lupus is found more often in women than in men, especially between the ages of 20 and 40.

There is no cure for lupus at present. Treatment is individual and usually involves taking steroids. It is best not to become pregnant while you are experiencing a flare-up. There is an increased risk of miscarriage and stillbirths in women with lupus, which requires extra care during pregnancy.

Babies born to women with lupus may have a rash, heart block and heart defects. These babies may be born prematurely or experience intrauterine-growth retardation. Consult your doctor before you become pregnant if you have lupus.

——— Pregnancy and Medications ———

During pregnancy, play it safe. Some general guidelines for medication use while you are trying to get pregnant include the following.

- Do not stop birth control unless you want to be pregnant.
- Take prescriptions exactly as they are prescribed.
- Notify your doctor if you think you might be pregnant or if you are not using birth control when a medication is prescribed.
- Do not self-treat or use medications you were given in the past for other problems.
- Never use someone else's medications to treat a current problem.
- If you are unsure about using a medication, ask your doctor.

——— ❈ ———

⌁ *Epilepsy and Seizures*

Epilepsy includes several different problems. There are different kinds of seizures, called *grand mal* and *petit mal* seizures. A mother-to-be with epilepsy has a 1 in 30 chance of having a baby with a seizure disorder. Babies also have a higher chance of birth defects, perhaps related to medications taken for epilepsy during pregnancy.

If you take medication for epilepsy, it is important to consult your doctor before you become pregnant. Discuss the amounts and the types of medication you take. Some medications are safe during pregnancy. Most doctors will have you switch to phenobarbital during the time you are trying to conceive and while you are pregnant.

Seizures can be dangerous to the mother and fetus. It is important for you to take your medication regularly and as prescribed by your doctor. Do not decrease or discontinue any medication on your own!

⟡ Migraine Headaches

About 15% to 20% of all pregnant women suffer from migraine headaches. Many women notice an improvement in their headaches while they are pregnant. If you must take medication for headaches during pregnancy, check with your doctor ahead of time so you'll know whether the one you take is safe to use.

⟡ Other Problems

Many other specific chronic illnesses can affect a pregnancy. If you have any chronic problem or take any medication on a regular basis, talk it over with your doctor.

Current Medications

It's important for you and your doctor to consider the possibility of pregnancy each time you are given a prescription or told to take a medication. When you are pregnant, everything changes with regard to medications.

Medications that are safe when you are not pregnant may have harmful effects when you are pregnant. There may not be a precise answer to whether a medication is safe during pregnancy. Ask your doctor before changing any medication. (Some effects of medications and chemicals are discussed in Week 9 and Week 17.)

Most organ development of the baby occurs in the first trimester. This is an important time to keep your baby from being exposed to unnecessary medications. You'll feel better and do better during pregnancy if you have medication use under control before you try to get pregnant.

Some medications are intended for short-term use, such as antibiotics for infections. Others are for chronic or long-lasting problems, such as high blood pressure or diabetes. Some medications are OK to take while you are pregnant and might even help make your pregnancy successful. Other medications may not be safe to take during pregnancy.

Vaccinations

The same rule applies to vaccinations as to X-ray tests—when you have a vaccination, use reliable contraception. Some vaccines are safe during pregnancy; some are not. A good rule of thumb is to complete vaccinations at least 3 months before trying to get pregnant. Most vaccinations can be most harmful to a pregnancy in the first trimester.

Genetic Counseling

If you're planning your first pregnancy, you are probably not considering genetic counseling. However, there may be circumstances in which genetic counseling could help you and your partner make informed decisions about childbearing.

Genetic counseling is an information session between you and your partner and a genetic counselor or group of counselors. Any information you share with or receive from a genetic counselor is confidential. It may involve one visit or several visits. Genetic counseling is available at most major universities. Your physician can advise you.

Through genetic counseling, you and your partner hope to understand the possibilities or probabilities of what might affect your ability to get pregnant or your future offspring. The information you receive is not given precisely. Answers may only be described as "chances" or "odds of a problem."

A decision will not be made for you in genetic counseling. You are provided information on tests you might take and what the results of those tests indicate. When speaking with a genetic counselor, don't hide information you feel is embarrassing or hard to talk about. It is important to give him or her as much information as possible.

Ask your doctor if you should seek genetic counseling. Most couples who need genetic counseling do not find out they needed it until after they have a child born with a birth defect. Groups of people who should seek genetic counseling include:

- women over 35 at the time of delivery
- any woman who has delivered a child with a birth defect
- when either partner has a birth defect
- if there is a family history of Down syndrome, mental retardation, cystic fibrosis, muscular dystrophy, bleeding disorders, skeletal or bone problems, dwarfism, epilepsy, congenital heart defects or blindness
- if you and your mate are related (consanguinity)
- women who have had recurrent miscarriages (usually three or more)
- if both partners are descended from Ashkenazi Jews

Some research indicates the father's age may be important. Medical information shows a father over 40 may have an increased chance of fathering a child with a birth defect.

Some of the information you need may be difficult to gather, especially if you or your partner were adopted. You may know little or nothing of your family's medical history. Discuss this with your doctor before you become pregnant. You will have a better idea of the chances of problems before getting pregnant, rather than becoming pregnant and then having to make choices. The primary goal in genetic counseling is the same as other goals in pregnancy—early diagnosis and prevention of problems.

The Older Pregnant Woman

More couples are choosing to start their families at a later age. Today, physicians are seeing more older first-time mothers.

We have found that an older woman considering pregnancy has two major concerns. She wants to know how the pregnancy will affect her and how her age will affect her pregnancy. There is a slight increase in the possibility of complications for the mother and baby when the mother is older. (See Week 15.) You may also want to read my book, *Your Pregnancy After 30,* which focuses primarily on pregnancy in older women.

࿘ *Down Syndrome*

Through medical research, we know older women are at higher risk of giving birth to a child with Down syndrome. Various tests are offered to an older woman during pregnancy to determine whether a baby will have Down syndrome.

The risk of delivering a baby with Down syndrome increases as you get older. Look at the following statistics:

- at age 25 the risk is 1 in 1,300 births
- at 30 it is 1 in 965 births
- at 35 it is 1 in 365 births
- at 40 it is 1 in 109 births
- at 45 it is 1 in 32 births
- at 49 it is 1 in 12 births

But there is also a positive way to look at these statistics. If you're 45, you have a 97% chance of *not* having a baby with Down syndrome. If you're 49, you have a 92% chance of delivering a child *without* Down syndrome.

࿘ *Father's Age*

Research shows a father's age may be important. Chromosomal abnormalities that cause birth defects occur more often in older women and in men over 40. Men over 55 have twice the normal risk of fathering a child with Down syndrome than younger men. The chance of chromosomal problems increases with the increase in the age of the father. Some researchers recommend that men father their children before age 40. However, there is still some controversy about this.

↭ *Maternal Problems*

An older woman considering pregnancy must deal with problems a younger woman might not face. A very broad simplification of this is that it is easier to be pregnant when you are 20 than it is when you are 40. Maternal problems with increasing age include most of the chronic illnesses that tend to appear as age increases. High blood pressure is one of the more common pregnancy complications in women over 35. There is also a higher incidence of pre-eclampsia (toxemia of pregnancy).

The chance of diabetes, as well as complications of diabetes, increases with age. Researchers cite figures showing that twice as many women over age 35 have complications with diabetes. In the past, hypertension and diabetes were major complications in any pregnancy. With today's advances, we can manage these complications of pregnancy quite well.

↭ *Your General Health*

Important questions to consider before getting pregnant when you are older include those about your general health. Are you fit for pregnancy? If you are an older woman, you can maximize your chances of having a successful pregnancy by being as healthy as possible before you become pregnant.

Most researchers recommend a baseline mammogram be performed at age 35. Have this done before you become pregnant. Paying attention to general recommendations for your diet and your health care are also important in preparing for pregnancy.

Nutrition before Pregnancy

Most people feel better and work better when they eat a well-balanced diet. Planning a good diet and carrying through with it before pregnancy ensures that your developing fetus receives good nutrition during the first few weeks or months of pregnancy. A balanced diet is part of good general health.

Usually a woman takes good care of herself once she knows she is pregnant. By planning ahead, you will guarantee your baby has a healthy environment for the entire 9 months of pregnancy, not just for 6 or 7 months. When you make your nutrition plan, you are preparing the environment in which your baby will be conceived, develop and grow.

Do *not* diet during pregnancy or while you are trying to conceive. Don't take diet pills either, unless you're using reliable contraception. Consult your doctor if you are considering a special diet for weight reduction or weight gain before you try to get pregnant. Dieting may cause temporary deficiencies in vitamins and minerals that may be important to your pregnancy.

๛ *Be Careful with Vitamins, Minerals and Herbs*

Don't self-medicate with large amounts or unusual combinations of vitamins, minerals or herbs. You can overdo it. In specific instances, certain vitamins can cause birth defects if used in excessive amounts. A good example is vitamin A. Its excessive use has been shown to increase birth defects.

As a general rule, it is wise to stop all extra supplementation at least 3 months before pregnancy. Eat a well-balanced diet and take one multivitamin or one prenatal vitamin a day. Most doctors are happy to prescribe prenatal vitamins if you are planning a pregnancy.

> *Tip for Prepregnancy*
> Even though you know you aren't pregnant, treat your body as if you were during this preparation period. When you do get pregnant, you'll be on the right track for eating, exercising and avoiding harmful substances.

๛ *Begin Good Eating Habits*

Your eating habits before pregnancy carry into your pregnancy. Many women eat on the run and pay little attention to what they eat most of the day. Before pregnancy, you may be able to get away with this. However, because of the increased demands on you and the requirements of your developing baby, this won't work when you do become pregnant.

The key to good nutrition is balance. Going to extremes with vitamins or fad diets can be harmful to you and to your developing baby. It could even make you feel run-down during pregnancy.

✍ *Specific Considerations*

Specific factors to consider with relation to nutrition before getting pregnant include whether you follow a vegetarian diet, the amount of exercise you do, whether you skip meals, your diet plan (are you trying to lose or gain weight?) and any special dietary needs you might have.

If you eat a special diet because of medical problems, consult your doctor about it. Much information is available through your doctor or your local hospital about good diets and healthful nutrition.

Many diets go to extremes that you may be able to tolerate, but these extremes can be harmful to a developing baby. It is important to discuss dieting with your doctor ahead of time. You don't want to find out when you are 8 weeks pregnant that you are malnourished because of dieting.

Exercise before Pregnancy

Exercise is good for you—before you become pregnant and during pregnancy. However, exercise can be carried to extremes, which can cause problems.

Begin exercising regularly before you become pregnant. Making adjustments in your lifestyle to include regular exercise will benefit you. Benefits may include weight control, a feeling of well-being and increased stamina or endurance, which will become important later in pregnancy.

While you are trying to get pregnant, don't be involved in intense training or try to increase your exercise program. This is not a good time to play competitive sports where you push yourself to the maximum.

It's important to find exercise you enjoy and will continue on a regular basis, in any kind of weather. Concentrate on improving the strength in your lower back and abdominal muscles to help during your pregnancy.

——— General Guidelines for Exercise ———

Here are some general guidelines to remember relating to exercise before and during pregnancy.

1. Before beginning any exercise program, consult with your doctor about past medical problems and past pregnancy problems.
2. Begin any exercise program before you are pregnant.
3. Exercise on a regular basis.
4. Begin exercising gradually.
5. Wear comfortable clothing during exercise, including clothing that is warm enough or cool enough, and good, comfortable shoes.
6. Avoid risky sports, such as horseback riding or water skiing.
7. Allow sufficient time to warm up and cool down.
8. Do not get overheated.
9. Start with 15-minute workout intervals, with 5-minute rest periods.
10. Take your pulse every 15 minutes. Don't let it exceed 140 beats a minute. An easy way to calculate your pulse is to count the number of heartbeats by feeling the pulse in your neck or wrist for 15 seconds. Multiply by four. If your pulse exceeds 140 beats a minute, rest until your pulse drops below 90.
11. Increase the number of calories you consume when you exercise regularly.
12. When you're pregnant, be careful about getting up and lying down.
13. After the fourth month of pregnancy (16 weeks), don't lie on your back while exercising. This can decrease the blood flow to the uterus and placenta.
14. When you finish exercising, lie on your left side for 15 to 20 minutes.
15. Stop exercising and consult your healthcare provider if you experience bleeding or loss of fluid from the vagina while exercising, shortness of breath, dizziness, severe abdominal pain or any other serious problem.
16. Consult your doctor and exercise only under supervision if you experience irregular heartbeat, high blood pressure, diabetes, thyroid disease, anemia or any other chronic medical problem.

——— ✳ ———

Some general guidelines for exercise before pregnancy and during pregnancy have been proposed by the American College of Obstetricians and Gynecologists (ACOG). Many hospitals and health clubs or spas have exercise programs for pregnant women. ACOG has videotapes available on exercise during pregnancy and after pregnancy. Ask your doctor how to obtain these tapes or the guidelines.

✎ *Exercise and Previous Pregnancy Problems*

Consult your doctor about exercise if you have a history of three or more miscarriages, an incompetent cervix, a history of intrauterine-growth retardation, premature labor or any abnormal bleeding during pregnancy. If you have other concerns about exercise before or during pregnancy, discuss them with your doctor. Exercise you tolerate well and easily before pregnancy may be difficult for you during pregnancy.

The best approach to exercise is a balanced one. Regular exercise that is enjoyable helps you feel better and helps you enjoy your pregnancy more. It will also provide your developing baby with a healthy environment.

Substance Use and Abuse before Pregnancy

In the past, little was understood about drug or alcohol abuse, and not a lot could be done to help a person with these problems. However, today healthcare providers are able to give suggestions and to provide care for those who use or abuse drugs, alcohol or other substances. Don't be embarrassed to confide information about substance abuse to your doctor. Your doctor's concern is for you and your developing baby.

We have learned much about the use and abuse of drugs and alcohol in recent years. We now believe the safest approach to drug or alcohol use during pregnancy is no use at all.

It makes sense to solve these problems before pregnancy. By the time you realize you're pregnant, you may already be 8 or 10 weeks along. Your developing baby goes through some of its most important stages in the first 13 weeks of pregnancy. You might use drugs and not realize you are pregnant. Few women would take these substances if they knew they were pregnant. Stop using any substance you don't need at least *3 months* before trying to get pregnant!

Information continues to be gathered showing that use of drugs or alcohol during pregnancy affects a child's IQ, attention span and learning ability. To date, no safe level of these substances has been identified.

Drug use before pregnancy is serious business. Fortunately, there is help for those who use drugs. Get help before you become pregnant. Preparing for pregnancy may be a good reason for you and your partner to change your lifestyle and your drug habits.

✑ *Cigarette Smoking*

We have known for a long time that smoking affects fetal development. Mothers who smoke during pregnancy are more likely to have low-birth-weight babies or babies with growth retardation. Ask for help in stopping smoking before you become pregnant. Your doctor should be receptive to this request.

✑ *Alcohol*

In the past, some believed a small amount of alcohol during pregnancy was OK. Today, we believe *no amount of alcohol is safe to drink* during pregnancy. Alcohol crosses the placenta and directly affects your baby. Heavy drinking during pregnancy can cause fetal alcohol syndrome (FAS), discussed in Weeks 1 & 2.

✑ *Cocaine*

Cocaine has a very definite effect on pregnancy and has been shown to affect the baby throughout pregnancy. Women who use cocaine during the first 12 weeks of pregnancy have more miscarriages. Cocaine has also been shown to cause birth defects. Women who use cocaine have a higher number of stillbirths and babies who later develop SIDS (sudden infant death syndrome).

In some parts of the country, it is estimated that more than 10% of all pregnant women use cocaine at some time during their pregnancy. If cocaine use is a problem for you, get help before you stop birth control and try to get pregnant.

↬ *Marijuana*

Marijuana (hashish) is dangerous during pregnancy because it crosses the placenta and enters the baby's system. It can have long-lasting effects on babies exposed before birth. Research has shown a mother's use of marijuana during pregnancy can affect cognitive function, the ability to make decisions and future-planning ability in her child. Use can also affect a child's verbal reasoning and memory.

Work and Pregnancy

You may need to consider your job when you plan a pregnancy. Many women do not know they are pregnant until the early stages of the pregnancy are already behind them. It's wise to plan ahead. Learn about things you are exposed to at work.

Some jobs might be considered dangerous or possibly harmful during pregnancy. Some substances you might be exposed to at work, such as chemicals, inhalants, radiation or solvents, could be a problem during pregnancy. Much of this chapter has discussed your lifestyle and how you take care of yourself. It is important to consider things you are exposed to at work as part of your lifestyle. Continue reliable contraception until you know the environment at work is safe.

Other important work-related considerations are the types of benefits or insurance coverage you have and your company's maternity-leave program. Most programs allow some time off work. It makes sense to check into this before getting pregnant. With the expense of medical care and having a baby, it could cost you several thousand dollars if you don't plan ahead.

Attention has been paid to women who must spend a lot of time standing at work. Women who stand for long periods have smaller babies. If you have had a premature delivery in the past or if you have an incompetent cervix, a job that requires you to stand a great deal may not be the wisest choice for you during pregnancy. Talk to your doctor about your work situation.

Sexually Transmitted Diseases

Infections or diseases passed from one person to another by sexual contact are grouped together and are called *sexually transmitted diseases (STDs)*. These infections can affect your ability to get pregnant and can harm your developing baby. The type of contraception you use may have an effect on the likelihood of your contracting an STD. Condoms and spermicides can lower the risk of getting an STD. You are more likely to get a sexually transmitted disease if you have more than one sexual partner.

✃ *Pelvic Inflammatory Disease*

Some STD infections can be very serious and can cause *pelvic inflammatory disease (PID)*. PID is serious because it can spread from the vagina and cervix through the uterus and involve the Fallopian tubes and ovaries. The result can be scarring and blockage of the tubes, making it difficult or impossible for you to become pregnant or making you more susceptible to an ectopic pregnancy.

✃ *Protecting Yourself from STDs*

Part of planning and preparing for pregnancy includes protecting yourself against STDs. You can help protect yourself by using a condom (regardless of what other type of contraception you might be using), limiting the number of sexual partners you have and by having sexual contact only with those you are sure do not have multiple sexual partners. Ask for treatment if you think you have a sexually transmitted disease.

Weeks 1 & 2

❧ Pregnancy Begins ❧

You might want to start
by reading the previous chapter.

❧❧❧✱❧❧❧

This is an exciting time for you—having a baby growing and developing inside you is an incredible experience! This book will help you understand and enjoy your pregnancy. You will learn what is going on in your body and how your baby is growing and changing.

One focus of this book is to help you see how your actions and activities affect your health and well-being and that of your growing baby. If you're aware of how a particular test at a particular time, such as an X-ray, will affect the growing baby, you may decide on another course of action. If you understand how taking a certain drug can harm your baby or cause long-lasting effects, you may decide not to use it. If you know a poor diet can cause heartburn or nausea in you or delayed growth in your baby, you may choose to eat nutritiously. If you are aware of how much your actions affect your pregnancy, you may be able to choose wisely, free yourself from worry and enjoy your pregnancy more.

Material in this book is divided into weeks of pregnancy. Illustrations help you see clearly how you and your baby are changing and growing each week. General topics are discussed each week, such as how big your baby is and how big you are. Areas of special concern are also discussed.

The information in this book is *not* meant to take the place of any discussion with your physician. Be sure you discuss any and all concerns with him or her. Use this material as a starting place in your dialogue with your medical-care provider. It may help you put your concerns or interests into words.

—— Signs and Symptoms of Pregnancy ——

Here are definite signs and symptoms to look for if you believe you might be pregnant:

- missed menstrual period
- nausea, with or without vomiting
- fatigue
- breast changes and breast tenderness
- frequent urination

What will you notice first? It's different for every woman. When your expected menstrual period does not begin, it may be the first sign of pregnancy.

—— ✳ ——

When Is Your Baby Due?

The beginning of a pregnancy is actually figured from the beginning of your last menstrual period. That means, for your doctor's computational purposes, you are pregnant 2 weeks before you actually conceive! This can be confusing, so let's examine it more closely.

✌ *Figuring Your Due Date*

Most women don't know the exact date of conception, but they are usually aware of the beginning of their last period. This is the point from which a pregnancy is dated. For most women, the fertile time of the month (ovulation) is around the middle of their monthly cycle or about 2 weeks before the beginning of their next period.

Pregnancy lasts about 280 days, or 40 weeks from the beginning of the last menstrual period. You can calculate your due date by counting 280 days from the first day of bleeding of your last period. Or count back 3 months from the date of your last period and add 7 days. This also gives you the approximate date of delivery. For example, if your last period began on February 20, your due date is November 27.

Calculating a pregnancy this way gives the gestational age or menstrual age. This is how most doctors and nurses keep track of time during pregnancy. It is different from ovulatory age or fertilization age, which is 2 weeks shorter and dates from the actual date of conception.

Many people count the time during pregnancy by using weeks. It's really the easiest way. But it can be confusing to remember to begin counting from when your period starts and that you don't become pregnant until about 2 weeks later. For example, if your doctor says you're 10 weeks pregnant (from your last period), conception occurred 8 weeks ago.

You may hear references to your stage of pregnancy by trimester. Trimesters divide pregnancy into three periods, each about 13 weeks long. This helps group together developmental stages. For example, your baby's body structure is largely formed and his or her organ systems develop during the first trimester. Most miscarriages occur during the first trimester. During the third trimester, most maternal problems with pregnancy-induced hypertension or pre-eclampsia occur.

You may even hear about lunar months, referring to a complete cycle of the moon, which is 28 days. Because pregnancy is 280 days from the beginning of your period to your due date, pregnancy lasts 10 lunar months.

✍ 40-Week Timetable

In this book, pregnancy is based on a 40-week timetable. Using this method, you actually become pregnant during the third week. Details of your pregnancy are discussed week by week beginning with Week 3. Your due date is the end of the 40th week.

Each weekly discussion includes the actual age of your growing baby. For example, under Week 8 you'll see:

> Week 8 (gestational age)
> Age of Fetus—6 Weeks (fertilization age)

In this way, you'll know how old your developing baby is at any point in pregnancy.

It's important to understand a due date is only an *estimate*, not an *exact date*. Only 1 out of 20 women delivers on her due date. It's a mistake to count on a particular day (your due date or an earlier date). You may see that day come and go, and still not have your baby. Think of your due date as a goal—a time to look forward to and to prepare for. It's helpful to know you're making progress. Understanding how time is recorded during pregnancy helps.

No matter how you count the time of your pregnancy, it's going to last as long as it's going to last. But a miracle is happening—a living human being is growing and developing inside you! Enjoy this wonderful time in your life.

∾ *Your Menstrual Cycle*

Menstruation is the normal, periodic discharge of blood, mucus and cellular debris from the cavity of the uterus. The usual interval for menstruation is 28 days, but this can vary widely and still be considered normal. The duration and amount of menstrual flow can also vary; the usual duration is 4 to 6 days.

Two important cycles actually occur at the same time—the ovarian cycle and the endometrial cycle. The ovarian cycle provides an egg for fertilization. The endometrial cycle provides a suitable site for implantation of the fertilized egg inside your uterus. Because endometrial changes are regulated by hormones made in the ovary, the two cycles are intimately related.

The ovarian cycle produces an egg (ovum) for fertilization. There are about 2-million eggs in a newborn girl at birth. This decreases to about 400,000 in girls just before puberty. The maximum number of eggs is actually present *before* birth. When a female fetus is about 5 months old (4 months before birth), she has about 6.8-million eggs.

Some women (about 25%) experience lower abdominal pain or discomfort on or about the day of ovulation, called *mittelschmerz*. It is believed to be caused by irritation from fluid or blood from the follicle when it ruptures. The presence or absence of this symptom is not considered proof that ovulation did or did not occur.

Your Health Can Affect Your Pregnancy

Your good health is one of the most important factors in your pregnancy. Good nutrition, proper exercise, sufficient rest and attention to how you care for yourself all affect your pregnancy. Throughout this book, I provide information about medications you may take, medical tests you may need, over-the-counter substances you might use and many other areas that may concern you. This information is presented so you will be aware of how your actions affect your health and the health of your developing baby.

The health care you receive can also affect your pregnancy and how well you tolerate being pregnant. Good health care is important to the development and well-being of your baby.

↣ *Your Healthcare Provider*

You have many choices when it comes time to choose your healthcare provider. An obstetrician is a doctor who specializes in the care of pregnant women, including delivering babies. Obstetricians are MDs (medical doctors who have graduated from an accredited medical school and have fulfilled the requirements for a medical license) or DOs (doctors of osteopathic medicine who have graduated from an accredited school of osteopathic medicine and have fulfilled the requirements for a medical license). Both have completed further training after medical school (residency).

Obstetricians who specialize in high-risk pregnancies are perinatologists. Few women require a perinatologist (1 out of 10). Ask your doctor if you need to see a specialist, if you're concerned about past health problems. Some women choose a family practitioner because he or she is the family doctor. In some cases, an obstetrician may not be available because a community is small or in a remote area. The family practitioner often serves as your internist, obstetrician/gynecologist and pediatrician. Many family practitioners deliver babies and are very experienced. If problems arise, a family practitioner may need to refer you to an obstetrician for your prenatal care. This also may be the case if a Cesarean section is required for delivery of your baby.

Pregnant women sometimes choose certified nurse-midwives for their care. A certified nurse-midwife is a trained professional who cares for women who are at low risk. A certified nurse-midwife delivers low-risk, uncomplicated pregnancies. These professionals are registered nurses with additional training and certification in nurse-midwifery. They require the immediate availability of a physician, in case complications arise.

——— What About the Hospital? ———

When you pick a healthcare provider, you usually pick a hospital also. Some considerations to keep in mind when choosing where to have your baby are:

- Is the facility close by?
- What are the policies regarding your partner and his participation?
- Can he be present if you have a Cesarean section?
- Can you have an epidural?
- Is it a birthing center (if that's what you want)?
- Does your HMO (health maintenance organization) or your insurance cover the doctor and the hospital?

——— ✳ ———

✌ Communication Is Important

It's important to be able to communicate well with your healthcare provider. Pregnancy and delivery are very individual experiences. You need to be able to ask your doctor any questions you have.

- What about natural childbirth? Does your doctor believe in it?
- Are there routines he or she performs on every patient? Does everyone "get" an enema, fetal monitor or more?
- Who covers patient care for your doctor when he or she is away?
- Are there other doctors you will meet or who will take care of you?

Express your concerns and talk about whatever is important to you. Your doctor has experience involving hundreds or thousands of deliveries and is drawing on this for your well-being. Your doctor has to consider what is best for you and your baby while he or she tries to honor any "special" requests you may have. Don't be afraid to ask any question; your doctor has probably already heard it. It may be that a request is unwise or risky for you, but it's important to ask about it ahead of time. If a request is possible, then you can plan for it together, barring unforeseen developments.

✌ Finding the "Right" Caregiver for You

How do you find someone who "fits the bill"? If you already have an obstetrician you're happy with, you may be all set. If you don't, call your local medical society. Ask for references to professionals who are taking new patients for pregnancy.

An added credential is board certification. Not all doctors who deliver babies are board-certified. It is not a requirement. Board certification means your doctor has put in extra time preparing for and taking exams to qualify him or her to care for pregnant women and to deliver their babies.

Board certification is administered by the American Board of Obstetrics and Gynecology, under the direction of the American College of Obstetricians and Gynecologists. If your doctor has passed his or her boards, it is often indicated by the initials

F.A.C.O.G. after the doctor's name. This means he or she is a Fellow of the American College of Obstetricians and Gynecologists. Your local medical society can also give you this information.

There are other ways to find a caregiver with whom you are happy. Ask friends who have recently had a baby about their experiences. Ask the opinion of a labor-delivery nurse at your local hospital. Various publications, such as the *Directory of Medical Specialties* or the *Directory of the American Medical Association,* are available at most U. S. libraries. In Canada, refer to the *Canadian Medical Directory.* Another doctor, such as a pediatrician or internist, may also provide a reference.

How Your Actions Affect Your Baby's Development

It's never too early to start thinking about how your activities and actions can affect your growing baby. Many substances you normally use may have adverse effects on the baby you carry. These substances include drugs, tobacco, alcohol and caffeine. Below is a discussion on drug abuse, cigarette smoking and alcohol use. Any of these activities can harm a developing baby.

⭒ Drug Use and Abuse

Drug abuse is more common today in our society than it once was, and drug abuse in pregnancy is occurring more frequently. Unfortunately, it affects a second, innocent party—the unborn baby. A baby exposed to drugs before birth can be affected developmentally or "born with a habit."

"Drug abuse" most often refers to drugs prohibited by law, but it can also include the use of legal substances, such as alcohol, caffeine and tobacco. Legal medications, such as benzodiazepines (Valium®) or barbiturates, may also have harmful effects.

Dependence on a particular drug may be physical, psychological or both. Physical dependence implies the drug must be taken to avoid unpleasant withdrawal symptoms. It does not necessarily mean addiction or drug abuse. For example, many caffeine users develop withdrawal symptoms if they stop drinking coffee, but they are not considered drug abusers or drug addicts. Psychological dependence means the user has an emotional need for a drug or medication. This need can be more compelling than a physical need and can provide the stimulus for continued drug use.

Many drug abusers primarily desire the enjoyable or pleasurable effects of a drug. They may develop a tolerance for it after continued use, requiring higher amounts of the medication to achieve the same effects.

Another trend in drug abuse is the use of more than one drug at a time. This is done in an attempt to heighten the effect of a particular agent or to avoid its undesirable effects.

Can drug use affect a pregnancy? The answer is a definite "Yes!" We know certain drugs can damage an unborn baby. In some cases, a woman who abuses drugs is more prone to certain complications of pregnancy. Nutritional deficiencies are common with the use of certain substances. Maternal anemia and fetal-growth retardation are also problems, and pre-eclampsia may be more likely.

Opioids, agents derived from opium and synthetic compounds with similar actions, produce euphoria, drowsiness or sleepiness and decreased sensitivity to pain. Habitual use often leads to physical dependence. Morphine, heroin, Demerol® and codeine all belong to this group. These drugs are associated with a variety of congenital abnormalities and complications of pregnancy that are difficult to separate from poor nutrition and lack of prenatal care. Women who use opioids during pregnancy are often at high risk for premature labor, intrauterine-growth retardation, pre-eclampsia and other problems. A baby born to a mother who uses opioids may experience withdrawal symptoms after birth.

A high incidence of sexually transmitted diseases and other infectious diseases may be part of the picture with drug abuse. Intravenous drug use is associated with hepatitis, endocarditis and acquired-immune-deficiency syndrome (AIDS). Any of these can present serious problems during pregnancy. Women with drug problems may not seek prenatal care.

Hallucinogens, such as LSD, mescaline and peyote, are still used but not as commonly as several years ago. Phencyclidine

(PCP; angel dust) is a powerful hallucinogen that can cause psychotic episodes. It causes abnormal development in some animals and possibly humans, although this has not definitely been proved.

Marijuana and hashish contain tetrahydrocannabinol (THC). Studies have shown that THC crosses the placenta and enters the baby's system. Exposure can cause problems, including attention deficit, memory problems and impaired decision-making ability in children. These problems can appear in a child between 3 and 12 years of age.

Information about effects of a specific drug on a human pregnancy comes from cases of exposure before the pregnancy is discovered. These "case reports" help researchers understand possible harmful effects but leave gaps in our knowledge. For this reason, it can be difficult or impossible to make exact statements about particular drugs and their effects.

Cocaine (and crack) has become a popular recreational drug. A large number of women use it. Cocaine use is an increasingly common complication of pregnancy. Often the drug is consumed over a long period, such as several days. During this time, very little is eaten or drunk, which can have dangerous consequences for an unborn baby. Cocaine intoxication may be associated with convulsions, arrhythmias, hypertension and hyperthermia in the mother-to-be. Continual or repeated use of cocaine can affect maternal nutrition and temperature control, which can be damaging to the baby. Cocaine use has been linked to miscarriage, placental abruption and congenital defects—important reasons for concern about its use during pregnancy. (Also see Week 4.)

Barbiturates may be associated with birth defects, although a cause-and-effect relationship has not been proved. Withdrawal in a newborn infant, along with poor feeding, seizures and other problems, has been seen.

Benzodiazepines include tranquilizing agents, such as diazepam (Valium®) and chlordiazepoxide (Librium®), along with newer agents. Several studies have related the use of these drugs to an increase in congenital malformations.

If you use drugs, be honest with your doctor. Ask questions about drugs and drug use. Tell your doctor about anything you take that may affect your baby.

The victim of drug use is your baby. A drug problem may have serious consequences that can be best dealt with if they are known about in advance.

↝ *Cigarette Smoking*

Smoking cigarettes has harmful effects on a pregnancy. A pregnant woman who smokes 20 cigarettes a day (one pack) inhales tobacco smoke more than 11,000 times during an average pregnancy.

Tobacco smoke contains many harmful substances—nicotine, carbon monoxide, hydrogen cyanide, tars, resins and some cancer-causing agents (carcinogens). These substances may be responsible singly or together for damaging your developing baby.

Scientific evidence has shown smoking during pregnancy increases the risk of fetal death or fetal damage. Smoking interferes with a woman's absorption of vitamins B and C and folic acid. Lack of folic acid can result in neural-tube defects and increases the risk of pregnancy-related complications in a mother-to-be. (See Week 3.)

For more than 20 years, we have known infants born to mothers who smoke weigh less by about 7 ounces (200g). That is why cigarette packages carry a warning to women about smoking during pregnancy. Decreased birth weight is directly related to the number of cigarettes the expectant mother smoked. These effects don't appear in her other babies if the mother doesn't smoke with other pregnancies. There is a direct relationship between smoking and impaired fetal growth.

Children born to mothers who smoked during pregnancy have been observed to have lower IQ scores and increased incidence of reading disorders than children of nonsmokers. The incidence of minimal-brain-dysfunction syndrome (hyperactivity) has also been reported higher among children of mothers who smoked during pregnancy.

Cigarette smoking during pregnancy increases the risk of miscarriage and fetal death or death of a baby soon after birth. The risk is also directly related to the number of cigarettes the pregnant woman smokes. The risk may increase as much as 35% in a woman who smokes more than one pack of cigarettes a day.

Smoking also increases the incidence of serious complications in a mother-to-be. An example of this is placental abruption, discussed in detail in Week 33. The risk of developing placental abruption increases by almost 25% in moderate smokers and more than 65% in heavy smokers.

Placenta previa, discussed in Week 35, also occurs more frequently among smokers. The rate of occurrence increases by 25% in moderate smokers and 90% in heavy smokers.

Known or suspected harmful effects to general health from smoking are numerous and include increased risk of:

- pulmonary diseases, such as chronic bronchitis, emphysema and cancer
- cardiovascular diseases, including ischemic heart disease, peripheral vascular disease or arteriosclerosis
- bladder cancer
- peptic-ulcer disease

In addition, smokers have a mortality rate 30% to 80% higher than nonsmokers.

What can you do? The answer sounds simple but isn't—quit smoking. In more realistic terms, a woman who smokes during pregnancy will benefit from reducing or stopping cigarette use before or during pregnancy; so will her developing baby. Some studies indicate a nonsmoker and her unborn baby exposed to secondary smoke (cigarette smoke in the environment) are exposed to nicotine and other harmful substances.

Perhaps pregnancy can serve as good motivation for everyone in the family to stop smoking!

——— Nicoderm® Patch and Nicorette® Gum ———

Many studies have shown the harmful effects of cigarette smoking during pregnancy. The *specific* effects of Nicoderm and Nicorette on fetal development are unknown. However, if you are pregnant, researchers advise avoiding both of these "stop-smoking" systems.

——— ✳ ———

❧ *Alcohol Use in Pregnancy*

Alcohol use by a pregnant woman carries risk. Moderate drinking has been linked to an increased chance of miscarriage. Excessive alcohol consumption during pregnancy often results in fetal abnormalities. Chronic use of alcohol in pregnancy can lead to abnormal fetal development called *fetal alcohol syndrome (FAS)*.

FAS is characterized by growth retardation before and after birth, and defects in limbs, the heart and facial characteristics of children born to women who are alcoholic. Facial characteristics are recognizable—the nose is upturned and short, the upper jawbone is flat and the eyes look "different." An FAS child may also have behavioral problems.

FAS children often have impaired speech, and their fine and gross motor functions are impaired. The perinatal (time before, during and immediately after birth) mortality rate is 15% to 20%.

Most studies indicate women would have to drink four to five drinks a day for FAS to occur. But mild abnormalities have been associated with two drinks a day (1 ounce of alcohol). This has led many researchers to conclude there is *no safe level of alcohol consumption* during pregnancy. For this reason, all alcoholic beverages in the United States carry warning labels similar to those on cigarette packages. The warning advises women to avoid alcohol during pregnancy because of the possibility of fetal problems, including fetal alcohol syndrome.

Taking drugs with alcohol increases the chances of damaging a baby. Analgesics, antidepressants and anticonvulsants cause the most concern.

Some researchers have suggested the father's heavy alcohol consumption prior to conception may also result in fetal alcohol syndrome. Alcohol intake by the father has been blamed for intrauterine-growth retardation.

As a precaution, be very careful about over-the-counter cough and cold remedies you may use. Many contain alcohol—some as much as 25%!

Some women want to know if they can drink socially. There is a great deal of disagreement about it because there is no known safe level of alcohol consumption during pregnancy. Why take chances? For the health and well-being of your developing baby, abstain from alcohol during pregnancy. Responsibility for preventing these problems rests squarely on your shoulders!

∼ *Hepatitis in Pregnancy*

Hepatitis is a viral infection of the liver. It is one of the most serious infections that can occur during pregnancy. Hepatitis B is responsible for nearly half of the cases of hepatitis in the United States. It is transmitted by sexual contact and reuse of hypodermic needles. Those at risk for contracting hepatitis B include people with a history of intravenous drug use, a history of sexually transmitted diseases or exposure to people or blood products that contain hepatitis B. The B type can be transmitted to the developing fetus of a pregnant woman.

Hepatitis symptoms include nausea, flulike symptoms and pain in around the liver or upper-right abdomen. A person with hepatitis may appear yellow or jaundiced, and urine may be darker than normal. Diagnosis of hepatitis is made by blood tests.

In most areas, women are tested for hepatitis B at the beginning of pregnancy. If you test positive, your baby may receive immune globulin (antibodies to fight hepatitis) following delivery. It is now recommended that all newborns receive hepatitis vaccine shortly after birth. Ask your pediatrician if this vaccine is available in your area.

> *Tip for Weeks 1 & 2*
> Over-the-counter pregnancy tests are reliable and can be positive (indicate pregnancy) as early as 10 days after conception.

Week 3

Age of Fetus ~ 1 Week

If you've just found out you're pregnant, you might
want to start by reading the previous chapters.

~~~~*~~~~

How Big Is Your Baby?

The embryo growing inside you is very small. At this point, it is
only a group of cells, but one that is multiplying and growing
very rapidly. The embryo is the size of the head of a pin and
would be visible to the naked eye if you could see it. The group
of cells doesn't look like a fetus or baby; it looks like the illustration on page 39. During this first week, the embryo is about
0.006 inch (0.150mm) long.

How Big Are You?

In this third week of pregnancy, you won't notice any changes.
It's too soon! Few women know they have conceived.
Remember, you haven't even missed a period yet.

How Your Baby Is Growing and Developing

A great deal is happening, even though your pregnancy is in its very earliest stage. Ovaries lie free in your pelvis or peritoneal cavity. They are close to the uterus and Fallopian tube. At the time of ovulation, the end of the tube (called the *fimbria*) lies close to the ovary. Some researchers believe this tube opening covers the area on the ovary where the egg (ovum) is released at the time of ovulation. The release site on the ovary is called the *stigma*.

During intercourse, an average of 0.06 to 0.15 ounce (2 to 5ml) of semen is deposited in the vagina. Each milliliter contains an average of 70-million sperm; each ejaculation contains 140- to 350-million sperm. Only about 200 sperm actually reach the egg in the tube. Fertilization is the joining together of one sperm and an egg.

✥ Fertilization of the Egg

Fertilization is believed to occur in the middle part of the tube called the *ampulla,* not inside the uterus. Sperm travel through the uterine cavity and out into the tube to meet the egg.

When the sperm and egg join, the sperm must pass through the outer layer of the ovum, the corona radiata. The sperm must then digest its way through another layer of the ovum, the zona pellucida. Although several sperm may penetrate the outer layers of the ovum, usually only one sperm enters the ovum and fertilizes it.

After the sperm penetrates the ovum, the sperm head attaches to its surface. The membranes of the sperm and ovum unite, enclosing them in the same membrane or sac. The ovum reacts to this contact with the sperm by making changes in the outer layers so no other sperm can enter.

Once the sperm gets inside the ovum, it loses its tail. The head of the sperm enlarges and is called the *male pronucleus;* the ovum is called the *female pronucleus.* The chromosomes of the male and female pronuclei intermingle. When this happens, extremely small bits of information and characteristics from each partner unite. This chromosomal information gives each of us

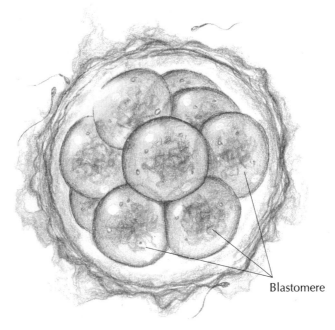

Blastomere

9-cell embryo 3 days after fertilization. The embryo is made up of many blastomeres; together they form a *blastocyst.*

our particular characteristics. The usual number of chromosomes in each human is 46. Each parent supplies 23 chromosomes. Your baby is a combination of chromosomal information from you and your partner.

∿ *Embryonic Development Begins*

The developing ball of cells is called a *zygote.* The zygote passes through the uterine tube on its way to the uterus as the division of cells continues. These cells are called a *blastomere.* As the blastomere continues to divide, a solid ball of cells is formed, called a *morula.* The gradual accumulation of fluid within the morula results in the formation of a *blastocyst,* which is very small.

During the next week, the blastocyst travels through the uterine tube to the cavity of the uterus (3 to 7 days after fertilization in the tube). The blastocyst lies free in the uterine cavity as it continues to grow and to develop. About a week after fertilization, it attaches to the uterine cavity (implantation). The cells burrow into the lining of the uterus.

──── **Boy or Girl?** ────

Your baby's sex is determined at the time of fertilization by the type of sperm (male or female) that fertilizes the egg. A Y-chromosome-bearing sperm produces a male, and an X-chromosome-bearing sperm produces a female.

──── ✳ ────

Changes in You

Some women can tell when they ovulate. They may feel mild cramping or pain, or they may have an increased vaginal discharge. Occasionally at the time of implantation of the fertilized egg into the uterine cavity, a woman may notice a small amount of bleeding.

It's too early for you to notice many changes. Your breasts haven't started to enlarge and you won't be starting to "show." That lies ahead!

How Your Actions Affect Your Baby's Development

Exercise is an important part of life for many women. The more we learn about health, the more the advantages of regular exercise become evident. Regular exercise may decrease your risk of developing several medical problems, including cardiovascular disease, osteoporosis (softening of bones), depression, premenstrual syndrome (PMS) and obesity.

There are many types of exercise or physical activity to choose from. Each offers its own advantages. Aerobic exercise is very popular with women today who want to keep in shape.

∾ *Aerobic Exercise*

For cardiovascular fitness, aerobic exercise is the best. Aerobic exercise must be performed at least 3 times a week at a sustained heart rate of 110 to 120 beats a minute and maintained for at

——— **Target Heart Rates** ———

Age (years) (beats/minute)	Target heart rate (beats/minute)	Maximum heart rate
20	120-150	200
25	117-146	195
30	114-146	190
35	111-138	185
40	108-135	180
45	105-131	175
50	102-131	170

(U.S. Department of Health and Human Services)

——— ✳ ———

least 15 continuous minutes. The rate of 110 to 120 beats a minute is an approximate target for people of different ages. Many tables show target heart rates; I often use the one above with my patients.

Nancy, pregnant for the first time, was concerned about exercising during pregnancy. She was healthy and her pregnancy was normal, but she hadn't exercised much in the past. I told her good choices for aerobic exercise during pregnancy include brisk walking, stationary bicycling, swimming and aerobic exercise designed especially for pregnant women. I helped Nancy design an exercise program that would work for her.

৵ *Muscle Strength*

Some women exercise for muscle strength. To strengthen a muscle, there has to be resistance against it. There are three different kinds of muscle contractions—isotonic, isometric and isokinetic. Isotonic exercise involves shortening the muscle as tension is developed, like lifting a barbell. Isometric exercise occurs when the muscle develops tension but doesn't change its length, such as pushing against a stationary wall. Isokinetic exercise occurs when the muscle moves at a constant speed, as when you swim.

Cardiac and skeletal muscles cannot usually be strengthened

at the same time. Strengthening skeletal muscles requires lifting heavy weights, but you can't lift these heavy weights long enough to strengthen the cardiac muscle.

Weight-bearing exercise is the most effective at promoting increased bone density to help avoid osteoporosis. Other advantages of exercise include flexibility, coordination, improvement in mood and alertness. Stretching and warming up muscles before and after exercise help you improve flexibility and avoid injury.

⁓ *Exercise during Pregnancy?*

As a pregnant woman, you are probably concerned about the risks of exercise. Can you or should you exercise when you're pregnant?

It's desirable for a pregnant woman to have cardiovascular fitness. Women who are physically fit are better able to perform the work of labor and delivery. Exercise during pregnancy is not without some risk, however. Risks to the developing baby can include increased body temperature, decreased blood flow to the uterus and possible injury to the mother's abdominal area.

You can exercise during pregnancy if you do it wisely. Avoid raising your body temperature above 102F (38.9C). Aerobic exercise can raise your body temperature higher than this, so be careful. A rise in body temperature can be increased by dehydration. Avoid prolonged aerobic exercise, particularly during hot weather.

While exercising aerobically, blood can be diverted to the exercising muscle or skin and away from other organs, such as the uterus, liver or kidneys. A lower workload during pregnancy is advised to avoid potential problems. Now is *not* the time to try to set new records or train for an upcoming marathon! During pregnancy, keep your pulse below 140 beats a minute.

If you exercised aerobically before pregnancy, you can probably continue exercising at a somewhat lower rate. If you have any problems, such as bleeding or

---

Tip for Week 3

Talk with your doctor before starting an exercise program during pregnancy. If you have been exercising, cut back your level of exercise to no more than 80% of your prepregnancy level.

premature labor, you and your doctor will have to choose another program.

It is unwise to start an aerobic exercise program during pregnancy or to increase training. If you haven't been involved in regular, strenuous exercise before pregnancy, walking and swimming are probably about as involved as you should get with exercise.

Before you begin, discuss exercising with your doctor. Together you can develop a program consistent with your current level of conditioning and your exercise habits.

You Should also Know

↷ *Bleeding during Pregnancy*

Bleeding during pregnancy causes concern. In the first trimester, bleeding can make you worry about the well-being of your baby and the possibility of a miscarriage. (Miscarriage is discussed in Week 8.)

Bleeding during pregnancy is *not* unusual. Some researchers estimate that 1 in 5 pregnant women bleeds during the first trimester. Although it makes you worry about possible problems, not all women who bleed have a miscarriage.

Bleeding at the time of implantation is mentioned on page 40. This can occur as the blastocyst "burrows" into the uterine lining. At this point, you won't know you are pregnant because you haven't missed a period. If this happens, you may just think your period is starting early.

As your pregnancy grows and the uterus grows, the placenta forms and vascular connections are made. Bleeding may occur at this time. Strenuous exercise or intercourse may also cause some bleeding. If this occurs, stop your activities and check with your doctor, who will advise you what to do.

If bleeding causes your doctor concern, he or she may order an ultrasound exam. Sometimes ultrasound can show a reason for bleeding, but during this early part of pregnancy, there may be no discernible reason for it.

Most doctors suggest rest, decreasing activity and avoiding intercourse when bleeding occurs. Surgery or medication are not helpful and are unlikely to make a difference.

Call your doctor if you experience any bleeding. He or she will advise you what to do.

✦ *Aspirin Use*

Almost any medication taken during pregnancy can have some effect on your baby. This includes aspirin, a drug taken frequently for many reasons, either alone or in combination with other medications.

Aspirin use can increase bleeding. Aspirin causes changes in the platelet function; platelets are important in blood clotting. This is particularly important to know if you are bleeding during pregnancy or if you are close to delivery at the end of your pregnancy. Small doses of aspirin may be acceptable during pregnancy; check with your physician.

Read labels on any medication you take to see if they contain aspirin. Avoid using aspirin or any products that contain aspirin during pregnancy unless you have discussed it with your doctor first.

If you need a pain reliever or a medication to reduce fever, and you cannot reach your physician for advice, acetaminophen (Tylenol®) is one over-the-counter medication you can use for a short while with little fear of complications or problems for you or your baby.

For further information about over-the-counter medication use during pregnancy (see Week 17.)

✦ *Folic Acid Use and Neural-Tube Defects*

Neural-tube defects are defective closures of the neural tube during early pregnancy. These birth defects occur in about 1 in 1000 births in the United States and Canada. In general, the cause of these defects is unknown. Defects include spina bifida, when the base of the spine remains open, exposing the spinal cord and nerves; anencephaly, congenital (present at birth) absence of the brain and spinal cord; and encephalocele, a protrusion of the brain through an opening in the skull.

Recent studies indicate taking folic acid during pregnancy may help prevent or decrease the incidence of neural-tube defects. However, these studies are continuing.

Recommended dietary allowance of folic acid during pregnancy is 0.4mg a day. The American College of Obstetricians and Gynecologists recommends any woman who has had a child born with a neural-tube defect take 4mg of folic acid a day, preferably beginning 1 month before she plans to become pregnant. Continue taking this amount through the first trimester of pregnancy. It is unnecessary to supplement beyond the first trimester because the neural tube closes within 4 weeks after conception.

Week 4

Age of Fetus ⁓ 2 Weeks

If you've just found out you're pregnant, you might want to start by reading the previous chapters.

⋰⋰⋰✳⋰⋰⋰

How Big Is Your Baby?

Your developing baby is still very small. Its size varies from 0.014 inch to about 0.04 inch (0.36mm to about 1mm) in length. One millimeter is half the size of a letter "o" on this page.

How Big Are You?

At this point, your pregnancy doesn't show at all. You haven't gained weight, and your figure hasn't changed. The illustration on page 48 gives you an idea of how small your baby still is, so you can see why you won't notice any changes yet.

How Your Baby Is Growing and Developing

Fetal development is still in the very early stages, but many great changes are taking place! The implanted blastocyst is imbedded more deeply into the lining of your uterus, and the amniotic cavity, which will be filled with amniotic fluid, is starting to form. The placenta, which plays an important role in hormone production and transport of oxygen and nutrients, is forming, and vascular networks that contain maternal blood are being established.

✧ *Germ Layers*

Different layers of cells are developing. These *germ layers* develop into specialized parts of your baby's body, such as various organs. There are three germ layers—the ectoderm, endoderm and mesoderm.

The ectoderm will become the nervous system (including the brain), the skin and the hair. The endoderm develops into the lining of the gastrointestinal tract, the liver, pancreas and thyroid. From the mesoderm comes the skeleton, connective tissues, blood system, urogenital system and most of the muscles.

Changes in You

You are probably expecting a period around the end of this week. When it doesn't occur, pregnancy may be one of the first things you think of!

✧ *The Corpus Luteum*

When you ovulate and the egg leaves the ovary, the area on the ovary where the egg comes from is called the *corpus luteum*. If you become pregnant, it is called the *corpus luteum of pregnancy*. The corpus luteum forms immediately after ovulation at the site of the ruptured follicle where the egg is released and looks like a small sac of fluid on the ovary. It undergoes rapid blood-vessel development in preparation for producing hormones, such as progesterone, to support a pregnancy before the placenta takes over.

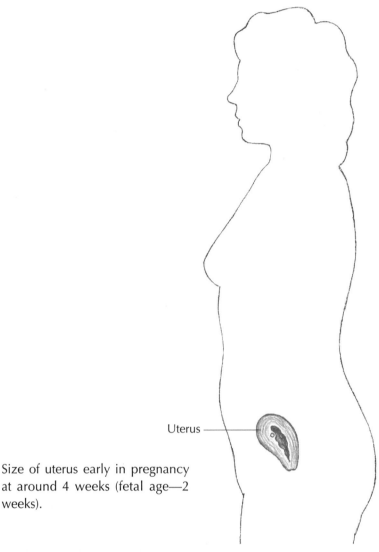

Uterus —

Size of uterus early in pregnancy at around 4 weeks (fetal age—2 weeks).

The importance of the corpus luteum is the subject of much debate. It is believed to be essential in the early weeks of pregnancy because it produces progesterone. The placenta takes over this function between 8 and 12 weeks of pregnancy. The corpus luteum lasts until about the sixth month of pregnancy, when it shrinks, although normal corpus lutea have been found with full-term pregnancies. Successful pregnancies have also occurred when the corpus luteum was removed because of a ruptured cyst as early as the 20th day after a menstrual period or about the time of implantation.

How Your Actions Affect Your Baby's Development

ᔰ HIV and AIDS

Women make up one of the fastest growing groups infected with the human immunodeficiency virus (HIV). Most affected women are of childbearing age.

HIV is the causative agent of acquired immune deficiency syndrome (AIDS). The exact number of people infected with HIV is unknown. Currently it is estimated that up to 2-million people in the United States alone may be infected. The AIDS epidemic among women has grown to 15% of all reported cases.

Infection with HIV can lead to a progressive debilitation of the immune system, which is AIDS. This can leave the individual susceptible to various infections and unable to fight them.

Women at greatest risk include current or former I.V. drug users and women whose sexual partners have used drugs intravenously or engaged in bisexual activities. Women with sexually transmitted diseases, those who engage in prostitution or those who received blood transfusions before screening began are also at higher risk. If you are unsure about your risk, seek counseling about testing for the AIDS virus.

When Helen came to see me for an HIV test, she wasn't pregnant but was planning a pregnancy in the next 6 months. I told her having the HIV test before she got pregnant was a good idea. She could be reassured she was not HIV-positive when she got pregnant. I also told her it was better to have the test *before* she got pregnant than after. She was relieved to receive negative test results. She entered her pregnancy with greater peace of mind.

A woman infected with HIV may not have symptoms. There may be a period of weeks or months when tests do not reveal the presence of the virus. In most cases, antibodies can be detected 6 to 12 weeks after exposure. In some cases, this latent period can be as long as 18 months. Once the test is positive, a person may remain without symptoms for a variable amount of time. For every patient with AIDS, there are 20 to 30 infected individuals who have no symptoms.

There is no evidence of transmission through casual contact with water, food or environmental surfaces. There is no evidence the virus can be transmitted with RhoGAM®. (See Week 16.) A mother can pass HIV to her baby before birth or during its birth.

Pregnancy may hide some AIDS symptoms, which makes the disease harder to discover. Because the illness is a serious threat to an unborn child, counseling and psychological support are critical.

There is some positive news for women who suffer from AIDS. We know if a woman is in the early course of the illness, she can usually have an uneventful pregnancy, labor and delivery. Her baby has a 20% to 30% risk of being infected during pregnancy, birth or breastfeeding. Research has also shown that taking AZT during pregnancy decreases the risk of giving birth to a baby infected with AIDS.

There is no indication that one method of delivery (C-section versus vaginal delivery) is safer for mother or infant. Because we know it is possible for the HIV infection to spread during breastfeeding, women with HIV are advised not to breastfeed.

↝ Testing for AIDS

Testing comprises two tests—the ELISA test and the Western Blot test. The ELISA is a screening test. If positive, it should be confirmed by the Western Blot test. Both tests involve testing blood to measure antibodies to the virus, not the virus itself. No test should be considered positive until the Western Blot test is done. It is believed to be more than 99% sensitive and specific.

You Should also Know

↝ Environmental Pollutants and Pregnancy

Some environmental pollutants may be harmful to a developing baby. They are particularly important for a pregnant woman to know about. Avoiding exposure to these pollutants can be very important to the well-being of a developing baby. See the list on the following page.

——— Some Pollutants to Avoid during Pregnancy ———

Lead
The toxicity of lead has been known for centuries. In the past, most lead exposure came from the atmosphere. Today, exposure may come from many sources, including some gasoline (now regulated), water pipes, solders, storage batteries, construction materials, paints, dyes and wood preservatives.

Lead is easily transported across the placenta to the baby. Toxicity can occur as early as the 12th week of pregnancy, which could result in lead poisoning in the baby.

Avoid exposure to lead. If you might be exposed in your workplace, discuss it with your physician.

Mercury
Mercury has a long history as a potential poison to a pregnant woman. Reports of fish contaminated with mercury have been linked to cerebral palsy and microcephaly.

PCBs
Our environment has been significantly contaminated with polychlorinated biphenyls (PCBs). PCBs are mixtures of several chemical compounds.

Most fish, birds and humans now have measurable amounts of PCBs in their tissues. Some experts have suggested that pregnant women limit their intake of fish (to avoid exposure to mercury and PCBs), particularly if a woman is exposed to PCBs where she works.

Pesticides
Pesticides cover a large number of agents used to control unwanted plants and animals. Human exposure is common because pesticides are used extensively. Those of most concern contain several agents—DDT, chlordane, heptachlor, lindane and others.

✑ *What Can You Do?*

There is a lack of clear information on the safety or lack of safety of many chemicals in our environment. The safest course of action is to avoid exposure when possible, whether by oral ingestion or through the air you breathe. It may not be possible to eliminate all contact.

If you know you will be around various chemicals, wash your hands well before eating. Not smoking cigarettes also helps.

One reassuring fact is that most of the chemicals tested have produced illness in the mother-to-be before damage to her growing baby occurred. An environment that is healthy for you will be healthy for your developing baby.

� Cocaine Use in Pregnancy

Many people use cocaine today. It can be introduced into the body by three primary routes—sniffing, smoking or injecting into a vein. When smoked, it is called *crack*. When it is injected directly into a vein, it is called *freebasing*.

> **Tip for Week 4**
> Secondary smoke may harm a nonsmoking woman and her developing baby. Ask those who smoke to refrain from smoking around you during your pregnancy.

Cocaine use by a pregnant woman can be very serious for the developing baby. Cocaine is a stimulant and increases the user's heart rate and blood pressure. Women who use the drug during pregnancy have a higher rate of placental abruption, the premature separation of the placenta from the uterus.

If you use cocaine during the first 12 weeks of pregnancy, you run a higher risk of miscarriage. Cocaine can also cause severe deformities in a fetus. The type of defect it causes depends on the point at which cocaine is used in the pregnancy.

Infants born to mothers who use cocaine during pregnancy have been found to have long-term mental deficiencies. Sudden infant death syndrome (SIDS) is also more common in these babies. Many babies born to women who use cocaine are stillborn.

Stop using cocaine before you stop using birth control. Damage to the embryo (later the fetus) can occur as early as 3 days after conception!

Week 5

Age of Fetus Ꭷ 3 Weeks

If you've just found out you're pregnant, you might
want to start by reading the previous chapters.

ᎧᎧᎧ❋ᎧᎧᎧ

How Big Is Your Baby?

Your developing baby hasn't grown a great deal. It's about 0.05
inch (1.25mm) long.

How Big Are You?

At this point, there are still no big changes in you. Even if you
are aware you're pregnant, it will be awhile before others notice
your changing figure.

How Your Baby Is Growing and Developing

As early as this week, a plate that will later become the heart has developed. The central nervous system (brain and spinal cord), and muscle and bone formation are beginning to take shape. During this time, your baby's skeleton is also starting to form.

Changes in You

Many changes are occurring now. You may be aware of some of them; others will be evident only after some kind of test.

∾ Pregnancy Tests

Pregnancy tests have become more sensitive, which makes early diagnosis of pregnancy more common. Tests detect the presence of human chorionic gonadotropin (HCG), a hormone of early pregnancy. A pregnancy test can be positive before you have even missed a period! Many tests can provide positive results (pregnant) 10 days after you become pregnant. But it's usually best to wait until you have missed a period before investing money and emotional energy in pregnancy tests, whether done at a hospital, in a clinic or at home.

Most home tests range in price from $12 to $30. They vary in how effective they are in helping you "diagnose" your pregnancy. Many hospitals or clinics offer free pregnancy testing, which can save you some money.

∾ Nausea and Vomiting

An early symptom of pregnancy for some women is nausea, with or without vomiting. This is often called *morning sickness,* whether it occurs in the morning or later in the day. It usually starts early in the day and improves during the day as you become active. Morning sickness can begin around the 6th week of pregnancy and usually improves by the end of the first trimester (around 13 weeks).

Many women have nausea. It doesn't usually cause enough

trouble to require medical attention. However, a condition called *hyperemesis gravidarum* (severe nausea and vomiting) causes a great deal of vomiting, which results in loss of nutrients and dehydration. The pregnant woman is often treated in the hospital with intravenous fluids and medications. Hypnosis has also been used successfully in treating the problem.

There is no completely successful treatment for the normal nausea and vomiting of pregnancy, nor are there currently any approved medications for it.

This is an extremely important period in the development of your baby. Don't expose your unborn baby to medication, herbs, over-the-counter treatments or any other "remedies" for nausea that neither you nor your doctor know to be safe during pregnancy. Discuss ways to deal with nausea with your health-care provider.

✌ *Other Changes You May Notice*

In early pregnancy, you may notice you need to urinate frequently. It can continue during most of your pregnancy and become particularly annoying near delivery, as your uterus enlarges and puts pressure on your bladder.

You may notice changes in your breasts. Tingling or soreness in the breasts or nipples is common. You may also see a darkening of the areola or an elevation of the glands around the nipple.

Another early symptom of pregnancy is tiring easily. This very common symptom may continue through pregnancy. Be sure to take your prenatal vitamins and any other medications prescribed by your doctor, and get enough rest.

How Your Actions Affect Your Baby's Development

✌ *When Should You Visit the Doctor?*

One of the first questions you may ask yourself when you suspect you're pregnant is, "When should I see a doctor?"

Good prenatal care is necessary to deliver a healthy baby from a healthy mother. Make an appointment to see your physician as soon as you are reasonably sure you're pregnant. This could be as early as a few days after a missed period. For the health of your baby, as well as your own health and well-being, seek care early.

⌖ *Getting Pregnant While Using Birth Control*

If you have been using some type of birth control, it's important to tell your doctor. No method is 100% effective. Occasionally a method fails, even oral contraceptives. If you are sure you're pregnant, stop taking the pill and see your doctor as soon as possible. Don't become overly alarmed if this happens to you; talk to your doctor about it.

Pregnancy can also occur with an IUD (intrauterine device) in place. If this happens, it's important to see your doctor immediately. Discuss whether you should remove the IUD or leave it in place. In most cases, an attempt is made to remove the IUD. If left in place, the risk of miscarriage increases slightly.

Spermicides used alone, or with a condom, sponge or diaphragm, are frequently in use when pregnancy occurs. They have not been shown to be harmful to a developing baby.

You Should also Know

⌖ *Ectopic Pregnancy*

As described in Weeks 1 & 2, fertilization occurs in the Fallopian tube. The fertilized egg travels through the tube to the uterus, where it implants on the cavity wall. An ectopic pregnancy occurs when implantation occurs outside the uterine cavity, usually in the tube itself. Ninety-five percent of all ectopic pregnancies occur in the tube (hence the term "tubal pregnancy"). Other possible sites of implantation are the ovary, cervix or other places in the abdomen. The illustration on page 57 shows some possible locations of an ectopic pregnancy.

Ectopic pregnancy occurs in 1 out of every 100 pregnancies. Chances of an ectopic pregnancy occurring increase with damage to the Fallopian tubes from pelvic inflammatory disease (PID), from other infections, such as a ruptured appendix, or from

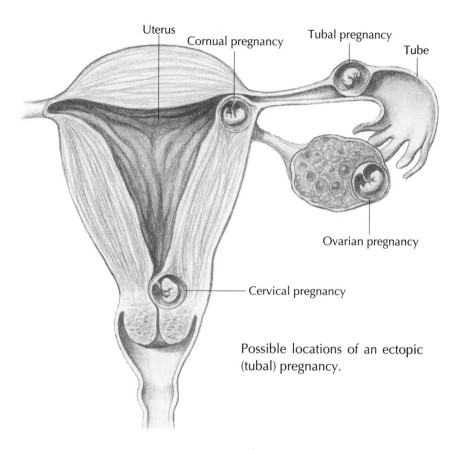

Uterus
Cornual pregnancy
Tubal pregnancy
Tube
Ovarian pregnancy
Cervical pregnancy

Possible locations of an ectopic (tubal) pregnancy.

abdominal surgery. If you have had a previous ectopic pregnancy, there is a 12% chance of recurrence. Use of an intrauterine device (IUD) also increases the chance of ectopic pregnancy.

✢ Symptoms of an Ectopic Pregnancy

Symptoms include vaginal bleeding, pain in the abdomen and other signs, such as tender breasts or nausea. However, it may be difficult for your doctor to diagnose an ectopic pregnancy because many of these symptoms can be present in a normal pregnancy.

✢ Diagnosing Ectopic Pregnancy

To test for an ectopic pregnancy, human chorionic gonadotropin (HCG), a hormone produced during pregnancy, is measured. The test is called a *quantitative HCG*. The level of HCG increases very rapidly in a normal pregnancy and doubles in value about every 2 days. If HCG levels do not increase as they should, an abnormal pregnancy is suspected. In the case of an ectopic pregnancy, the woman may have a high HCG level with no sign of a pregnancy inside the uterus.

Ultrasound testing is also helpful in diagnosing an ectopic pregnancy. (Ultrasound is discussed in detail in Week 11.) A tubal pregnancy may be seen in the tube during ultrasound examination. Doctors may see blood in the abdomen from rupture and bleeding or a mass in the area of the Fallopian tube or the ovary.

Our ability to diagnose an ectopic pregnancy has improved with use of laparoscopy. Very small incisions are made in the area of the bellybutton and in the lower-abdominal area. Doctors view the inside of the abdomen and the pelvic organs with a small instrument (called a *laparascope*). They can see an ectopic pregnancy if one is present.

An attempt is made to diagnose a tubal pregnancy before it ruptures and damages the tube, which could make it necessary to remove the entire tube. Early diagnosis also attempts to avoid the risk of internal bleeding from a ruptured, bleeding tube.

Most ectopic pregnancies are detected around 6 to 8 weeks of pregnancy. The key in early diagnosis involves communication between you and your doctor about symptoms and their severity.

↬ Treatment for Ectopic Pregnancy

With an ectopic pregnancy, the doctor's goal is to remove the pregnancy while preserving fertility. Surgical treatment requires general anesthesia and laparoscopy or laparotomy (a larger incision and no scope), and recovery from surgery. In many instances, it is necessary to remove the Fallopian tube, which affects future fertility.

A new, nonsurgical treatment of an unruptured ectopic pregnancy involves the use of a cancer drug, methotrexate. Methotrexate is given through an I.V. in the hospital or outpatient clinic. Methotrexate is *cytotoxic;* it terminates the pregnancy. HCG levels should decrease after this treatment, which indicates the pregnancy has been terminated. Symptoms should improve.

❧ **What Sex Will Your Baby Be?**

You can guess the sex of your child as well as your doctor—often better! As I've mentioned, the sex of your baby is determined when the egg is fertilized by the baby's father's sperm.

Many couples ask for ways to "get a boy" or "get a girl" before they try to get pregnant. In a few cases, sperm separation is used. Male and female sperm are separated, and artificial insemination deposits the selected sperm in the woman. It's not a foolproof method, and it is expensive. This procedure may be done when there is a sex-specific problem, such as a family history of hemophilia.

——— Health of the Baby's Father ———

Some women are concerned about the health of the baby's father. Can his health and his drug or alcohol use affect the health of the developing baby?

In recent years, more attention has been given to the paternal contribution in pregnancy. We now believe if a father is older than 40, it may increase risk of Down syndrome, although there is not a great deal of evidence to support this theory. A father's drug habit at the time of conception may also influence the outcome of your pregnancy. Evidence is scanty, but there does appear to be an effect.

——— ✳ ———

❧ **Artificial Sweetener Use during Pregnancy**

Many women use artificial sweeteners. Aspartame and saccharin are the two most common artificial sweeteners added to foods and beverages. Are they safe to use during pregnancy?

Aspartame (sold under the brand names Nutrasweet® and Equal®) may be the most popular, widely used artificial sweetener. It is used in many "low-calorie" foods and beverages to help reduce calorie content. Aspartame is a combination of phenylalanine and aspartic acid, two amino acids.

Recently, there has been controversy as to the safety of aspartame. I advise you to substitute foods that do not contain the sweetener. At this point we are unsure about aspartame's safety for pregnant women and their developing babies. Also, pregnant women who suffer from phenylketonuria must follow a low-phenylalanine diet or their babies may be adversely affected. The phenylalanine in aspartame contributes to phenylalanine in the diet.

Saccharin is another artificial sweetener used in many foods and beverages. Although it is not used as much today as in the past, it still appears in many foods, beverages and other substances. The Center for Science in the Public Interest reports testing of saccharin does not indicate that it is safe to use during pregnancy. It would probably be better to avoid using this product while you're pregnant.

Don't use artificial sweeteners or food additives during pregnancy if you can avoid them. I recommend eliminating *any* substance you don't really need from the foods you eat and the beverages you drink. Do it for the good of your baby.

One of my patients, Joy, was a little upset when I advised her to watch her artificial sweetener intake. She had told me she regularly drank a 2-liter bottle of diet soda every day. I told her she didn't have to give up the soda completely—she could have one can a day. I suggested she substitute unsweetened fruit juice and water flavored with lemon or other citrus juice for the rest of the day.

❧ Weight Gain during Pregnancy

The amount of weight women gain during pregnancy varies greatly. It may actually range from weight loss to a total gain of 50 pounds or more.

We know complications arise at the extremes of these weight changes. Because of this, it's difficult to set one figure as an "ideal" weight gain during pregnancy. How much weight you gain is affected by your weight before you became pregnant. Many quote a weight-gain figure of 2/3 of a pound (10 ounces) a week until 20 weeks, then 1 pound a week from 20 to 40 weeks.

Other researchers have suggested weight-gain amounts acceptable for underweight, normal weight and overweight women. See the chart on page 61.

———— **Weight Gain during Pregnancy** ————

Body Type	Acceptable Gain (pounds)
Underweight	28 to 40
Normal Weight	25 to 35
Overweight	15 to 25

———— ❋ ————

If you have any questions about your weight gain during pregnancy, discuss them with your physician. He or she will advise you and guide you about how much weight you should gain during pregnancy.

Dieting during pregnancy is not a wise idea, but that doesn't mean not watching your caloric intake. You should! It's important for your baby to get proper nutrition from the foods you eat. Choose your foods for the nutrition they provide for you and your growing baby.

Tip for Week 5
Precaution! Be careful about using over-the-counter cough and cold remedies. Many contain alcohol—some as much as 25%!

Week 6

Age of Fetus ~ 4 Weeks

If you've just found out you're pregnant, you might
want to start by reading the previous chapters.

ﾉﾉﾉ✳ﾉﾉﾉ

How Big Is Your Baby?

The crown-to-rump length of your growing baby is 0.08 to 0.16
inch (2 to 4mm). *Crown-to-rump* is the sitting height or distance
from the top of the baby's head to its rump or buttocks. This
measurement is used more often than crown-to-heel length
because the baby's legs are most often bent, making that determination difficult.

Occasionally, with the proper equipment, a heartbeat can be
seen on ultrasound by the 6th week. Ultrasound is discussed in
detail in Week 11.

How Big Are You?

You may have gained a few pounds by now. If you have been
nauseated and not eating well, you may have lost weight. You

have been pregnant for 1 month, which is enough time to notice some changes in your body. If this is your first pregnancy, your abdomen may not have changed much. Or you may notice your clothes are getting a little tighter around the waist. You may be gaining weight in your legs or other places, such as your breasts.

If you have a pelvic exam, your healthcare provider can usually feel your uterus and note some change in its size.

How Your Baby Is Growing and Developing

This is the beginning of the embryonic period (to 10 weeks of pregnancy; 8 weeks of development). It is a period of extremely important development in your baby! At this time, the embryo is most susceptible to factors that can interfere with its development. Most malformations originate during this critical period.

As the illustration on page 64 shows, the result of this growth is a body form showing the head and tail area. Around this time, the neural groove closes, and early brain chambers form. The eyes are also forming. Limb buds are seen.

The heart tubes fuse, and heart contractions begin. This can be seen on ultrasound.

Changes in You

∽ **Suffering from Heartburn**

Heartburn discomfort (pyrosis) is one of the most common complaints of pregnancy. It may begin early, although generally it becomes more severe later in pregnancy. It is usually caused by the backing up (reflux) of gastric and duodenal contents into the esophagus. This occurs more frequently during pregnancy for two reasons—food moves more slowly through the intestines and the stomach is compressed by the uterus as it enlarges and moves up into the abdomen.

Symptoms are not severe for most women. It helps to eat small meals frequently and to avoid some positions, such as

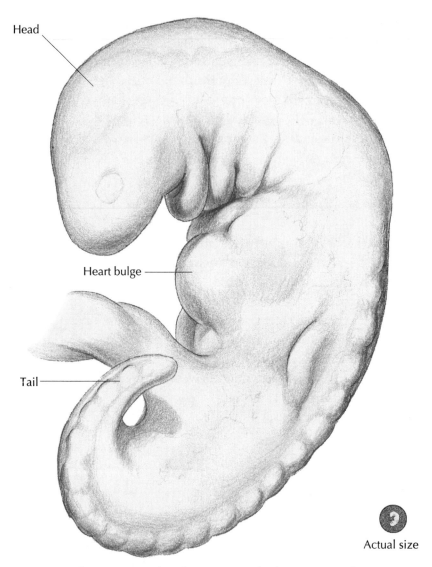

Head

Heart bulge

Tail

Actual size

Embryo at 6 weeks of pregnancy (fetal age—4 weeks).
It is growing rapidly.

bending over or lying flat. One sure way to get heartburn is to eat a large meal and then lie down! (This is true for anyone, not just pregnant women.)

Some antacids provide considerable relief, including aluminum hydroxide, magnesium trisilicate and magnesium hydroxide (Amphojel®, Gelusil®, Milk of Magnesia® and Maalox®).

Follow your doctor's orders or the instructions on the package relating to pregnancy. Don't overdo taking antacids! Avoid sodium bicarbonate because it contains excessive amounts of sodium that may cause you to retain water.

Cissy, pregnant for the first time, was having trouble sleeping because of stomach problems. She and her husband Robbie often ate out after work. We talked about not eating late or lying down soon after eating. I suggested five or six small meals a day might be a better plan for her. I also advised her that using antacids occasionally was OK.

Try to find foods (and amounts of foods) that don't give you heartburn, but don't go overboard on them. If you find chocolate malts don't cause you problems, for example, don't have one at every meal!

⚬ Food Cravings

Food cravings have long been considered a nonspecific sign of pregnancy. Craving a particular food doesn't mean you are pregnant, but when added together with many other signs, it might mean you're pregnant.

Cravings for certain foods during pregnancy can be good and bad. Don't eat foods that aren't good for you. Add foods that benefit you and your growing baby. Some women find they can't stand foods they usually enjoy.

⚬ Constipation

It's common for your bowel habits to change during pregnancy. Most women notice some constipation, often accompanied by irregular bowel movements. Hemorrhoids may occur more often.

You can help yourself avoid constipation problems during pregnancy. Increase your fluid intake. Exercise also helps. Many doctors suggest a mild laxative, such as milk of magnesia or prune juice, if you have problems. Certain foods, such as bran and prunes, can increase the bulk in your diet, which may help relieve constipation.

Do not use laxatives, other than those mentioned, without your doctor's OK. If constipation is a continuing problem, discuss treatment with your doctor.

Try not to strain when you have a bowel movement, if you are constipated. Straining can lead to hemorrhoids.

How Your Actions Affect Your Baby's Development

During pregnancy, a sexually transmitted disease (STD) can harm your growing baby. Any STD must be taken care of as soon as possible.

ஓ *Genital Herpes Simplex Infection*

Usually a herpes infection during pregnancy is a reinfection, not a primary infection. Infection in the mother is associated with higher risks of premature delivery and low-birth-weight infants. We believe an infant can be infected when traveling through the birth canal. When membranes rupture, the infection may also travel upward to the uterus.

There is no safe treatment during pregnancy for genital herpes. When a woman has an active herpes infection late in pregnancy, a Cesarean section is done to deliver the baby.

ஓ *Monilial Vulvovaginitis*

Monilial (yeast) infections are more common in pregnant women than in nonpregnant women. They have no major negative effect on pregnancy, but they may cause discomfort and anxiety.

Yeast infections are sometimes harder to control when you're pregnant. They may require frequent retreatment or longer treatment (10 to 14 days instead of 3 to 7 days). Creams used for treatment are usually safe during pregnancy. Your partner does not need to be treated.

A newborn infant can get thrush after passing through a birth canal infected with monilial vulvovaginitis. Treatment with nystatin is effective. Avoid the use of fluconazole; it may not be safe to use during pregnancy.

ஓ *Trichomonal Vaginitis*

This infection has no major effects on pregnancy. However, a problem in treatment may arise because some doctors believe metronidazole, the drug of choice, shouldn't be taken in the first trimester of pregnancy. Most healthcare providers will prescribe metronidazole for a bad infection after the first trimester.

✎ *Condylomata Acuminatum*

This condition is commonly called *venereal warts*. If you have extensive venereal warts, a Cesarean delivery may be necessary to avoid heavy bleeding.

Warty skin tags often enlarge during pregnancy. In rare instances, they have blocked the vagina at the time of delivery. Infants have also been known to get laryngeal papillomas (small benign tumors on the vocal cords) after delivery.

✎ *Gonorrhea*

Gonorrhea presents risks to a woman and her partner, and to her baby when it passes through the birth canal. The baby may contract gonorrheal ophthalmia, a severe eye infection. Eyedrops are used in newborns to prevent this problem. Other infections may also result. Gonorrheal infections are easily treated with penicillin or other medications that are safe to use during pregnancy.

✎ *Syphilis*

Detection of a syphilis infection is important for you, your partner and your infant. Fortunately this rare infection is also very treatable. If you notice any open sore on your genitals during pregnancy, have your doctor check it out. Syphilis can be treated effectively with penicillin and other medications that are safe in pregnancy.

You Should also Know

✎ *Your First Visit to the Doctor*

Your first visit to your doctor may be your longest visit. There's a lot to be accomplished. If you saw your doctor before you got pregnant, you may have already discussed some of your concerns.

Feel free to ask questions to get an idea of how this person will relate to you and to your needs. This factor is important as your pregnancy progresses. During pregnancy, there should be an exchange of ideas. Consider what your doctor suggests and why. It's important to share your feelings and ideas. You also need to remember your doctor has experience that can be valuable to you during pregnancy.

⤳ What Will Happen?

What should you expect at this first visit? First, you will be asked for a history of your past medical health. This includes general medical problems and any problems relating to your gynecological and obstetrical history. You will be asked about your periods and recent birth-control methods. If you've had an abortion or a miscarriage, tell your doctor. If you've been in the hospital for surgery or for some other reason, it's important information. If you have old medical records, bring them with you.

Your doctor needs to know about any medication you take or any medication you are allergic to. Your family's past medical history may also be important, such as the occurrence of diabetes or other chronic illness.

A physical exam, including a pelvic exam and Pap smear, will be performed. This exam determines if your uterus is the appropriate size for how far along in your pregnancy you are.

Laboratory tests may be done at this first visit or on a subsequent visit. Lab tests are discussed in depth in Week 8.

If you have questions, ask them. If you think you may have a "high-risk" pregnancy, discuss it with your doctor.

In most cases, you will be asked to return every 4 weeks for the first 7 months, then every 2 weeks until the last month, then every week. If problems arise, you may be scheduled for more frequent visits.

> *Tip for Week 6*
> If you have questions between your prenatal visits, call and ask your doctor or a nurse. It's OK to call, and you'll probably feel more comfortable when your questions are answered.

Week 7

Age of Fetus ౼ 5 Weeks

*If you've just found out you're pregnant, you might
want to start by reading the previous chapters.*

౼౼౼*౼౼౼

How Big Is Your Baby?

Your baby has an incredible growth spurt this week! At the
beginning of the 7th week, the crown-to-rump length of your
growing baby is 0.16 to 0.2 inch (4 to 5mm). This is about the
size of a BB pellet. By the end of the week, your baby has grown
to 0.44 to 0.52 inch (11 to 13mm).

How Big Are You?

Although you are probably quite anxious to show the world
you're pregnant, there still may be little change. Changes will
come soon, though.

How Your Baby Is Growing and Developing

Leg buds are beginning to appear as short fins. As you can see on page 71, arm buds have grown longer; they have divided into a hand segment and an arm-shoulder segment. The hand and foot have a digital plate where the fingers and toes will develop.

The heart bulges from the body. By this time, it has divided into right and left heart chambers. The primary bronchi are present in the lungs; *bronchi* are air passages in the lungs.

The cerebral hemispheres, which make up the brain, are also growing. Eyes and nostrils are developing.

Intestines are developing, and the appendix is present. The pancreas, which produces the hormone insulin, is also present. Part of the intestine bulges into the umbilical cord. Later in your baby's development, it will return to the abdomen.

Changes in You

Changes are occurring gradually. You still probably won't "show," and people won't be able to tell you're pregnant unless you tell them. You may be gaining weight throughout your body, but you should have gained only a couple of pounds this early in your pregnancy.

If you haven't gained weight or if you have lost a couple of pounds, it isn't unusual. It will go the other direction in the weeks to come. You may still experience morning sickness and other symptoms of early pregnancy.

How Your Actions Affect Your Baby's Development

◦ Good Nutrition Is Important

Many factors can influence the development of your baby. What you eat is an important contributing factor. If your diet is deficient, it could affect your baby's development.

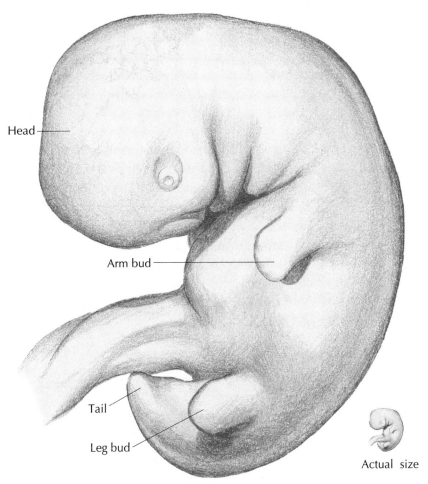

Head

Arm bud

Tail

Leg bud

Actual size

Your baby's brain is growing and developing. The heart has divided into right and left chambers.

Increase the number of calories you consume by 300 to 800 calories a day, depending on your prepregnancy weight. The extra calories provide extra energy for tissue growth in you and your baby. You also need more body fat during pregnancy and after your baby's birth for nursing. (Even if you don't breastfeed, you need the additional body fat during pregnancy.)

Your baby uses the energy you provide to create and to store protein, fat and carbohydrates, and to provide energy for its body processes to function. If enough calories aren't available, your body may metabolize protein as a source of energy instead of using it for your baby's growth and development.

Below is a discussion of how your body uses protein, carbohydrate and fat during pregnancy. Discuss any questions you have with your doctor. Good nutrition and a healthful nutrition plan are essential for you and your growing baby.

✢ Protein

The nonpregnant woman needs protein to repair tissues. During pregnancy, the body also needs protein for growth and repair of the embryo/fetus, placenta, uterus and breasts. Most protein should come from animal sources, such as meat, milk, eggs, cheese, poultry and fish. These protein sources supply amino acids in the best combinations. The recommendation during pregnancy is 6 to 7 ounces (168 to 196g) of protein a day. If you're a vegetarian, discuss the situation with your healthcare provider. Protein is very important for your diet, and you may need to eat different foods.

✢ Carbohydrates

There is no recommended dietary allowance (RDA) for carbohydrate intake during pregnancy. Calories from carbohydrates should make up about 60% of the total number of calories in your diet. Adequate carbohydrate intake can help avoid formation of ketones, which accumulate in the blood when carbohydrate intake is low. High levels of ketones may be harmful to the growing baby.

✢ Fat

There is no recommended daily requirement for fat consumption. Most of us don't need to worry about inadequate fat intake. On the contrary, fat intake is usually excessive.

The issue of cholesterol levels has been widely discussed. Elevated cholesterol levels are a risk factor for heart disease. However, pregnancy and nursing are *not* times to check your blood cholesterol. Cholesterol levels increase during pregnancy and nursing because of increased hormone levels. Sometimes this increase can be as high as 25%.

ﺽ *Do You Need Extra Minerals?*

Nearly all diets that supply a sufficient number of calories for appropriate weight gain contain enough minerals (except iron) to prevent mineral deficiency.

During pregnancy, your iron requirement increases. Very few women have sufficient iron stores to meet pregnancy demands. During a normal pregnancy, blood volume increases by about 50%. A large amount of iron is required to produce those additional blood cells.

Iron needs are most important in the latter half of pregnancy. Most women don't need to take iron supplements during the first trimester. If prescribed at this time, they can worsen symptoms of nausea and vomiting.

The iron content of prenatal vitamins can irritate your stomach. Iron supplements may also cause constipation. You may not be able to take iron supplements until after the first trimester.

> *Tip for Week 7*
> If you experience leg cramps during pregnancy, don't stand for long periods, and rest on your side as often as possible.

Some doctors prescribe calcium supplementation. Calcium is important for every pregnant woman. It helps build strong bones and teeth in the baby and helps keep the woman's bones healthy. During pregnancy, you need 1200 to 1500mg a day. That's about 3 to 4 glasses of skim milk a day.

Calcium supplementation may help control blood pressure. It can help reduce hypertension and the risk of pre-eclampsia. Some substances interfere with the body's absorption of calcium. Salt, protein foods, tea, coffee and unleavened bread should not be consumed with calcium-containing foods.

Research has also found that zinc can be helpful to a thin or underweight woman during pregnancy. We believe this mineral helps a thin woman increase her chances of giving birth to a bigger, healthier baby.

The value of fluoride and fluoride supplementation in a pregnant woman is unclear. Some researchers believe fluoride supplementation during pregnancy results in improved teeth in the child; not everyone agrees. Some prenatal vitamins contain fluoride. Fluoride supplementation in a pregnant woman has not been proved to harm her baby.

ᔗ *Folic Acid during Pregnancy*

Folic acid (vitamin B-9) may be very important to you during pregnancy. A folic-acid deficiency can result in anemia. Additional folic acid may be necessary with multiple fetuses or if the mother suffers from Crohn's disease or alcoholism.

Spina bifida may be prevented if the mother-to-be takes 0.4mg of folic acid a day, beginning before pregnancy and continuing through the first 13 weeks. This is suggested for all pregnant women, especially those who have previously given birth to a baby with spina bifida.

────── **Prenatal Vitamins** ──────

Prenatal vitamins are usually prescribed for a pregnant woman by her doctor. Some women like to begin taking prenatal vitamins while they are trying to get pregnant. They contain the daily amounts of vitamins and minerals recommended for you during pregnancy. For your good health and your baby's benefit, do not consider them a substitute for food.

Your prenatal vitamin is different from a regular multivitamin because of its iron and folic-acid content. Prenatal vitamins are probably the most important supplement for you in pregnancy. Prenatal vitamins are usually best tolerated if you take them with meals or at night before bed.

──────── ✳ ────────

You Should also Know

~ Sexual Intimacy during Pregnancy

Andrea was very upset at her second visit. Crying, she told me, "Todd doesn't find me attractive now. We haven't had sex since I got pregnant." Todd, who was with her, said that wasn't true; he thought she was more beautiful than ever. But he was afraid sex would hurt the baby.

I explained to them that intimacy during pregnancy is natural and OK. It wouldn't hurt the baby as long as Andrea's pregnancy was normal and uncomplicated.

Many couples question whether it is wise or permissible to have sexual intercourse during pregnancy. Sexual relations are acceptable for a healthy pregnant woman and her partner. However, when miscarriage or premature labor threaten, avoid intercourse.

Some doctors recommend abstinence from intercourse during the last 4 weeks of pregnancy, but not all physicians agree with this. Discuss it with your doctor.

~ Cancer Before Pregnancy

If you are now pregnant and you have had any type of cancer in the past, tell your doctor as soon as you discover you are pregnant. He or she may need to make decisions about individualized care for you during this pregnancy.

Week 8

Age of Fetus — 6 Weeks

If you've just found out you're pregnant, you might
want to start by reading the previous chapters.

ૐૐૐ✳ૐૐૐ

How Big Is Your Baby?

By your 8th week of pregnancy, the crown-to-rump length of
your baby is 0.56 to 0.8 inch (14 to 20mm). This is about the
size of a pinto bean.

How Big Are You?

Your uterus is getting bigger, but it probably still isn't big enough
for you to be showing, especially if this is your first pregnancy.
You will notice a gradual change in your waistline and the fit of
your clothes. Your doctor will see that your uterus is enlarged if
you have a pelvic exam.

How Your Baby Is Growing and Developing

Your baby is continuing to grow and to change rapidly during these early weeks. Compare the illustration on page 80 with the illustration for the 7th week of pregnancy. Can you see the incredible changes?

Eyelid folds are forming on the face. The tip of the nose is present. Ears are forming, internally and externally.

In the heart, the aortic and pulmonary valves are present and distinct. Tubes leading from the throat to the functioning part of the lungs are branched, like the branches of a tree. The body's trunk area is getting longer and straightening out.

Elbows are present, and the arms and legs extend forward. Arms have grown longer. They bend at the elbows and curve slightly over the heart. The digital rays, which become fingers, are notched. Toe rays are present on the feet.

Changes in You

✃ Changes in Your Uterus

Before pregnancy, your uterus was about the size of your fist. After 6 weeks of growth, it is about the size of a grapefruit. As the uterus grows, you may feel cramping or even pain in your lower abdomen or your sides. Some women feel tightening or contractions of the uterus.

The uterus tightens or contracts throughout pregnancy. If you don't feel this, don't worry. However, when contractions are accompanied by bleeding from the vagina, consult your physician.

✃ Sciatic-Nerve Pain

Many women experience an occasional excruciating pain in their buttocks and down the back or side of their legs as pregnancy progresses. This is called *sciatic-nerve pain*. The sciatic nerve runs behind the uterus in the pelvis to the legs. We believe pain is caused by pressure on the nerve from the growing, expanding uterus.

The best treatment for the pain is to lie on your opposite side. This helps relieve pressure on the nerve.

How Your Actions Affect Your Baby's Development

✥ Use of Accutane

Some women notice an improvement in their acne during pregnancy. But this doesn't happen for everyone.

Accutane® (isotretinoin) is commonly prescribed for the treatment of acne. Do not take Accutane during pregnancy! Taken during the first trimester, Accutane is responsible for a higher frequency of miscarriage and malformation of the fetus.

If you are pregnant or think you might be pregnant, don't take Accutane. Use reliable birth control to avoid pregnancy if you do use it.

✥ Miscarriage

Miscarriage occurs when a pregnancy ends before the embryo or fetus can survive on its own outside the uterus. Nearly every pregnant woman thinks about miscarriage during pregnancy, but it occurs in only about 15% of all pregnancies.

✥ What Causes a Miscarriage?

We don't usually know and are often unable to find out what causes a miscarriage. The most common finding in early miscarriages is an abnormality in the development of the early embryo. Studies indicate more than half of all early miscarriages have chromosomal abnormalities.

Many factors can affect the embryo and its environment, including radiation, chemicals (drugs or medications) and infections. Called *teratogens,* these adverse factors are discussed in depth in Week 9.

We believe various maternal factors are important in some miscarriages. Unusual infections, such as listeria, toxoplasma and syphilis, have been implicated in miscarriages.

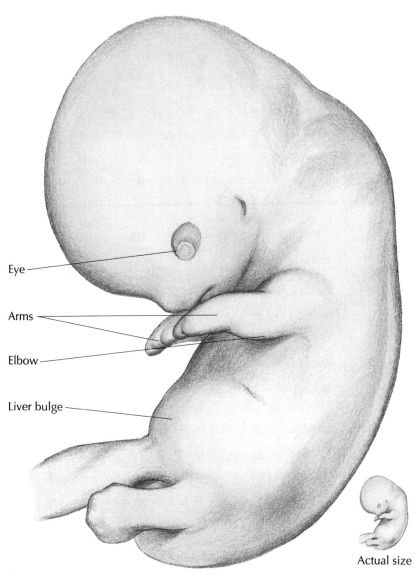

Eye

Arms

Elbow

Liver bulge

Actual size

Embryo at 8 weeks (fetal age—6 weeks). Crown-to-rump length is about 0.8 inch (20mm). Arms are longer and bend at the elbows.

We have no concrete evidence that deficiency of any particular nutrient or even a moderate deficiency of all nutrients causes a miscarriage. Women who smoke have a higher rate of miscarriage. Alcohol is also blamed for an increase in miscarriages.

Ruby, 8 weeks pregnant, was upset when she came for her first prenatal visit. Her last pregnancy had ended in miscarriage at

8 weeks, and she was scared she would have a miscarriage with this pregnancy. I assured her there were no indications it would happen this time. She left the office looking forward to her next visit, when she could probably hear the baby's heartbeat.

The trauma of an accident or major surgery has been related to an increase in miscarriages, although this is difficult to verify. An incompetent cervix (see Week 24) is a cause of pregnancy loss after the first trimester. Many women have blamed emotional upset or trauma for a miscarriage, but this is hard to prove.

Below is a discussion of different types of and causes of miscarriage. It is included to alert you about what to watch for if you have any symptoms of a miscarriage. If you have questions, discuss them with your doctor.

∽ Threatened Miscarriage

A threatened miscarriage may be presumed when there is a bloody discharge from the vagina during the first half of pregnancy. Bleeding may last for days or even weeks. There may or may not be any cramping or pain. Pain may feel like a menstrual cramp or a mild backache. Resting in bed is about all you can do, although being active does not cause miscarriage. No procedures or medication can keep a woman from miscarrying.

Threatened miscarriage is a common diagnosis because 20% of all women experience bleeding during early pregnancy but not all miscarry.

∽ Inevitable Miscarriage

An inevitable miscarriage occurs with the rupture of membranes, dilatation of the cervix and passage of blood clots and even tissue. Miscarriage is almost certain under these circumstances. The uterus usually contracts, expelling the fetus or *products of conception* (so-called when no embryo or fetus is present).

∽ Incomplete Miscarriage

With an incomplete miscarriage, the entire pregnancy may not be passed at once. Part of the pregnancy is passed while part of it remains in the uterus. Bleeding may be heavy and continues until the uterus is empty.

᠅ *Missed Miscarriage*

A missed miscarriage can occur with prolonged retention of an embryo that died earlier. There may be no symptoms or bleeding. The time period from when the pregnancy failed to the time the miscarriage is discovered is usually weeks.

᠅ *Habitual Miscarriage*

This term usually refers to three or more consecutive miscarriages.

᠅ *If You Have Problems*

If you have problems, notify your doctor immediately! Bleeding usually appears first, followed by cramping. Ectopic pregnancy must be considered a possibility. A quantitative HCG may be useful in identifying a normal pregnancy, but a single test report usually won't help. Your doctor needs to repeat the test over a period of days.

Ultrasound may help if you are more than 5 gestational weeks into your pregnancy. You may continue to bleed, but seeing your baby's heart beat and a normal-appearing pregnancy may be reassuring. If the first ultrasound is not reassuring, you may be asked to wait a week or 10 days and then repeat the ultrasound.

The longer you bleed and cramp, the more likely you are to be having a miscarriage. If you pass all of the pregnancy and bleeding stops and cramping goes away, you may be done with it.

However, if everything is not expelled, it may be necessary to perform a D&C (dilatation and curettage) to empty the uterus. It is preferable to do this so you won't bleed for a long time, risking anemia and infection.

Some women are given the hormone progesterone to help them keep a pregnancy. The use of progesterone to prevent miscarriage is controversial. Doctors do not agree on its use or its effectiveness.

᠅ *Rh-Sensitivity and Miscarriage*

If you're Rh-negative and you have a miscarriage, you will need to receive RhoGAM. This applies *only* if you are Rh-negative. RhoGAM is given to protect you from making antibodies to Rh-positive blood. (This is discussed in Week 16.)

✎ *If You Have a Miscarriage*

One miscarriage can be traumatic; two in a row can be very difficult to deal with. Repeated miscarriages occur due to chance or "bad luck" in most cases.

Most doctors don't recommend testing to find a reason for miscarriage unless you have three or more. Chromosome analysis can be done, and other tests investigate the possibility of infections, diabetes and lupus.

Don't blame yourself or your partner for a miscarriage. It is usually impossible to look back at everything you've done, eaten or been exposed to and find the cause of a miscarriage.

You Should also Know

✎ *Lab Tests Your Doctor May Order*

At your first or second visit, routine lab tests are performed. You will have a pelvic exam, including a Pap smear. Other tests include a CBC (complete blood count), urinalysis and urine culture, a test for syphilis (VDRL or ART) and cervical cultures, as indicated. Many doctors test blood sugar (to look for diabetes). They also test for your immunity against rubella and your blood type and Rh-factor. Other tests are done as needed. Tests are not performed at each visit; they are done at the beginning of pregnancy and as needed. Tests for hepatitis are now standard.

✎ *Rubella during Pregnancy*

It's a good idea to be checked for immunity to rubella before you get pregnant. Rubella (German measles) during pregnancy can be responsible for miscarriage or fetal malformation. Because there is no known treatment for rubella, the best approach is prevention. If you're not immune, you can receive a vaccination while you take reliable birth control. Do not have a vaccination shortly before or during pregnancy because of the possibility of exposing the baby to the rubella virus.

∽ *Toxoplasmosis*

If you have a cat, you may be concerned about toxoplasmosis. The disease is spread by eating raw, infected meat or by contact with infected cat feces. It can cross the placenta to your baby. Usually an infection in the mother has no symptoms.

Infection during pregnancy can lead to miscarriage or an infected infant at birth. Antibiotics, such as pyrimethamine, sulfadiazine and erythromycin, can treat toxoplasmosis, but the best plan is prevention. Hygienic measures prevent transmission of the disease.

Avoid exposure to cat feces (get someone else to change the kitty litter). Wash hands thoroughly after petting your cat, and keep your cat off counters and tables. Wash your hands after contact with meat and soil, and cook meat thoroughly.

Tip for Week 8

Wash your hands thoroughly throughout the day, especially after handling raw meat or using the bathroom. This simple activity can help prevent the spread of many bacteria and viruses that cause infection.

Week 9

Age of Fetus ᐧ 7 Weeks

If you've just found out you're pregnant, you might
want to start by reading the previous chapters.

༉༉༉❈༉༉༉

How Big Is Your Baby?

The crown-to-rump length of the embryo is 0.9 inch to 1.2
inches (22 to 30mm). This is close to the size of a medium green
olive.

How Big Are You?

Each week your uterus grows larger with the baby growing
inside it. You may begin to see your waistline growing thicker by
this time. A pelvic exam will detect a uterus a little bigger than a
grapefruit.

How Your Baby Is Growing and Developing

If you could look inside your uterus, you'd see many changes in your baby. The illustration on page 88 shows some of them.

Your baby's arms and legs are longer. Hands are flexed at the wrist and meet over the heart area. They continue to extend in front of the body. Fingers are longer, and the tips are slightly swollen where touch pads are developing. The feet are approaching the midline of the body and may be long enough to meet in front of the torso.

The head is more erect, and the neck is more developed. The eyelids almost cover the eyes. Up to this time, the eyes have been uncovered. External ears are evident and well-formed.

Your baby now moves its body and limbs. This movement may be seen during an ultrasound exam.

The baby looks more recognizable as a human being, although it is still extremely small. It still is probably impossible to distinguish a male from a female. External organs (external genitalia) of the male and female appear very similar and will not be distinguishable for another few weeks.

Changes in You

✂ *Weight Gain*

Most women are very interested in their weight during pregnancy; many watch their weight closely. As strange as it may seem, gaining weight is an important way to monitor the well-being of your developing baby. Even though your weight gain may be small, your body is changing. See the chart on the next page.

——— How is Pregnancy Weight Distributed? ———

7 pounds	Maternal stores (fat, protein and other nutrients)
4 pounds	Increased fluid volume
2 pounds	Breast enlargement
2 pounds	Uterus
7-1/2 pounds	Baby
2 pounds	Amniotic fluid
1-1/2 pounds	Placenta (tissue connecting mother and baby that brings nourishment and takes away waste)

(Modified from: A.C.O.G. *Guide to Planning for Pregnancy, Birth and Beyond;* 1990, American College of Obstetricians and Gynecologists)

——— ✳ ———

Beatrice was upset when she came to my office. She had heard she would gain between 25 and 35 pounds during her pregnancy, but she didn't want to be "that fat." I told her, "Changes to your body—increased size of the uterus, breast tissue, blood volume and body fluid—account for the largest part of your weight gain. To support a pregnancy, your body stores nutrients and increases the volume of blood and other fluids it produces. One reason for the extra fat is to prepare you to produce milk for breastfeeding." She felt better knowing that the weight she gained was for the good of the baby.

✍ *Increased Blood Volume*

Your blood system changes dramatically during pregnancy. Your blood volume increases greatly—to about 50% more than before you became pregnant. However, this amount varies from woman to woman.

Increased blood volume is important. It is designed to meet the demands of your growing uterus. This increase does not include the blood in the embryo, whose circulation is separate (fetal blood does not mix with your blood). It protects you and your baby from harmful effects when you lie down or stand up. It is also a safeguard during labor and delivery when some blood is lost.

Eye

Fingers

Actual size

Toes

Embryo at 9 weeks of pregnancy (fetal age—46 to 49 days). Toes are formed, and feet are more recognizable. Crown-to-rump length is 1 inch (25mm).

The increase in blood volume starts during the first trimester. The largest increase occurs during the second trimester. It continues to increase at a slower rate during the third trimester.

Blood is composed of fluid (plasma) and cells (red blood cells and white blood cells). Plasma and cells play an important role in your body's function.

Fluid and cells increase to different degrees. Usually there is an initial rise in plasma volume followed by an increase in red blood cells. The increase in red blood cells increases your body's demand for iron.

Red blood cells and plasma both increase during pregnancy; plasma increases more. This increase in plasma can cause anemia. If you're anemic, especially during pregnancy, you may feel tired, fatigue easily or experience a general feeling of ill health. (See Week 22 for a discussion of anemia.)

How Your Actions Affect Your Baby's Development

During pregnancy, nearly every woman worries whether her baby will be perfect. Most women worry unnecessarily. Major birth defects are apparent in only about 3% of all newborns at birth. Of those 3%, are causes of these abnormalities known? Could they have been prevented?

✌ *Abnormal Fetal Development*

Teratology is the study of abnormal fetal development. An exact cause or reason for a birth defect is found in less than half of all cases. Obstetricians and other doctors providing care to pregnant women are often asked about substances (*teratogens*) that may be harmful. We believe some agents may be harmful, but researchers have not been able to prove this. However, other agents *have* been proved to be harmful.

Some agents cause major defects if exposure occurs at a specific, critical time in fetal development. But they may not be harmful at other times. Once major development has been completed in the fetus, usually by the 13th week, the effect of a certain substance may be only growth retardation or smaller organ size rather than large structural defects. One example is rubella. It can cause many anatomical defects, such as heart malformations, if the fetus is infected during the first trimester of pregnancy. A rubella infection occurring later is less serious.

❧ *Individual Response to Exposure*

There is a great deal of individual variation in response to the size of a dose of an agent and to particular agents. Alcohol is a good example. Large amounts appear to have no effect on some fetuses, while other fetuses may be harmed by low amounts.

Animal studies provide much of our information about possible harmful agents. This information can be helpful but cannot always be applied directly to humans. Other information comes from situations in which women were exposed who did not know they were pregnant or who did not know a particular medication could be harmful. Information gathered from these instances is difficult to apply directly to a particular pregnancy.

A list of known teratogens and the effects they may have on an embryo or fetus follows. If you have taken any of these substances, discuss them as soon as possible with your doctor for your peace of mind. If testing or follow-up is necessary, your doctor will advise you.

❧ *Effects of Medications and Chemicals on Your Baby*

Many substances can affect the your baby's early development. Below is a list of some medications and chemicals, and their possible effects on a developing baby.

Drugs and Chemicals	Effects on Fetus
Alcohol	Growth and mental retardation Microcephaly Various major malformations
Androgens (male hormones)	Ambiguous genital development (depends on dose given and when given)
Anticoagulants (warfarin)	Bone and hand abnormalities Intrauterine-growth retardation Central-nervous-system and eye abnormalities
Antithyroid drugs (propylthiouracil, iodide, methimazole)	Hypothyroidism Fetal goiter

Chemotherapeutic drugs (methotrexate, aminopterin)	Increased risk of miscarriage
Diethylstilbestrol (DES)	Abnormalities of female reproductive organs Female and male infertility
Isotretinoin (Accutane)	Increased miscarriage rate Nervous-system defects Facial defects Cleft palate
Lead	Increased miscarriage and stillbirth rates
Lithium	Congenital heart disease
Organic mercury	Cerebral atrophy Mental retardation Spasticity Seizures Blindness
Phenytoin (Dilantin®)	Growth retardation Mental retardation Microcephaly
Streptomycin	Hearing loss Cranial-nerve damage
Tetracycline	Hypoplasia of tooth enamel Discoloration of permanent teeth
Thalidomide	Severe limb defects
Trimethadione	Cleft lip Cleft palate Growth retardation Miscarriage
Valproic acid	Neural-tube defects
X-ray therapy	Microcephaly Mental retardation Leukemia

(Modified from A.C.O.G. Technical Bulletin #84, *Teratology*, February, 1985, American College of Obstetricians and Gynecologists)

You Should also Know

~ Effects of Infections on Your Baby

Some infections and illnesses a woman contracts can also affect her baby's development during this growth period. Below is a list of some infections and diseases, and the effects they may have on a developing baby.

Infections	Effects on Fetus
Cytomegalovirus (CMV)	Microcephaly Brain damage Hearing loss
Rubella (German measles)	Cataracts Deafness Heart lesions Can involve all organs
Syphilis	Fetal death Skin defects
Toxoplasmosis	Possible effects on all organs
Varicella	Possible effects on all organs

Tip for Week 9

It's an old wives' tale that your hair won't curl if you have a permanent during pregnancy. My only precaution is that if odors affect you, the fumes from a permanent or hair coloring could make you feel ill.

Week 10

Age of Fetus ✦ 8 Weeks

If you've just found out you're pregnant, you might
want to start by reading the previous chapters.

❧❧❧❀❧❧❧

How Big Is Your Baby?

By the 10th week of pregnancy, the crown-to-rump length of
your growing baby is about 1.25 to 1.68 inches (31 to 42mm).
At this time, we can start measuring how much the baby weighs.
Before this week, weight was too small to measure weekly differences. Now that the baby is starting to put on a little weight,
weight is included in this section. The baby weighs close to 0.18
ounce (5g) and is the size of a small plum.

How Big Are You?

Changes are gradual, and you may still not show much. You may
be thinking about and looking at maternity clothes, but you
probably don't need them just yet.

✌ *Molar Pregnancy*

A condition that can make you grow too big too fast is a molar pregnancy, sometimes called *gestational trophoblastic neoplasia (GTN)* or *hydatidiform mole.*

The occurrence of GTN is easily monitored by checking HCG levels (see Week 5). Molar pregnancy can be cured with medications or by surgery.

When a molar pregnancy occurs, an embryo does not usually develop. Other tissue grows, which is abnormal placental tissue. The most common symptom is bleeding during the first trimester. Another symptom is the discrepancy between the size of the mother-to-be and how far along she is supposed to be in pregnancy. Half the time, a woman is too large. Twenty-five percent of the time, she is too small. Excessive nausea and vomiting are other symptoms. Cysts may also occur on the ovaries.

The most effective way to diagnose a molar pregnancy is by ultrasound. The ultrasound picture has a "snowflake" appearance. A molar pregnancy is usually found when ultrasound is done early in pregnancy to determine the cause of bleeding or rapid growth.

When a molar pregnancy is diagnosed, a D&C (dilatation and curettage) is usually done as soon as possible. After a molar pregnancy occurs, effective birth control is important to be sure the molar pregnancy is completely gone. Most doctors recommend using reliable birth control for 1 year before pregnancy is attempted again.

In addition to D&C, hysterectomy may be considered when childbearing is concluded. This is uncommon, but it is a treatment. Ovaries are usually left untouched. Some medications, such as methotrexate and Actinomycin D®, are effective in the treatment of molar pregnancy.

The good news about molar pregnancy is that treatment is very effective. Cure rates are close to 100%!

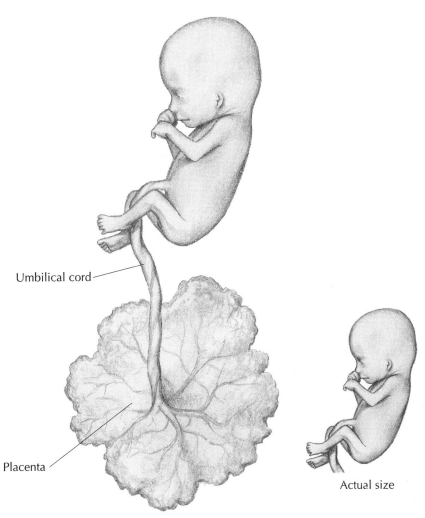

Umbilical cord

Placenta

Actual size

Baby is shown attached to the placenta by its umbilical cord. Eyelids are fused and remain closed until week 27 (fetal age—25 weeks).

How Your Baby Is Growing and Developing

The end of week 10 is the end of the embryonic period. At this time, the fetal period begins. It is characterized by rapid growth of the fetus when the three germ layers are established. (See Week 4 for further information.) During the embryonic period, the embryo was most susceptible to things that could interfere with its development. Most congenital malformations occur before the end of week 10. It is encouraging to know that a critical part of your baby's development is safely behind you.

Few malformations occur during the fetal period. However, drugs and other harmful exposures, such as severe stress or radiation (X-ray), can destroy fetal cells at any time during pregnancy. Continue to avoid them.

By the end of week 10, development of organ systems and the body are well under way. Your baby is beginning to look more human.

Changes in You

↜ *Pregnancy Brings Many Changes*

When your pregnancy is confirmed by an exam or a pregnancy test, you may be affected in many ways. Pregnancy can change many of your expectations. Some women see pregnancy as a sign of womanhood. Some consider it a blessing. Still others feel it is a problem to be dealt with.

You will experience many changes in your body. You may wonder if you are still attractive. Will your partner still find you desirable? (Many men believe pregnant women are very beautiful and desirable.) Will your partner help you? Clothing may become an issue. Can you look attractive? Can you learn to adapt?

If you aren't immediately excited about pregnancy, don't feel alone. You may question your condition—that's common. Some of this reaction is because you're not sure of what lies ahead.

When and how you begin to regard the fetus as a person is different for everyone. Some women have told me it is when their pregnancy test is positive. Others say it occurs when they hear the fetal heartbeat, usually at around 12 weeks. For still others, it happens when they first feel their baby move, at between 16 and 20 weeks.

You may find you are very emotional about many things. You may feel moody, cry at the slightest thing or drift off in daydreams. Emotional swings are normal and continue to some degree throughout your pregnancy.

✌ *Dealing with Emotional Changes*

How can you help yourself deal with emotional changes? One of the most important things you can do is to get good prenatal care. Follow your doctor's recommendations. Keep all your prenatal appointments. Establish good communication with your doctor and his or her office staff. Ask questions. If something bothers you or worries you, discuss it with someone reliable.

How Your Actions Affect Your Baby's Development

✌ *Vaccinations and Immunizations*

Many vaccines are available that help prevent illness. A vaccine is a substance given to provide you with protection against foreign substances (infection). A vaccine is usually given by injection or taken orally.

Most women of childbearing age in the United States and Canada should be immune to measles, mumps, rubella, tetanus and diphtheria. Most people born before 1957 were exposed to and infected naturally with measles, mumps and rubella and can be considered immune. They have antibodies and therefore are protected.

For women born after 1957, the situation may not be quite so clear. A physician-diagnosed case of measles, documentation of vaccination with measles vaccine or a positive blood test for measles is necessary to determine immunity. The diagnosis of rubella is difficult without a blood test because many other illnesses may have similar symptoms. Physician-diagnosed mumps or mumps vaccination is necessary evidence of immunity.

Vaccination for measles, mumps and rubella (MMR) should be administered *only* when a woman is practicing birth control. She must continue to use contraception for at least 3 months after receiving this immunization. Other vaccinations are also important, such as the tetanus (DPT; diphtheria, pertussis [whooping cough], tetanus) vaccine.

Marcia called my office very upset. She had cut her leg on a rusty piece of pipe and thought she might need a tetanus shot.

We checked her records and assured her she was up to date on her vaccinations. A person is considered immune to tetanus, diphtheria and whooping cough if she has received at least three doses of the DPT vaccine and if the last dose was given at least a year after the previous dose. A booster is required every 10 years. Marcia had had a booster shot 2 years before. If you aren't sure when or if you've been vaccinated, check with your doctor.

ᨔ Risk of Exposure

It's important to consider your risk of exposure to various diseases when you are deciding whether to have a particular vaccination. Try to decrease your chance of exposure to disease and illness. Avoid visiting areas known to have prevalent diseases. Avoid people (usually children) with known illnesses.

It's impossible to avoid all exposure to disease. If you have been exposed, or if exposure is unavoidable, the risk of the disease must be balanced against the potential harmful effects of vaccination.

After that, the vaccine must be evaluated in terms of its effectiveness and its potential for complicating pregnancy. There is little information available on harmful effects on the developing fetus from vaccines. In general, killed vaccines are safe.

Live-measles vaccine should never be given to a pregnant woman. The only immunizing agents recommended for use during pregnancy is the DPT vaccine. MMR vaccine should be given before pregnancy or after delivery. A pregnant woman should receive primary vaccination against polio only if her risk of exposure to the disease is high; only inactivated polio vaccine should be used.

You Should also Know

ᨔ Chorionic Villus Sampling

Chorionic villus sampling (CVS) is a test used to detect genetic abnormalities before delivery. Sampling is done early in pregnancy, usually between the 9th week and the 11th week.

CVS is done for many reasons. The test helps identify problems related to genetic defects, such as Down syndrome.

This test offers an advantage over amniocentesis because it is done much earlier in pregnancy; results are available in about 1 week. If the pregnancy will be terminated, it can be done earlier and may carry fewer risks to the woman.

Chorionic villus sampling involves placing an instrument through the cervix or abdomen to remove fetal tissue from the placenta. There is a small risk of miscarriage after this procedure, so the test should be performed only by someone experienced in the technique.

If your doctor recommends you have CVS, ask about its risks. The risk of miscarriage is small—between 1% and 2%.

✧ *Fetoscopy*

Fetoscopy provides a view of the baby and placenta inside your uterus. In some cases, abnormalities and problems can be detected and corrected.

The goal of fetoscopy is to correct a defect before the problem worsens, which could prevent a fetus from developing into a normal baby. A doctor can see the problem more clearly with fetoscopy than with ultrasound.

The test is done by placing a scope, like the one used in laparoscopy or arthroscopy, through the abdomen. The procedure is similar to amniocentesis, but the fetoscope is larger than the needle used for amniocentesis.

If your doctor suggests fetoscopy to you, discuss possible risks, advantages and disadvantages of the procedure with him or her. The test should be done only by someone experienced in the technique. Risk of miscarriage is 3% to 4% with this procedure. It is not available everywhere.

> *Tip for Week 10*
> It's common for your breasts to tingle and to feel sore early in pregnancy. In fact, it may be one of the first signs of pregnancy.

✒ *Dieting during Pregnancy?*

Don't diet to lose weight during pregnancy! You should be gaining weight now; it can be harmful to your baby if you don't. As I've stated before, a woman of normal weight can expect to gain between 25 and 35 pounds while pregnant. Watching your weight gain gives your doctor an indication of your well-being and that of your baby.

Pregnancy is not a time to experiment with different diets or cut down on calories. However, this doesn't mean you have the go-ahead to eat anything you want, any time you want.

Exercise and a proper nutrition plan, without "junk food," will help you manage your weight. Be smart about food choices. It's true you're eating for two—however, you must eat wisely for both of you!

Week 11

Age of Fetus ✈ 9 Weeks

How Big Is Your Baby?

By this week, the crown-to-rump length of your baby is 1.75 to 2.4 inches (44 to 60mm). Fetal weight is about 0.3 ounce (8g). Your baby is about the size of a large lime.

How Big Are You?

While big changes are occurring in your baby, changes are probably happening more slowly with you. You are almost at the end of the first trimester; your uterus has been growing along with the fetus inside it. It is almost big enough to fill your pelvis and may be felt in your lower abdomen, above the middle of your pubic bone.

You won't be able to feel your baby moving yet. If you think you feel your baby move at this time, you either have gas or are further along in your pregnancy than you thought.

How Your Baby Is Growing and Developing

Fetal growth is rapid now. The crown-to-rump length of your baby doubles in the next 3 weeks. As you can see in the illustration on page 103, the head is almost half the baby's entire length. As the head extends (uncurls or tips backward toward the spine), the chin rises from the chest and the neck develops and lengthens. Fingernails appear.

External genitalia are beginning to show distinguishing features. Development of the fetus into a male or female is complete in another 3 weeks. If a miscarriage occurs after this point, it may be possible to tell if it is male or female.

All embryos begin life looking very much the same, as far as outward appearances are concerned. Whether the embryo develops into a male or female is determined by the genetic information contained in the embryo.

Changes in You

Some women notice changes in their hair, fingernails or toenails during pregnancy. This doesn't happen to everyone, but if it happens to you, don't worry about it. Some fortunate women notice an increase in hair and nail growth during pregnancy. Others find they lose some hair during this time.

Some doctors believe these changes occur during pregnancy because of increased circulation throughout your body. Others credit the hormonal changes occurring in you. Still others explain these differences with a change in "phase" of the growth cycle of the hair or nails.

In any event, these differences are rarely permanent. There is little or nothing you can do about them.

Actual size

By week 11 of gestation (fetal age—9 weeks),
fingernails are beginning to appear.

How Your Actions Affect Your Baby's Development

ᕦ *Traveling during Pregnancy*

Pregnant women frequently ask whether travel during pregnancy can hurt their baby. If your pregnancy is uncomplicated and you are not at high risk, travel is usually acceptable. Ask your doctor about any travel you are considering before making firm plans or buying tickets.

Whether you travel by car, bus, train or airplane, it's wise to get up and walk at least every 2 hours. Regular visits to the bathroom may take care of this requirement.

The biggest risk of traveling during pregnancy is development of a complication while you are away from those who know your medical and pregnancy history. If you do decide to take a trip, be sensible in your planning. Don't overdo it. Take it easy!

You Should also Know

∾ Ultrasound in Pregnancy

By this point, you may have discussed ultrasound with your doctor. Or you may already have had an ultrasound test. Ultrasound (also called *sonography* or *sonogram*) is one of our most valuable methods for evaluating a pregnancy. Although doctors, hospitals and insurance companies (yes, they get involved in this, too) don't agree as to when ultrasound should be done or if every pregnant woman should have an ultrasound test during pregnancy, it definitely has its place. The test has proved useful in improving the outcome in pregnancy. It is a noninvasive, safe test, and there are no known risks associated with it.

Ultrasound involves the use of high-frequency soundwaves made by applying an alternating current to a transducer. A lubricant is placed on the skin to improve contact with the transducer. The transducer passes over the abdomen above the uterus. Soundwaves are projected from the transducer through the abdomen, into the pelvis. Soundwaves bounce off tissues they are directed toward and back to the transducer. The reflection of soundwaves can be compared to "radar" used by airplanes or ships.

Different tissues of the body reflect ultrasound signals differently, and we can distinguish among them. Motion can be distinguished, so we can detect motion of the baby or parts of the baby, such as the heart. With ultrasound, a fetal heart can be seen beating as early as 5 or 6 weeks into the pregnancy.

Ultrasound can detect fetal motion. Your baby's body and limbs can be seen moving as early as 7 weeks of embryonic growth (9th week of pregnancy).

You will be asked to drink a lot of water before an ultrasound examination. If you have had an ultrasound exam during a previous pregnancy, one of the main things you may remember is how uncomfortable you were with your bladder full to overflowing!

—— Ultrasound ——

Your doctor can use ultrasound in many ways in relation to your pregnancy. These include:

- helping in the early identification of pregnancy
- showing the size and rate of growth of the embryo or fetus
- identifying the presence of two or more fetuses
- measuring the fetal head, abdomen or femur to determine the stage of pregnancy
- identifying some fetuses with Down syndrome
- identifying fetal abnormalities, such as hydrocephalus and microcephaly
- identifying abnormalities of internal organs, such as the kidneys or bladder
- measuring the amount of amniotic fluid, to help determine fetal well-being
- identifying the location, size and maturity of the placenta
- identifying placental abnormalities
- identifying uterine abnormalities or tumors
- detecting an IUD
- differentiating between miscarriage, ectopic pregnancy and normal pregnancy
- in connection with amniocentesis, percutaneous blood-cord sampling (PUBS) and chorionic villus sampling (CVS), to select the correct place to position the needle for each test

——— ✳ ———

Your bladder is in front of your uterus. When your bladder is empty, your uterus is harder to see because it is farther down inside the pelvic bones. Bones disrupt ultrasound signals and make the picture harder to interpret. With your bladder full, your uterus rises out of the pelvis and can be seen more easily. The bladder acts as a window to look through to see the uterus and the fetus inside.

The ultrasound vaginal probe, also called the *transvaginal ultrasound*, can be used in early pregnancy for a better view of the baby and placenta. A probe is placed inside the vagina, and the pregnancy is viewed from this angle. You don't have to have your bladder full for this one!

Some couples ask for ultrasound to determine whether they are carrying a boy or girl. If the baby is in a good position and it is old enough for the genitals to have developed and they can be seen clearly, determination *may* be possible. However, many doctors feel this reason alone is not a good reason to do an ultrasound exam. Discuss it with your doctor. Understand ultrasound is a test, and tests can occasionally be wrong.

✍ Physical Injury during Pregnancy

Trauma (physical injury) occurs in about 6% to 7% of all pregnancies. Accidents involving motor vehicles account for 66% of these cases; falls and assaults account for the remaining 34%. More than 90% of these are minor injuries.

If you experience trauma during pregnancy, you may be taken care of by emergency-medicine personnel, trauma surgeons, general surgeons and your obstetrician.

Most experts recommend observing a pregnant woman for a few hours after an accident. This provides adequate time to monitor the baby. Longer monitoring may be necessary in a more serious accident.

Tip for Week 11
You may be able to get a "picture" of your baby before birth from an ultrasound test. Some facilities can even make a videotape for you. Ask about it before the test, if you're scheduled to have one.

✂ *Dental Care*

Don't avoid your dentist or ignore your teeth while you're pregnant. It's a good idea to see your dentist at least once during pregnancy. Tell your dentist you're pregnant. If you need dental work, postpone it until after the first 12 weeks, if possible. You may not be able to wait if you have an infection. An untreated infection could be harmful to you and your baby.

Antibiotics or pain medications may be necessary. If you need medication, consult with your physician before taking anything.

Be careful with regard to anesthesia for dental work during pregnancy. Avoid general anesthesia. If general anesthesia is necessary, make sure it's administered by an experienced anesthesiologist who knows you are pregnant.

Sally called the office because she had problems with bleeding gums. She was sure something was wrong with her teeth. I told her that a pregnant woman's gums can change during pregnancy. Gums may be affected by the hormones of pregnancy and become sensitive and bleed more easily. I advised Sally to floss and to brush regularly, and that using mouthwash and gargles was also OK.

✂ *Bringing Children to an Office Visit*

Some women bring their children with them to an office appointment. Most office personnel don't mind if you bring your children with you occasionally. They understand it may not always be possible to find someone to watch your children. However, if you are having problems or have a lot to discuss with your doctor, don't bring your child.

Think twice before bringing your children to the office. If a child is sick, has just gotten over chickenpox or is getting a cold, leave him or her at home. Don't expose everyone else in the waiting room.

Some women like to bring one child at a time to a visit if they have more than one child. That makes it special for you and for them. Crying or complaining children can create a difficult situation. Ask your doctor when it's good to bring family members with you before you come in with them.

Week 12

Age of Fetus ✑ 10 Weeks

Your baby weighs between 0.3 and 0.5 ounce (8 to 14g), and crown-to-rump length is almost 2.5 inches (61mm). As you can see on page 110, your baby's size has almost doubled in the past 3 weeks! Length of the baby is a better measure at this time than fetal weight.

By the end of 12 weeks, your uterus is too large to remain completely in your pelvis. You may feel it above your pubic bone (pubic symphysis). The uterus has a remarkable ability to grow while you're pregnant. During pregnancy, it grows upward to fill the pelvis and abdomen, and returns to its usual size within a few weeks after delivery.

Before pregnancy, your uterus is almost solid. It holds about 0.3 ounce (10ml) or less. The uterus changes during pregnancy into a comparatively thin-walled, muscular container big enough to hold the fetus, placenta and amniotic fluid. The uterus increases its capacity 500 to 1000 times during pregnancy!

The weight of the uterus also changes. When your baby is born, your uterus weighs almost 40 ounces (1100g) compared to 2.5 ounces (70g) before pregnancy.

The uterine wall grows during the first few months of pregnancy due to hormonal stimulation by estrogen and progesterone. Later in your pregnancy, the growth of the baby and the placenta stretch and thin the uterine wall.

How Your Baby Is Growing and Developing

Few, if any, structures in the baby are formed after this week in pregnancy. However, the structures already formed continue to grow and to develop.

At your 12-week visit (or close to that time), you'll probably be able to hear your baby's heart beat! It can be heard with *doppler,* a special listening machine (not a stethoscope). It magnifies the sound of your baby's heartbeat so you can hear it.

The skeletal system now has centers of bone formation (ossification) in most bones. Fingers and toes have separated, and nails are growing. Scattered rudiments of hair appear on the body. External genitalia are beginning to show distinct signs of male or female sex characteristics.

The digestive system (small intestine) is capable of producing contractions that push food through the bowels. It is also able to absorb glucose (sugar).

At the base of your baby's brain, the pituitary gland is beginning to make many hormones. Hormones are chemicals that are made in one part of the body, but their action is exerted on another part of the body.

Other things are also happening. The fetal nervous system has developed further. Your baby is moving inside your uterus, but

Your baby is growing rapidly. It has doubled in
length in the last 3 weeks.

you probably won't feel it for a while yet. Stimulating the fetus in
certain spots may cause it to squint, open its mouth and move
fingers or toes.

The amount of amniotic fluid is increasing. Total volume is
now about 1.5 ounces (50ml). At this time, the fluid is similar to
maternal plasma (the noncellular portion of your blood), except it
contains much less protein.

Changes in You

You are probably starting to feel better than you have for most of your pregnancy. At this point, morning sickness often begins to improve. You aren't extremely big and are probably still quite comfortable.

You may be wearing maternity clothes. If it's your first pregnancy, you may still be wearing regular clothes. If you've had other pregnancies, you may start to show earlier and to feel more comfortable in looser clothing.

You may be getting bigger in places besides your tummy. Your breasts are probably getting larger. They may have been sore for some time. You may also notice weight gain in your hips, legs and at your sides.

✺ Skin Changes

Your skin may change during pregnancy. In many women, skin along the midline of the abdomen becomes markedly darker or pigmented with a brown-black color. It forms a vertical line called the *linea nigra.*

Occasionally irregular brown patches of varying size appear on the face and neck called *chloasma* or *mask of pregnancy.* These disappear or get lighter after delivery. Oral contraceptives may cause similar pigmentation changes.

Pamela was concerned with a red rash on her neck, face, upper chest and arms. After examining her, I told her she had vascular spiders (also called *telangiectasias* or *angiomas*). They are small, red elevations on the skin, with branches extending outward. The condition develops in about 65% of white women and 10% of black women during pregnancy. She was relieved when I reassured her it wasn't serious.

A similar condition is redness of the palms, called *palmar erythema.* It is seen in 65% of white women and 35% of black women.

Vascular spiders and palmar erythema often occur together. Symptoms are temporary and disappear shortly after delivery. The occurrence of either condition is probably caused by high levels of estrogen during pregnancy.

How Your Actions Affect Your Baby's Development

Some women have the false notion they can eat all they want during pregnancy. Don't fall into this trap! First, it's unhealthy for you and your baby if you gain a great deal of weight during pregnancy. It makes carrying your baby more uncomfortable, and delivery may be more difficult. Second, it will be hard to shed the extra pounds after pregnancy. After their baby is born, most women are anxious to return to "normal" clothes and to look the way they did before pregnancy. Having to deal with extra weight can interfere with reaching this goal.

✈ Junk Food

Is junk food your kind of food? Do you eat it several times a day? Pregnancy is the time to break that habit!

Now that you're pregnant, your dietary habits affect someone besides just yourself—your growing baby. If you're used to skipping breakfast, getting something "from a machine" for lunch, then eating dinner at a fast-food restaurant, it could be harmful to your pregnancy.

What and when you eat becomes more important when you realize how your actions affect your baby. Proper nutrition takes some planning on your part, but you can do it.

If you work, take healthful foods that you like with you for lunches and snacks. Stay away from fast food and junk food.

✈ Late-Night Snacks

Late-night, nutritious snacks are beneficial for some women. However, for many women, snacking at night is unnecessary. If you're used to ice cream or other goodies before bed, you may pay for it during pregnancy with excessive weight gain. Food in your stomach late at night may also cause you more distress if you suffer from heartburn or nausea and vomiting.

You Should also Know

↬ *Fifth Disease*

Fifth disease, also called *parvo virus B19,* was the fifth disease to be described with a certain kind of rash. It is a mild, moderately contagious airborne infection. Fifth disease spreads easily through groups, such as classrooms or day-care centers.

The rash looks like reddened skin caused by a slap. The reddening fades and recurs, and lasts from 2 to 34 days. There is no treatment.

This virus is important during pregnancy because it interferes with the production of red blood cells in the woman and the fetus. If you believe you have been exposed to fifth disease during pregnancy, contact your healthcare provider. A blood test can determine whether you have had the virus. If you haven't, your healthcare provider can monitor you to detect fetal problems. Some fetal problems can be dealt with before the baby is born.

↬ *Auto Safety during Pregnancy*

Women often ask me about driving and about using seat belts and shoulder harnesses during pregnancy. Wearing safety restraints dramatically decreases the incidence of injury in an accident. More than 50,000 deaths and 2-million injuries are directly related to auto accidents every year. Wearing a seat belt and shoulder harness can decrease these losses.

——— The Proper Way to Wear a Lap Belt ——— and Shoulder Harness

There is a proper way for you to wear a seat belt during pregnancy. Place the lap-belt portion under your abdomen and across your upper thighs. It should be as snug as is comfortably possible. The shoulder belt should also be snug but comfortable. Adjust your position so the belt crosses your shoulder without cutting into your neck. Position the shoulder belt between your breasts. This belt should *not* be slipped off your shoulder. If it's a long trip, adjust the belt as needed for comfort. (For an illustration, see page 190.)

——— ✳ ———

Many women have told me they believe using a safety restraint might be harmful to their pregnancy. Here are some excuses I commonly hear (and my answers) about using seat belts and shoulder harnesses in pregnancy.

"Using a safety belt will hurt my baby."

There is no evidence their use will increase the chance of fetal or uterine injury. Your chance of survival with a seat belt is better than without one. Your survival is important to your unborn baby.

"I don't want to be trapped in my car if there is a fire."

Few automobile accidents result in fires. Even if a fire did occur, you could probably undo the restraint and escape if you were conscious. Ejection from a car accounts for about 25% of all deaths in automobile accidents. Seat-belt use prevents this.

"I'm a good driver."

Defensive driving helps but doesn't prevent an accident.

"I don't need to use a safety belt; I'm just going a short distance."

Most injuries occur within 25 miles of home.

A few studies have been done on pregnant women who used seat belts. In one California study, only 14% of all pregnant women used seat belts compared to 30% of nonpregnant women. We know the lap/shoulder seat-belt system is safe to wear during pregnancy, so buckle up for you *and* your baby.

✧ Infant-Restraint Seats

It isn't too early to think about infant- and child-restraint systems. Some people believe they can hold their baby safely in an accident. Others say their child won't sit still in a restraint.

In an accident, an unrestrained child becomes a missile. The force of a crash can literally pull a child out of an adult's arms! One study showed *more than 30 deaths a year* occur to unrestrained infants going home from the hospital after birth. In nearly all cases, if the baby had been in an approved infant-restraint system, he or she would have survived the accident.

Start early to teach your child safety. If you always place your child in a restraint system in the car, it will become a natural thing to do. You can increase your child's acceptance of a restraint if you wear seat belts, too!

Many states now have infant-restraint laws. Call your local police department or hospital for further information.

Many hospitals require you to take your baby home from the hospital in an approved infant-restraint system. If you want additional information, a pediatrician or the American Academy of Pediatrics can provide a list of safe child- and infant-restraint systems. Consumer magazines rate them quite frequently. Check your local library.

Tip for Week 12

If you have diarrhea that doesn't go away in 24 hours, or if it keeps returning, call your doctor. You can take milk of magnesia for 24 hours to help deal with the problem, but don't self-medicate for longer than this time.

Week 13

Age of Fetus ↝ 11 Weeks

How Big Is Your Baby?

Your baby is growing rapidly! Its crown-to-rump length is 2.6 to 3.1 inches (65 to 78mm), and it weighs between 0.5 and 0.7 ounce (13 to 20g). It is about the size of a peach.

How Big Are You?

Your uterus has grown quite a bit. You can probably feel its upper edge above the pubic bone in the lowest part of your abdomen, about 4 inches (10cm) below your bellybutton. At 12 to 13 weeks, your uterus fills your pelvis and starts growing upward into your abdomen. It feels like a soft, smooth ball.

You have probably gained some weight by now. If morning sickness has been a problem and you've had a hard time eating, you may not have gained much weight. As you feel better and as your baby rapidly starts to gain weight, you'll gain weight.

How Your Baby Is Growing and Developing

Fetal growth is particularly striking from now through about 24 weeks of pregnancy. The baby has doubled in length since the 7th week. Changes in fetal weight have also been tremendous during the last 8 to 10 weeks of your pregnancy.

One interesting change is the relative slowdown in the growth of your baby's head compared to the rest of its body. In week 13, the head is about half the crown-to-rump length. By week 21, the head is about one-third of the baby's body. At birth, your baby's head is only one-fourth the size of its body. Fetal body growth accelerates as fetal head growth slows.

Your baby's face is beginning to look more humanlike. Eyes, which started out on the side of the head, move closer together on the face. The ears come to lie in their normal position on the sides of the head.

External genitalia have developed enough so a male can be distinguished from a female if examined outside the womb.

Intestines initially develop within a large swelling in the umbilical cord outside the fetal body. About this time, they withdraw into the fetal abdominal cavity. If this doesn't occur and the intestines remain outside the fetal abdomen at birth, a condition called an *omphalocele* occurs. It is rare (occurs in 1 of 10,000 births). The condition can usually be repaired with surgery, and babies do well afterward.

Changes in You

You are losing your waist! Clothing fits snugly. It's time to start wearing loose-fitting clothing.

∾ **Stretch Marks**

Stretch marks, called *striae distensae,* are seen often and in varying degrees during pregnancy. They may appear early in your pregnancy, usually on the abdomen, breasts, and hips or buttocks. After pregnancy, they may fade to the same color as the rest of your skin, but they won't go away.

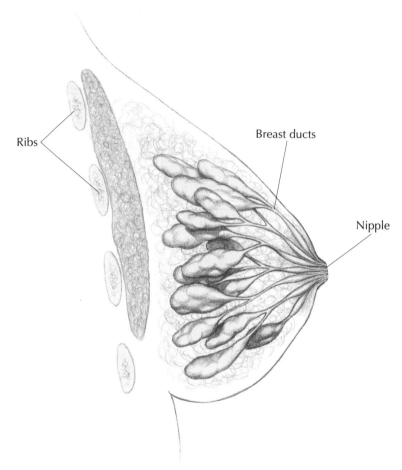

Ribs

Breast ducts

Nipple

Development of the maternal breast by end of
the first trimester (13 weeks pregnancy).

Hillary was concerned about stretch marks that had begun to appear on her abdomen and breasts. She wanted to know what to do about them. I told her there is no known prevention or cure for stretch marks. Women have tried many kinds of lotions with ingredients ranging from lanolin to aloe vera to mineral oil. It doesn't hurt to try lotions, but it probably won't make much difference.

If you use steroid creams, such as hydrocortisone or topicort, to treat stretch marks during pregnancy, you absorb some of the steroid into your system. The substance can then pass to your developing baby. Don't use steroid creams during pregnancy without first checking with your doctor. (See Week 26 for additional information.)

——— Itching ———

Itching *(pruritus gravidarum)* is a common symptom during pregnancy. There are no bumps or lesions on the skin; it just itches. Nearly 20% of all pregnant women suffer from itching, usually in the last weeks of pregnancy, but it can occur at any time. It may occur with each pregnancy and may also appear when you use oral contraceptives. The condition doesn't present any risk to you or your baby.

Treatment for the itching consists of antihistamines or cooling lotions containing menthol or camphor. Often no treatment is needed.

——— ✳ ———

❧ *Changes in Your Breasts*

You have probably noticed your breasts are changing. See the illustration on page 118. The mammary gland (another name for the breast) got its name from the Latin term for breast—*mamma.*

Your breast is made up of glands, connective tissue to provide support and fatty tissue to provide protection. Milk-producing sacs connect with the ducts leading to the nipple.

Before pregnancy, the average breast weighs about 7 ounces (200g). During pregnancy, breasts increase in size and weight. Near the end of pregnancy, each breast may weigh 14 to 28 ounces (400 to 800g). During nursing, each breast may weigh 28 ounces (800g) or more!

Size and shape of women's breasts vary greatly. Breast tissue usually projects under the arm. Glands that make up the breast open into ducts in the nipple. Each nipple contains nerve endings, muscle fibers, sebaceous glands, sweat glands and about 20 milk ducts.

The nipple is surrounded by the areola, a circular, pigmented area. Before pregnancy, the areola is usually pink. It turns brown or red-brown and enlarges during pregnancy and lactation. A darkened areola may act as a visual signal for the breastfeeding infant.

Breasts undergo many changes during pregnancy. In the early weeks, a common symptom of pregnancy is tingling or soreness of the breasts. After about 8 weeks of pregnancy, your breasts may grow larger and become nodular or lumpy as glands and ducts inside the breasts grow and develop. As your breasts change during pregnancy, you may notice veins appear just beneath the skin.

During the second trimester, a thin yellow fluid called *colostrum* begins to form. It can sometimes be expressed from the nipple by gentle massage. If your breasts have grown, you may notice stretch marks on your breasts similar to those on your abdomen.

Mammary glands begin to develop in the 6-week-old embryo. By the time of birth, milk ducts are present. After birth, a newborn's breasts may be swollen and may even secrete a small amount of milk. This can occur in both male and female infants and is caused by the secretion of estrogen.

How Your Actions Affect Your Baby's Development

⌁ Working during Pregnancy

Today, many women work outside the home, and many continue to work during pregnancy. It is common for employers and patients to ask doctors about work and pregnancy.

"Is it safe to work while I'm pregnant?"

"Can I work my entire pregnancy?"

"Am I in danger of harming my baby if I work?"

More than half of all women work or are seeking work. In the United States, more than 1-million babies are born to women who have been employed at some time during pregnancy. These women have understandable concerns about safety and occupational health.

⌁ Legislation that May Affect You

The U.S. Pregnancy Discrimination Act prohibits job discrimination on the basis of pregnancy or childbirth. It states pregnancy and related conditions should be treated the same as any other disability or medical condition. A doctor may be asked to certify a pregnant woman can work without endangering herself or her pregnancy. Pregnancy-related disability comes from:

- the pregnancy itself
- complications of pregnancy, such as pre-eclampsia, premature labor or other medical problems
- job exposures to chemicals, inhalants, gases, solvents or radiation

The Family and Medical Leave Act was passed in 1993. If you or your husband have spent at least 1 year working for a company, the law allows each of you to take up to 12 weeks of unpaid leave in any 12-month period for the birth of your baby. Leave may be taken intermittently or all at once.

Under the law, you must be restored to an equivalent position with equal benefits when you return. However, the act applies only to companies that employ 50 or more people within a 75-mile radius. States may allow an employer to deny job restoration to those in the top 10% compensation bracket.

At this time, about half the states have passed state legislation that deals with parental leave. Some states provide disability insurance if you have to leave work because of pregnancy or birth.

In Canada, unpaid parental leave is available. The length of time you may take off from work varies from province to province.

——— State or Provincial Laws and Parental Leave ———

State laws about parental leave differ, so check with your state labor office or consult the personnel director in your company's human resources department. You may also receive a summary of state laws on family leave, available from:

The Women's Bureau Publications
U.S. Department of Labor
Box EX
200 Constitution Avenue, NW
Washington, DC 20210

In Canada, contact the Human Resources office for information:

Human Resources
Tele-Center of Canada
(416) 730-1211
(800) 227-9914

——— ✳ ———

✍ Risks If You Work during Pregnancy

It may be difficult to know the exact risk of a particular job. In most cases, we don't have enough information to know all the specific substances that can harm a developing baby.

The goal is to minimize the risk to the mother and baby while still enabling the woman to work. A normal woman with a normal job should be able to work throughout her pregnancy. However, she may need to modify or to change her job somewhat. For example, she may need to spend less time standing. Studies show that women who stand in the same position for prolonged periods are more likely to give birth to premature babies and babies with low birth weight.

Work with your doctor and your employer. If problems arise, such as premature labor or bleeding, listen to your doctor. If bed rest at home is suggested, follow your doctor's advice. As your pregnancy progresses, you may have to work fewer hours or do lighter work. Be flexible. It doesn't help you or your baby if you "wear yourself out" and make complications of pregnancy worse.

You Should also Know

✍ Caffeine Use during Pregnancy?

Caffeine is a central-nervous-system stimulant found in many beverages and foods, including coffee, tea, cola drinks and chocolate. It is also found in some medications, particularly diet aids and headache medications. To date, no benefits to you or your unborn baby have been found with the use of caffeine.

As little as 4 cups of coffee (800mg of caffeine) a day have been associated with a decreased birth weight and

> **Tip for Week 13**
> When cutting down on caffeine during pregnancy, read labels. More than 200 foods, beverages and over-the-counter medications contain caffeine!

a smaller head size in newborns. Some researchers believe there is an association between caffeine use and miscarriage or premature labor.

Caffeine crosses the placenta to the baby. It can affect calcium metabolism of the mother and the baby. Your caffeine consumption may also increase the chances of breathing problems in your newborn. Caffeine passes to breast milk, which can cause irritability and sleeplessness in a breastfed baby. An infant metabolizes caffeine slower than an adult, and caffeine can collect in the infant.

Effects of caffeine on you during pregnancy may include irritability, sleeplessness and jitters. Smoking may compound the stimulant effect of caffeine.

Limit the amount of caffeine you consume. Read labels on over-the-counter medications for caffeine. Eliminate as much as you can from your diet. It's healthy for your baby, and you'll probably feel better, too.

ᴄ⁓ *Nursing with Silicone Breast Implants*

Women have nursed with breast implants. Implants may make it more difficult to nurse. Doctors don't agree as to whether it is safe or possibly harmful to nurse with implants. If you are concerned, discuss the matter with your doctor; ask him or her for the latest information.

ᴄ⁓ *Silicone Breast Disease*

Research continues into silicone breast implants and how they affect women. In 1995, the American College of Rheumatology issued a statement that there was no demonstrable risk between silicone breast implants and connective-tissue diseases or rheumatic disease. In contrast, other studies have shown a small but significant risk of developing a connective-tissue disorder with silicone breast implants.

Some labs in the U.S. offer diagnostic tests to screen for silicone breast disease. However, none of these tests have been approved by the Food and Drug Administration. Check with your physician if you are concerned.

Week 14

Age of Fetus ⇝ 12 Weeks

The crown-to-rump length is 3.2 to 4.1 inches (80 to 93mm). Your baby is about the size of your fist and weighs almost 1 ounce (25g).

Maternity clothes may be a "must" by now. Some women try to get by for a while by not buttoning or zipping their pants all the way or by using rubber bands or safety pins to avoid having to wear maternity clothing. Others wear their partner's clothing, but that usually works for only a short time. You're going to get even bigger. You'll enjoy your pregnancy more and feel more comfortable with clothing that fits comfortably and provides you room to grow.

How your body responds to this growth is influenced by previous pregnancies and the changes your body experienced then. Your skin and muscles stretched to accommodate your uterus, placenta and baby, and that changed them permanently. Skin and muscles may give way faster to accommodate your growing uterus and baby. This means you show sooner and feel bigger.

How Your Baby Is Growing and Developing

As you can see in the illustration on page 126, by this week your baby's ears have moved from the neck to the sides of the head. Eyes have been moving gradually to the front of the face from the side of the head. The neck continues to get longer, and the chin no longer rests on the chest.

Sexual development continues. The external genitalia are more developed, and it is becoming easier to determine male from female by looking at external genitalia.

Changes in You

✂ Skin Tags and Moles

Pregnancy can make skin tags and moles change and/or grow. Skin tags are small tags of skin that may appear for the first time or may grow larger during pregnancy. Moles may appear for the first time during pregnancy, or existing moles may grow larger and darken during pregnancy. If a mole changes, it must be checked. If you notice any changes, show it to your doctor!

How Your Actions Affect Your Baby's Development

✂ X-Rays, CT Scans and MRIs during Pregnancy

Some women are concerned about tests that use radiation during pregnancy. Can they hurt the baby? Can you have them at any time in pregnancy?

Your baby continues to change. Ears and eyes move to a more normal position by this week.

I remember getting a call from Lucy, who was in the emergency room. She had fallen in her driveway and hurt her ankle. The doctors wanted to do an X-ray; she wouldn't let them until she checked with me first. There are valid medical reasons for

X-rays, but in each case, the need must be weighed against the risk to a pregnancy. After talking with the emergency-room personnel, we determined Lucy could have her ankle X-rayed if her abdomen was shielded with a lead apron.

No known amount of radiation is safe for a developing baby. Dangers to your baby include an increased risk of mutations and an increased risk of cancer later in life. Some doctors believe the only safe amount of X-ray during pregnancy is *none*.

Researchers are becoming more aware of the potential dangers of radiation to a developing fetus. At present, they believe the fetus appears to be at greatest risk between 8 and 15 weeks gestation (between the fetal age of 6 weeks and 13 weeks).

Problems such as pneumonia or appendicitis can and do occur in pregnant women and may require an X-ray to treat properly. Discuss the need for X-rays with your doctor. It is your responsibility to let your doctor and others involved in your health care know you are pregnant or may be pregnant before you undergo *any* medical test. It's easier to deal with the questions of safety and risk before a test is performed.

If you have an X-ray or series of X-rays, then discover you are pregnant, talk to your doctor about the possible risk to your baby. He or she will be able to advise you.

Computerized tomographic scans, also called *CT scans,* are a form of very specialized X-ray. This technique combines X-ray with computer analysis. Many researchers believe the amount of radiation received by a fetus from a CT scan is much lower than that received from a regular X-ray. However, these tests should be undertaken with caution until we know more about the effects even this small amount of radiation has on a developing fetus.

Magnetic resonance imaging, also called *MRI,* is another diagnostic tool widely used today. At this time, no harmful effects in pregnancy have been reported from the use of MRI. However, it is probably best to avoid MRI during the first trimester of pregnancy.

ૐ *Dental Emergencies*

Dental emergencies do occur; emergencies you might face include root canal, tooth extraction, a large cavity, an abscessed tooth or problems resulting from an accident or injury. Any of these emergencies can occur during pregnancy. It might be unwise to postpone treatment until after your baby is born.

> **Tip for Week 14**
>
> If you must have dental work or diagnostic tests, tell your dentist or your physician you are pregnant so extra care can be taken with you.

If you have a dental problem, contact your dentist *and* your physician before doing anything else. It may be helpful for your dentist and doctor to talk before any decisions are made.

Dental X-rays are necessary sometimes and can be done during pregnancy. Your abdomen must be shielded with a lead apron before X-rays are taken. If possible, wait until after the end of the first trimester to have any dental work done.

Avoid gas or general anesthesia for a dental procedure during pregnancy. Local anesthetics are OK, and so are many antibiotics and pain medications. Be sure to consult your healthcare provider before taking any medications.

A serious dental problem, such as an abscess, must be treated. Problems that could result from not treating it are more serious than the risks you might be exposed to with treatment.

You Should also Know

⌁ *Partner Involvement*

Some men get jealous of all the attention given to the woman and her developing baby. New maternity clothes, baby toys and equipment, and conversations with friends or family often center around the pregnancy, making him feel left out. Make him feel he is an important part of your pregnancy. It's important to involve your partner in the miracle that is happening. He can be a big support to you. It helps if you make him feel part of what is going on. Take him to your prenatal appointments. Ask him to help you plan your meals.

✍ *Taking Others to Your Doctor Visits*

Take your partner with you to an appointment with your doctor. It's nice for your partner and doctor to meet before labor begins. Maybe your mother or the other grandmother-to-be would like to go with you to hear their grandchild's heartbeat. Or you may want to take a tape recorder, and record the heartbeat for others to hear. Things have changed since your mother carried you; many grandmothers-to-be enjoy this type of visit.

It's a good idea to wait until you have heard your baby's heartbeat before bringing other people. You don't always hear it the first time, and this can be frustrating and disappointing.

Week 15

Age of Fetus ᧦ 13 Weeks

The fetal crown-to-rump length by this week of pregnancy is 4.1 to 4.5 inches (93 to 103mm). The fetus weighs about 1.75 ounces (50g). It's close to the size of a softball.

You can easily tell you're pregnant by the changes in your lower abdomen, which alter the way your clothes fit. You may be able to feel your uterus about 3 or 4 inches (7.6 to 10cm) below your bellybutton (also called the *umbilicus* or *navel*).

Pregnancy may not be obvious to other people when you wear regular street clothes. But it may become obvious if you start wearing maternity clothes or put on a swimming suit.

It's still a little early to feel movement, although you should feel your baby move in the next few weeks!

How Your Baby Is Growing and Developing

Your baby's rapid growth continues. Its skin is very thin. Blood vessels can be seen through the skin at this point in its development. Fine hair called *lanugo hair* covers the baby's body.

By this time, your baby may be sucking its thumb. This has been seen with ultrasound examination. Eyes continue to move to the front of the face but are still widely separated.

Ears continue to develop externally. As you can see in the illustration on page 132, they now look more like normal ears. In fact, your baby looks more human all the time.

Bones already formed are getting harder and retaining calcium *(ossifying)* very rapidly. If an X-ray were performed at this time, the baby's skeleton would be visible.

↝ Triple-Screen Test

Tests are now available that go beyond alpha-fetoprotein testing in helping your healthcare provider determine if you might be carrying a child with Down syndrome. With the triple-screen test, your alpha-fetoprotein level is checked, along with the amounts of human chorionic gonadotropin (HCG; a pregnancy hormone) and unconjugated estriol (a form of estrogen produced by the placenta).

The levels of these three chemicals in your blood may indicate the presence of Down syndrome. For older mothers, the detection rate of the problem is higher than 60%, with a false-positive rate of nearly 25%.

If you have an abnormal result with a triple-screen test, an ultrasound and amniocentesis are usually recommended.

Changes in You

↝ Pap Smear during Pregnancy

During your first visit to your doctor, you probably had a Pap smear. A Pap smear is usually done at the beginning of pregnancy. By now, the result is back, and you have discussed it with your doctor, particularly if it was abnormal.

By week 15 of pregnancy (fetal age—13 weeks), your baby may suck its thumb. Eyes are at the front of the face but are still widely separated.

The Pap smear (short for *Papanicolaou smear*) is a screening test done at the time of a pelvic exam. It identifies cancerous or precancerous cells coming from the cervix, which is located at the top of the vagina. This test has contributed to a significant decrease in mortality from cervical cancer because of early detection and treatment.

❧ An Abnormal Pap Smear

If you have had an abnormal Pap smear or have been treated for an abnormal Pap test, continue to get checked as your doctor suggests.

Pap smears are screening tests. If a test is abnormal, findings must be verified and treatment decided upon by your doctor. If you are not pregnant, most doctors will suggest a biopsy of the cervix if your Pap smear is abnormal.

An abnormal Pap smear during pregnancy must be handled individually. When abnormal cells are "not too bad" (premalignant or not as serious), it may be possible to watch them during pregnancy with colposcopy or Pap smears; biopsies are not usually done at this time. The cervix bleeds easily during pregnancy because of changes in circulation. This situation must be handled very carefully.

❧ When Is a Biopsy Necessary?

A biopsy of the cervix is done in your doctor's office, without anesthesia, with colposcopy. Colposcopy is a procedure that uses an instrument similar to a pair of binoculars or a microscope to look at the cervix. This enables your doctor to see where abnormal areas are so biopsies can be taken. Most obstetricians/gynecologists are able to do this procedure without sending you to a specialist.

A biopsy provides a better idea of the nature and extent of the problem. If there is a possibility that abnormal cells could spread to other parts of the body, a cone biopsy may need to be done. A cone biopsy precisely determines the extent of more severe disease and removes abnormal tissue. This surgery is done with anesthesia but is not usually performed during pregnancy.

❧ Treating Abnormal Cells

There are several ways to treat abnormal cells on the cervix, but most treatment methods cannot be performed during pregnancy. These treatments include surgically removing the abnormal spot (if it can be seen), electric cautery to remove or "burn" small abnormal spots, cryocautery to freeze small lesions, laser treatment to destroy abnormal areas on the cervix and cone biopsy for more-involved lesions.

How Your Actions Affect Your Baby's Development

✍ *Genetic Counseling*

For some couples, genetic counseling may be important. If you have reasons to be concerned, genetic counseling can help you make informed decisions about childbearing.

Couples who may be advised to seek genetic counseling include those who have already had an infant with problems, those with a family history of inherited diseases, women who have had recurrent miscarriages (usually three or more), any woman whose age will be 35 or more at the time of birth or if you are married to a relative.

Questions asked may include things about both partners' family histories of Down syndrome, spina bifida, hemophilia and muscular dystrophy. If either partner is black, screening for the sickle-cell trait may be suggested. If both partners are descended from Ashkenazi Jews, they may be tested to see if they are carriers of the trait for Tay-Sachs disease.

If genetic counseling is recommended for you and your partner, you will meet with a group of counselors. Data is gathered by these specially trained healthcare professionals. Information is then interpreted and used by you and your partner to help you make decisions about childbearing.

Tip for Week 15

Some of the foods you normally love to eat may make you sick to your stomach during pregnancy. You may need to substitute with other nutritious foods you tolerate better.

You Should also Know

⌁ *Pregnancy After 30*

Today, many women are waiting until they have worked awhile and established a career before they get married and start their families. Older women who give birth have a slightly higher risk of abnormalities and problems, including premature labor, pelvic pressure and pelvic pain. For a detailed discussion of pregnancy in the older woman, read my book *Your Pregnancy After 30*. An older pregnant woman may be more likely to face increased risks of:

- a baby born with Down syndrome
- high blood pressure
- Cesarean delivery
- multiple births
- pre-eclampsia
- placental abruption
- bleeding and other complications

It's also harder to be pregnant when you're older. Chances are you have a job or other children making demands on your time. You may find it harder to rest, exercise and eat right.

⌁ *Down Syndrome*

Until a woman is 30 years old, her chance of giving birth to a baby with Down syndrome is less than 1 in 800. It increases to 1 in 100 by the age of 40 and 1 in 32 by age 45. Although the actual number of pregnancies affected by Down syndrome is higher, many of these pregnancies end in miscarriage or stillbirth.

The risk of giving birth to a Down syndrome infant, according to the mother's-to-be age, is shown in the table on page 136. However, this risk can also be looked at in a different way. At age 40, a woman still has less than a 1% chance of having a baby with Down syndrome. At 49, that risk is still fairly low; a woman has a 93% chance of having a normal baby.

Down syndrome is the most common chromosomal defect detected by amniocentesis. (See Week 17 for more information about amniocentesis.) If you are concerned about the risk of Down syndrome because of your age or family history, discuss it with your doctor.

——— Maternal Age and Down Syndrome ———

Maternal Age	Frequency of Down syndrome
25 years	1 in 1300 births
30 years	1 in 964 births
35 years	1 in 365 births
40 years	1 in 109 births
45 years	1 in 320 births
49 years	1 in 12 births

——— ✱ ———

Week 16

Age of Fetus ❧ 14 Weeks

How Big Is Your Baby?

The crown-to-rump length of your baby by this week is 4.3 to 4.6 inches (108 to 116mm). Weight is about 2.8 ounces (80g).

How Big Are You?

As your baby grows, your uterus and placenta are also growing. Six weeks ago, your uterus weighed about 5 ounces (140g). Today, it weighs about 8.75 ounces (250g). The amount of amniotic fluid around the baby is also increasing. There is now about 7.5 ounces (250ml) of fluid. You can easily feel your uterus about 3 inches (7.6cm) below your bellybutton.

How Your Baby Is Growing and Developing

There is fine lanugo hair on your baby's head. The umbilical cord is attached to the abdomen; this attachment has moved lower on the body of the fetus than before.

Fingernails are well formed. The illustration on page 139 shows legs are longer than arms. Arms and legs are moving. You can see this movement during an ultrasound examination. You may also be able to feel your baby move at this point in your pregnancy.

Many women describe feelings of movement as a "gas bubble" or "fluttering." Often, it's something you have noticed for a few days or more, but you didn't realize what you were feeling. Then it occurs to you: You're feeling the baby moving inside you!

～～～✳～～～

If you haven't felt your baby move yet, don't worry. Fetal movement, also called *quickening,* is usually felt between 16 and 20 weeks of pregnancy. The time is different for every woman. It can also be different from one pregnancy to another. One baby may be more active than another and produce more movement. The size of the baby or the number of fetuses can also affect what you feel.

～～～✳～～～

Changes in You

～ *Alpha-fetoprotein Testing*

As your baby grows inside you, it produces alpha-fetoprotein. This protein is found in increasing amounts in the amniotic fluid coming from the fetal urine. Some alpha-fetoprotein crosses fetal membranes and enters your circulation. The amount of this protein found in your blood is much lower than in the fetus or the amniotic fluid, but it does increase as your pregnancy progresses.

It is possible to measure the amount of alpha-fetoprotein in the amniotic fluid (by amniocentesis) and in maternal blood (by drawing your blood). The level of this protein can be meaningful during pregnancy. An alpha-fetoprotein (AFP) test is usually done between 16 and 18 weeks of gestation. The timing of the

By this week, fine lanugo hair covers the baby's body and head.

test is important and must be correlated to the gestational age of your pregnancy and to your weight.

An elevated level of alpha-fetoprotein can indicate problems with the fetus, such as spina bifida (spinal-cord problem) or anencephaly (serious central-nervous-system defect). Some researchers have even found an association between a low level of alpha-fetoprotein and Down syndrome. In the past, testing for Down syndrome could only be done with amniocentesis.

If the level of alpha-fetoprotein is abnormal, it may be confirmed with another alpha-fetoprotein test or by amniocentesis. A careful ultrasound examination is also done to look for spina bifida or anencephaly, and to determine how far along in pregnancy you are.

This test is not done on all pregnant women, although it is required in some states in the United States. It is not used routinely in Canada. If the test isn't offered to you, ask about it. There is relatively little risk to you, and it tells your doctor how your fetus is growing and developing.

ᴐ *Rh-Sensitivity*

In the lab tests you've already had, your blood type and Rh-factor were determined. You may know this information by now. Your blood type, such as O, A, B, AB, and the Rh-factor are important. In the past, Rh-negative women who carried an Rh-positive child faced complicated pregnancies, which could result in a very sick baby.

Your blood is separate from your baby's blood. If you are Rh-positive, you don't have to worry about any of this. If you are Rh-negative, you need to know about it.

If you are Rh-negative and your baby is Rh-positive or if you have had a blood transfusion or received blood products of some kind, there's a risk you could become Rh-sensitized or isoimmunized. *Isoimmunized* means you make antibodies that circulate inside your system which don't harm you but can attack the Rh-positive blood of your growing baby. (If your baby is Rh-negative, there is no problem.) Your antibodies can cross the placenta and attack your baby's blood. This can cause blood disease of the fetus or newborn. It can make your baby very anemic while still inside the uterus, and it can be very serious.

Fortunately, this reaction is preventable. The use of RhoGAM (Rh-immune globulin) has alleviated many problems. It is given at 28 weeks gestation to prevent sensitization before delivery. Very few women are seen today who are sensitized. If you are Rh-negative and have a pregnancy, a RhoGAM injection should be part of your pregnancy. RhoGAM is a product that is extracted from human blood. If you have religious, ethical or personal reasons for not using blood or blood products, consult your physician and/or minister.

RhoGAM is also given to you within 72 hours after delivery, if your baby is Rh-positive. If your baby is Rh-negative, you don't need RhoGAM after delivery and you didn't need the shot during pregnancy. But it's better not to take that risk and to have the RhoGAM injection during pregnancy.

If you have an ectopic pregnancy and are Rh-negative, you should receive RhoGAM. This applies to miscarriage and abortions as well. If amniocentesis is performed during pregnancy and you are Rh-negative, you should receive RhoGAM.

How Your Actions Affect Your Baby's Development

❧ *Amniocentesis*

If it is necessary, the amniocentesis test is usually performed for prenatal evaluation around 16 to 18 weeks of pregnancy. By this point, your uterus is large enough and there is enough fluid surrounding the baby to make the test possible. Doing the procedure at this time allows the woman enough time to make a decision about terminating the pregnancy, if that is what she desires.

With amniocentesis, ultrasound is used to locate a pocket of fluid where the fetus and placenta are not in the way. The abdomen over the uterus is cleaned. Skin is numbed, and a needle is placed through the abdominal wall into the uterus. Fluid is withdrawn from the amniotic cavity (area around the baby) with a syringe. About 1 ounce (30ml) of amniotic fluid is needed to perform various tests.

Fetal cells that float in the amniotic fluid can be grown in cultures. They are the cells used to identify fetal abnormalities. We know of more than 400 abnormalities a child can be born with—amniocentesis identifies about 40 (10%) of them. Abnormalities that can be identified include:

- chromosomal problems, particularly Down syndrome
- fetal sex, if sex-specific problems such as hemophilia must be identified
- skeletal diseases, such as osteogenesis imperfecta
- fetal infections, such as herpes or rubella
- central-nervous-system diseases, such as anencephaly
- hematologic (blood) diseases, such as erythroblastosis fetalis
- inborn errors of metabolism (chemical problems or deficiencies of enzymes), such as cystinuria or maple-syrup-urine disease

Risks from amniocentesis include injury to the fetus, placenta or umbilical cord, infection, miscarriage or premature labor.

The use of ultrasound to guide the needle helps avoid complications but doesn't eliminate all risk. There can be bleeding from the fetus to the mother. This can be important because fetal and maternal blood are separate and may be different types. As I've just discussed, this is important to an Rh-negative mother carrying an Rh-positive baby. This type of bleeding can cause isoimmunization. An Rh-negative woman should receive RhoGAM at the time of amniocentesis to prevent isoimmunization.

Fetal loss from amniocentesis complications is estimated to be less than 3%. The procedure should be done only by someone who has experience doing it.

✎ Saunas and Hot Tubs

Some women are concerned about using saunas, hot tubs and spas during pregnancy. They want to know if it is OK to relax in this way.

Your baby relies on you to maintain the correct body temperature. If your body temperature is elevated a few degrees and stays there for an extended period, it may damage the baby if it occurs at critical times in its development. Don't take a chance with a hot tub or sauna until more medical research can tell us it won't hurt your baby.

✎ Tanning Booths

Phoebe always had a tan. She told me she maintained her tan at a tanning booth by regular weekly visits. She wanted to know if she could continue these visits during her pregnancy. I advised her that we don't yet know the effects on the growing fetus of a pregnant woman lying in a tanning booth. It has not been studied by medical researchers. "Until medical studies indicate it's safe to get in a tanning booth," I told Phoebe, "it's best to avoid using them while you're pregnant."

You Should also Know

✧ *Change Sleeping Positions Now*

Some women have questions and concerns about their sleeping positions and sleep habits while they're pregnant. Some want to know if they can sleep on their stomachs. Others want to know if they should stop sleeping on their waterbed.

As you grow during pregnancy, you'll find it more difficult to find comfortable positions to sleep. Don't lie on your back when you sleep. As your uterus gets larger, lying on your back can place the uterus on top of important blood vessels (the aorta and the inferior vena cava) that run down the back of your abdomen. This can decrease circulation to your baby and parts of your body. Some pregnant women also find it harder to breathe when lying on their backs.

Lying on your stomach when you sleep puts extra pressure on your growing uterus. This is another reason to learn to sleep on your side. Some women have commented to me that their favorite thing after delivery was to be able to sleep on their stomachs again!

Try to find comfortable ways to sleep. As time passes and you grow larger, it will become more important to you.

Tip for Week 16

Start now to learn to sleep on your side. It will pay off later as you get bigger. Sometimes it helps to use a few extra pillows. Put one behind you so if you roll onto your back, you won't lie flat. Put another pillow between your legs, or rest your "top" leg on it. Some manufacturers make a "pregnancy pillow" that supports your entire body easily and effectively.

Week 17

Age of Fetus ❧ 15 Weeks

The crown-to-rump length of your baby is 4.4 to 4.8 inches (110 to 120mm: 11 or 12cm). Fetal weight has doubled in 2 weeks and is about 3.5 ounces (100g). By this week, your baby is about the size of your hand spread open wide.

Your uterus is 1.5 to 2 inches (3.8 to 5cm) below your bellybutton. You are showing more now and have an obvious "swelling" in your lower abdomen. By this time, stretchy or maternity clothing is a must for comfort's sake. When your partner gives you a hug, he may feel the difference in your lower abdomen.

The rest of your body is still changing. A 5- to 10-pound gain (2.25 to 4.5kg) by this time is normal.

How Your Baby is Growing and Developing

If you look at the illustration on page 146, then look at earlier chapters, very big changes are obviously occurring.

Fat begins to form during this week and the weeks that follow. Also called *adipose tissue,* fat is important to the body's heat production and metabolism.

At 17 weeks of development, water makes up about 3 ounces (89g) and fat 0.018 ounce (0.5g) of your baby's body. In a baby at term, fat makes up about 5.25 pounds (2.4kg) of the total average weight of 7.7 pounds (3.5kg).

You have felt your baby move, or you will soon. You may not feel it every day. As pregnancy progresses, movements become stronger and probably more frequent.

Changes in You

Feeling your baby move can reassure you that things are going well with your pregnancy. This is especially true if you've had problems.

As your pregnancy advances, the top of the uterus becomes almost spherical. It increases more rapidly in length (upward into your abdomen) than in width, so the uterus becomes more oval than round. The uterus fills the pelvis and starts to grow into the abdomen. Your intestines are pushed upward and to the sides. The uterus eventually reaches almost to your liver.

The uterus is not fixed in one place. Most attachments are located around the cervix (lower part of the uterus) and by the lower part of the body of the uterus. The uterus doesn't float around, but it is not firmly attached to one spot.

When you stand, the uterus touches the abdominal wall in the front. It may be felt most easily in this position. When you lie down, it can fall backward onto your spine and blood vessels (vena cava and aorta).

Round ligaments are attached to each side of the upper uterus and to the pelvic side wall. During pregnancy and the growth of

Your baby's fingernails are well formed. The baby
is beginning to accumulate a little fat.

the uterus, these ligaments are stretched and pulled. They
become longer and thicker. Your sudden or mild movements can
stretch and pull these ligaments, causing pain or discomfort
called *round-ligament pain*. It doesn't signal a problem; it indicates your uterus is growing. Pain may occur on one side only or
both sides, or it may be worse on one side than another. This
pain does not harm you or the baby.

If you experience pain, it may feel better to lie down and rest. Talk to your doctor about the pain if it is severe or if other symptoms arise. Warning signs of serious problems include bleeding from the vagina, loss of fluid from the vagina or severe pain.

How Your Actions Affect Your Baby's Development

ᢌ Quad-Screen Test

The quad-screen test can help your healthcare provider determine if you might be carrying a baby with Down syndrome. This blood test can also help rule out other problems in your pregnancy, such as neural-tube defects.

The quad-screen test is similar to the triple-screen (see the discussion in Week 15). Levels of alpha-fetoprotein, HCG and unconjugated estriol are checked. In addition, a fourth measurement, the level of inhibin-A, is determined. This fourth measurement raises the sensitivity of the standard triple-screen test by 20% in determining whether a fetus has Down syndrome.

The quad-screen test is able to identify 79% of those fetuses with Down syndrome. It has a false-positive result of 5%.

ᢌ Using Over-the-Counter Medications and Preparations

Many people don't consider over-the-counter (OTC) preparations as medication and take them at will, pregnant or not. Some researchers believe nonprescription or over-the-counter medication usage increases during pregnancy.

OTC medications and preparations may not be safe during pregnancy. Use them with as much caution as any other drug! Many over-the-counter preparations are combinations of medications. For example, pain medication can contain aspirin, caffeine and phenacetin. Cough syrups or sleep medications can contain as much as 25% alcohol. This is no different than drinking wine or beer during pregnancy.

My patient Catherine called because she had a chronic knee problem, and she used aspirin for pain and swelling. She asked if it was OK to use it during pregnancy. I told her that full doses of aspirin are not advised because aspirin use can increase bleeding. This could cause problems for Catherine or her baby if she bled during pregnancy or delivery. Under medical supervision, small doses may be used, but always discuss the situation with your healthcare provider.

> *Tip for Week 17*
> Don't take any over-the-counter medications for longer than 48 hours without consulting your healthcare provider. If a problem doesn't resolve, your doctor may have another treatment plan for you.

Another medication to be careful with is ibuprofen, a popular product available in prescription and nonprescription forms. Experience with this medication during pregnancy is limited; it hasn't been available that long. There are no known benefits of taking ibuprofen during pregnancy, and there have been reports of possible harmful effects. Why take a chance? Ibuprofen products include Advil®, Motrin® and Rufen®.

Other popular over-the-counter products include naprosyn (Aleve®) and ketoprofen (Orudis®), both used to relieve pain or to reduce fever. Experience with these medications during pregnancy is limited. It is best to use them only under your doctor's supervision.

Talk to your doctor about taking any medication *before* you use it! Read package labels and package inserts about safety during pregnancy—nearly all medications contain this information. Some antacids contain sodium bicarbonate, which increases your intake of sodium (this can be important if you have water-retention problems) and can cause constipation and increased gas. Some antacids contain aluminum, which can cause constipation and affect the metabolism of other minerals (phosphate). Others contain magnesium; excessive use of these may cause magnesium poisoning.

Some over-the-counter medications and preparations can be used safely during pregnancy, if you use them wisely. Those you may safely use for a short period of time include acetaminophen (Tylenol), some antacids (Amphojel, Gelusil, Maalox, milk of magnesia), throat lozenges (Sucrets®), some decongestants (Sudafed®) and some cough medicines (Robitussin®).

If you think your symptoms or discomfort are more severe than they should be, call your doctor. Follow his or her advice. In addition, take good care of yourself. Exercise, eat right and keep a positive mental attitude about your pregnancy.

You Should also Know

～ *Having a Baby Costs Money!*

Every couple wants to know what it will cost to have a baby. There are really two answers to that question—it costs a lot, and cost varies from one part of the country to another.

In determining how much it costs to have a baby in your area, you'll need to consider several different factors. It makes a big difference if you have insurance. If you don't, you will pay for everything.

If you do have insurance, you need to check out some things. Ask your employer the following questions.

- What type of coverage do I have?
- Are there maternity benefits? What are they?
- Do maternity benefits cover Cesarean deliveries?
- What kind of coverage is there for a high-risk pregnancy?
- Do I have to pay a deductible? If so, how much is it?
- How do I submit claims?
- Is there a cap (limit) on total coverage?
- What percentage of my costs are covered?
- Does my coverage restrict the kind of hospital accommodations I may choose, such as a birthing center or a birthing room?
- What procedures must I follow before entering the hospital?
- Does my policy cover a nurse-midwife?
- Does coverage include medications?
- What tests during pregnancy are covered?
- What tests during labor and delivery are covered?
- What types of anesthesia are covered during labor and delivery?
- How long can I stay in the hospital?

- Does payment go directly to my healthcare provider or to me?
- What conditions or services are *not* covered?
- What kind of coverage is there for the baby after it is born?
- How long can the baby stay in the hospital?
- Is there an additional cost to add the baby to the policy?
- How do I add the baby to the policy?
- Can we collect a percentage of a fee from my husband's policy and the rest from mine?

Your insurance dictates a lot of the costs and decisions for you.

Having a baby generates different costs. One is the hospital. Much of the covered amount for the hospital is determined by the length of stay and the "services" you use. In some cases, having an epidural or Cesarean section adds to this bill. Your doctor's bill is separate from this except under some plans. A pediatrician usually examines the baby, does a physical and sees the baby each day in the hospital. This is another cost.

When my first daughter was born in 1974, a normal delivery and 2-day hospital stay for my wife (no C-section, anesthesia or complications) cost a total of $600 for hospital, doctor, nursery and pediatrician. When my youngest daughter was born in 1985, a similar stay (again no anesthesia, C-section or complications) cost about $3500—an increase of almost 600% in 11 years! Across the United States, 1997 prices for a delivery range from $6000 to $14,000, depending on complications and the type of delivery.

It would be nice to think about costs before pregnancy and be sure to have insurance to help out. However, many pregnancies are surprises.

What can you do? First, find the answers to your questions. Talk to your insurance carrier. Then talk to someone in your doctor's office who handles insurance claims. This person may have answers or know of resources you haven't thought about. Don't be embarrassed to ask questions. You will be happier if you get these issues resolved early. Pregnancy is not the time to cut corners to save money.

Call around so you can compare hospitals and prices. Sometimes it's worth spending a little more money to get more.

When you call, ask for specifics about what is included in the prices you are quoted. You may get a price that seems lower and better than others but really doesn't cover everything you will want and need.

Today, some hospitals and medical centers offer "pregnancy packages." A package can cover many services for one fee. Ask about it in your area.

You want to be prepared well in advance. The last thing you need at this time is an unpleasant surprise about what is covered or how much you will have to pay for medical services.

❧ Costs of Having a Baby in Canada

The Canadian healthcare system is different from the healthcare system in the United States. Canadians pay a healthcare premium on a monthly basis. Cost varies depending on the province you live in. The doctor who delivers your baby is paid by the government. He or she submits the bill to the government, not you.

Week 18

Age of Fetus ⋙ 16 Weeks

How Big Is Your Baby?

The crown-to-rump length of your growing baby is 5 to 5.6 inches (12.5 to 14cm) by this week. Weight of the fetus is about 5.25 ounces (150g).

How Big Are You?

Your uterus can be felt just below your bellybutton. If you put your fingers sideways and measure, it is about two finger widths below your bellybutton (about 1 inch below).

Your uterus is the size of a cantaloupe or a little larger. Your weight gain to this point should be 10 to 13 pounds (4.5 to 5.8kg). However, this can vary widely. If you have gained more weight than this, talk to your doctor. You may need to see a nutritionist. You still have more than half of your pregnancy ahead of you, and you're going to gain even more weight.

Gaining more than the recommended weight can make pregnancy and delivery harder on you. Extra pounds are hard to lose afterward.

Dieting during pregnancy is not a wise idea, but that *doesn't* mean you don't have to watch what you eat. You should! It's important for your baby to get proper nutrition from the foods you eat. Choose food for the nutrition it provides you and your growing baby.

How Your Baby Is Growing and Developing

Your baby is continuing to grow and to develop, but now the very rapid growth rate slows down a little. As you can see in the illustration on page 154, your baby has a very human appearance now.

⌇ *Development of the Heart and Circulatory System*

At about the third week of fetal development, two tubes join to form the heart. The heart begins to contract by day 22 of development or about the beginning of the 5th week of gestation. A beating heart can be seen as early as 5 to 6 weeks of pregnancy during an ultrasound examination.

The heart tube divides into bulges. These bulges develop into heart chambers, called *ventricles* (left and right) and *atria* (left atrium and right atrium). These divisions occur between weeks 6 and 7. During week 7, tissue separating the left and right atria grows and an opening between the atria called the *foramen ovale* appears. This opening lets blood pass from one atrium to the other, allowing it to bypass the lungs. At birth, the opening closes.

The ventricles, the lower chambers of the heart (lying below the atria), also develop a partition. The ventricle walls are very muscular. Blood is pumped from the left ventricle to the body and brain, and from the right ventricle to the lungs.

Heart valves develop at the same time as the chambers. These valves fill and empty the heart. Heart sounds and heart murmurs are caused by blood passing through these valves.

Your baby gets oxygen from you. Blood from your baby flows to the placenta through the umbilical cord. In the placenta,

Your baby continues to grow. By this week, it is about 5 inches (12.5cm) from crown to rump. It looks much more human now.

oxygen and nutrients are transported from your blood to the fetal blood. Although the circulation of your blood and that of your baby come close, there is no direct connection. These circulation systems are completely separate.

At birth, the baby has to go very rapidly from depending entirely on you for oxygen to depending on its own heart and lungs. The foramen ovale closes, and blood goes to the right ventricle, the right atrium and to the lungs for oxygenation for the first time. It is truly a miraculous conversion.

At 18 weeks of gestation, ultrasound can detect some abnormalities of the heart. This can be helpful in identifying problems such as Down syndrome. A skilled ultrasonographer looks for specific heart defects. If an abnormality is suspected, further ultrasound exams may be ordered to follow a baby's development as pregnancy progresses.

Changes in You

✎ Does Your Back Ache?

Nearly every pregnant woman experiences backache at some time in pregnancy. It may have occurred already, or it may come later as you get bigger. Some women have severe back pain following excessive exercise, walking, bending, lifting or standing. It is more common to have mild backache than severe problems. Some women need to take special care getting out of bed or getting up from sitting. In severe instances, some women find it difficult to walk.

A change in joint mobility may contribute to the change in your posture and may cause discomfort in the lower back. This is particularly true in the latter part of pregnancy.

The growth of the uterus moves your center of gravity forward, over your legs. Your joints are looser, and the joints around the pelvis can be affected. Changes are believed to be caused by hormonal increases.

Tina came to the office after a long day at the grocery store, where she was a clerk. She told me her back ached a lot, and she wanted to know what to do. I told her that backache can often be helped with heat, rest and analgesics, such as acetaminophen

(Tylenol). Special maternity girdles are available that can provide some support. Keeping weight under control and exercising may also help. In a severe case, physical therapy or a consultation with an orthopedic surgeon might be necessary.

Watch your diet and weight gain. Continue exercising within guidelines during pregnancy. Get in the habit of lying on your side when you sleep. Find time to get off your feet and lie down for 30 minutes on your side. If you have other children, find ways to get some rest during the day. If they take a nap, get some rest of your own. Start early to do these things; it'll pay off as your pregnancy progresses.

—— Nasal Problems ——

Some women complain of stuffiness in their nose or frequent nose-bleeds during pregnancy. Some researchers believe these symptoms occur because of changes in circulation due to hormonal changes during pregnancy. This can cause the mucous membranes of your nose and nasal passageways to swell and to bleed more easily.

Don't try different medications to help, such as decongestants or nasal sprays. Many of these are combinations of several medications and may be ill-advised during pregnancy.

It may help to use a humidifier, particularly during the winter months when heating may dry out the air. Some women get relief from increasing their fluid intake and using a gentle lubricant, such as petroleum jelly. As for other relief, you may have to wait until your baby is born to breathe normally through your nose again.

———— ❋ ————

How Your Actions Affect Your Baby's Development

Some women are very involved in fitness activities. They want to know what they can do and what to avoid while pregnant.

Pregnant women can participate safely in many sports and other activities. This is a very different attitude from the ones 20, 30 and 40 years ago. Bed rest and decreased activity were common then. Today, we believe exercise and activity can benefit you and your growing baby.

As with any activity, discuss your particular activities with your doctor. If you are a high-risk patient or have had several miscarriages, it's particularly important to discuss exercise with your doctor before starting an activity. Now is not the time to train for any sport or to increase activity.

What about specific sports? Below is a discussion of various activities you might be interested in. (Aerobic exercise is discussed in Week 3.)

ꜰ *Swimming*

Swimming can be very good for you when you're pregnant. It may also make you feel comfortable. The support and buoyancy of the water can be relaxing.

If you swim, you are encouraged to swim throughout pregnancy. If you can't swim, exercising in a swimming pool in the shallow end can be very enjoyable. Classes are offered in many places. Ask at local spas or health clubs.

ꜰ *Bicycling*

Now is not the time to learn to ride a bike. If you're comfortable riding and have safe places to ride, it can be an exercise you can enjoy with your partner or family.

Your balance will change as your body changes. This can make getting on and off a bicycle difficult. And a fall from a bicycle could injure you or possibly injure your baby.

A stationary bicycle is good for bad weather and for later in pregnancy. Many doctors suggest you ride a stationary bike to avoid the danger of a fall in the last 2 to 3 months of pregnancy.

ꜰ *Walking*

Walking is a very desirable exercise during pregnancy. If you are just starting, gradually increase the time and distance you walk. Two miles of walking at a good pace is adequate.

Walking can be a good time for you and your partner to talk. Even when the weather is bad, you can walk in places such as enclosed shopping malls to get a good workout. As pregnancy progresses, you may need to decrease your speed and distance.

✥ *Jogging*

Many women continue to jog during pregnancy. Jogging may be permitted during pregnancy, but check with your doctor first. If you are a high-risk pregnancy, jogging is not a good idea.

Pregnancy is not the time to increase mileage or to train for a race. Wear comfortable clothing and shoes with good cushioning. Allow plenty of time to cool down.

During the course of your pregnancy, you'll probably need to slow down and to decrease the number of miles you run. You may even change to walking. If you notice pain, contractions, bleeding or other symptoms during or after jogging, call your doctor immediately.

✥ *Other Sports Activities*

Tennis and golf are safe but may provide little actual exercise. Horseback riding is not advisable during pregnancy. Avoid water skiing while you're pregnant. Bowling is OK, although the amount of exercise you get varies. Be careful in late pregnancy; back strain could occur. Your balance changes, which could make bowling difficult for you.

Talk to your doctor about snow skiing *before* you hit the slopes. Again, in the latter part of pregnancy, your balance changes significantly. A fall could be harmful to you and your baby. Most physicians agree that skiing in the second half of pregnancy is not a good idea. Some doctors may allow skiing in early pregnancy, but only if there are no complications with this or previous pregnancies.

Riding snowmobiles and motorcycles is not advised. Some doctors may allow you to ride if it is not strenuous. However, most believe the risk is too great, especially if you have had problems during this or other pregnancies.

Tip for Week 18

During exercise, your oxygen demands increase. Your body is heavier, and your balance may change. You may also tire more easily. Keep these points in mind as you adjust your fitness program.

You Should also Know

✂ *Bladder Infections*

One of the first symptoms you may notice early in pregnancy is frequent urination. This will continue during pregnancy and may get you up frequently at night.

It is more common to get urinary-tract infections during pregnancy. Other names for urinary-tract infections are *bladder infections* and *cystitis*. Symptoms of a bladder infection include painful urination, particularly at the end of urination, the feeling of urgency to urinate and frequent urination.

Most doctors will test your urine at your first visit. Your doctor will check it at other times during pregnancy and for infection if and when bothersome symptoms arise.

You can help avoid infection by not "holding" your urine. Empty your bladder as soon as you feel the need to. Drink plenty of fluid; cranberry juice may help avoid infections. For some women, it helps to empty the bladder after having intercourse.

See your doctor if you think you have a bladder infection. It should be treated. Some antibiotics are safe to use during pregnancy for this problem.

If left untreated, urinary-tract infections can get worse. They can even lead to *pyelonephritis,* a serious kidney infection. If you have pyelonephritis, you may have to be hospitalized to treat the infection.

A urinary-tract infection during pregnancy may also be a possible cause of premature labor or a low-birth-weight infant. If you think you have an infection, talk to your doctor. If you are diagnosed as having a urinary-tract infection, take the full course of antibiotics prescribed by your doctor.

Week 19

Age of Fetus ↣ 17 Weeks

How Big Is Your Baby?

Crown-to-rump length of the growing fetus is 5.2 to 6 inches (13 to 15cm) by this week. Your baby weighs about 7 ounces (200g). It's incredible to think your baby will increase its weight more than 15 times between now and delivery.

How Big Are You?

Your uterus can be felt about 0.5 inch (1.3cm) below your umbilicus. The illustration on page 162 gives you a good idea of the relative size of you, your uterus and your developing baby. A side view really shows the change in you!

Total weight gain at this point is between 8 and 14 pounds (3.6 and 6.3kg). Of this weight gain, only about 7 ounces (200g) is your baby! The placenta weighs about 6 ounces (170g); the amniotic fluid weighs another 11 ounces (320g). The uterus weighs 11 ounces (320g). Your breasts have each increased in weight by 6.3 ounces (180g).

How Your Baby Is Growing and Developing

✨ Your Baby's Nervous System

The beginning of the baby's nervous system (brain and other structures, such as the spinal cord) is seen as early as week 4 as the neural plate begins to develop. By week 6 of gestation, the main divisions of the central nervous system are established. These divisions consist of the forebrain, midbrain, hindbrain and spinal cord. In week 7, the forebrain divides into the two hemispheres that will become the two cerebral hemispheres of the brain.

✨ Hydrocephalus

Organization and development of the brain continues from this early beginning. Cerebral spinal fluid (CSF), which circulates around the brain and the spinal cord, is made by the choroid plexus. Fluid must be able to flow without restriction. If openings are blocked and flow is restricted for any reason, it can cause hydrocephalus (water on the brain).

Hydrocephalus causes enlargement of the head. Occurring in about 1 in 2000 babies, it is responsible for about 12% of all severe fetal malformations found at birth.

Hydrocephalus is often associated with spina bifida and occurs in about 33% of those cases. It is also associated with meningomyelocele and omphalocele (hernias of the spine and navel). Between 15 and 45 ounces of fluid (500 to 1500ml) can accumulate but much more than that has been found. Brain tissue is compressed by all this fluid, which is a major concern.

Diagnosis of the problem is best made by ultrasound. Hydrocephalus can usually be seen on ultrasound by 19 weeks of pregnancy. Occasionally it is found by routine exams and "feeling" your uterus.

In the past, nothing could be done about hydrocephalus until after delivery. Today, intrauterine therapy—treatment while the fetus is still in the uterus—can be performed in some cases.

There are two methods of treating hydrocephalus in utero (in the uterus). In one method, a needle passes through the mother's abdomen into the area of the baby's brain where fluid is collecting.

Comparative size of the uterus at 19 weeks of pregnancy (fetal age—17 weeks). The uterus can be felt just under the umbilicus (bellybutton).

Some fluid is removed to relieve pressure on the baby's brain. In another method, a small plastic tube is placed into the area where fluid collects in the baby's brain. This tube is left in place to drain fluid continuously.

Tip for Week 19
Fish can be a healthful food choice during pregnancy, but don't eat shark, swordfish or tuna (fresh or frozen) more than once a week.

Hydrocephalus is a high-risk problem. These procedures are highly specialized and should be performed only by someone experienced in the latest techniques. This requires consultation with a perinatologist specializing in high-risk pregnancies.

Changes in You

✒ Feeling Dizzy

Feeling dizzy during pregnancy is a fairly common symptom, often caused by hypotension (low blood pressure). It doesn't usually appear until the second trimester but can occur earlier.

There are two common reasons for hypotension during pregnancy. It can be caused by the enlarging uterus putting pressure on your aorta and vena cava. This is called *supine hypotension* and occurs when you lie down. It can be alleviated or prevented by not sleeping or lying on your back.

The second cause of hypotension is rising rapidly from a sitting, kneeling or squatting position. This is called *postural hypotension.* Your blood pressure drops when you rise rapidly as blood leaves your brain because of gravity. This problem is cured by rising slowly from a sitting or lying position.

If you are anemic, you may feel dizzy, faint or tired, or you may fatigue easily. Your blood is checked routinely during pregnancy. Your doctor will tell you if you have anemia.

Pregnancy also affects your blood-sugar level. High blood sugar (hyperglycemia) or low blood sugar (hypoglycemia) can make you feel dizzy or faint. Many doctors routinely test pregnant women for problems with blood sugar during pregnancy, particularly if they have problems with dizziness. Most people can avoid or improve the problem by eating a balanced diet, by not skipping meals and by not going a long time without eating. It's a good idea to carry a piece of fruit or several crackers with you for a quick boost in blood sugar when you need it.

How Your Actions Affect Your Baby's Development

✣ *Allergies May Be Affected during Pregnancy*

If you suffer from allergies, occasionally they get a little worse during pregnancy. To help deal with the problem, drink plenty of fluid. If you have allergy medication, don't assume it's safe to take. Ask your doctor about your medicine, whether prescription or nonprescription. Some types of allergy medication may not be advised. Many allergy medicines are combinations of several medicines, including aspirin. This advice also applies to nasal sprays.

Some women notice their allergies get better during pregnancy, and symptoms improve. Certain things they had trouble with before pregnancy are no longer a problem.

You Should also Know

✣ *Warning Signs during Pregnancy*

Missy was nervous because she didn't think she would know if something important or serious happened during pregnancy. Most women have few, if any, problems during pregnancy. If you are concerned, read the list below that I shared with Missy. She told me it was helpful. This list includes the most important symptoms to be aware of during pregnancy. Call your doctor if you experience any of them:

- vaginal bleeding
- severe swelling of the face or fingers
- severe abdominal pain
- loss of fluid from the vagina, usually a gush of fluid, but sometimes a trickle or continual wetness
- a big change in the baby's movement or a lack of movement
- high fever (more than 101.6F; 38.7C) or chills
- severe vomiting or an inability to keep food or liquid down
- blurring of vision

- painful urination
- a headache that won't go away or a severe headache
- an injury or accident, such as a fall or automobile accident, that causes you concern about the well-being of your pregnancy

One way to get to know your doctor is to ask his or her opinion about your concerns. When you talk to your doctor, don't be embarrassed to ask questions about *anything*. Your doctor would rather know about problems while they are small.

If problems warrant it, you may be referred to a perinatologist, an obstetrician who has spent an additional 2 years or more in specialized training. These specialists have experience caring for women with high-risk pregnancies. They spend most of their time taking care of these women and their babies.

You may not have a high-risk pregnancy at the beginning of your pregnancy. However, if problems develop, you may need to be referred for consultation for a problem with you, such as premature labor, or a problem with the baby, such as spina bifida. A perinatologist may provide your care during pregnancy. You may be able to return to your regular doctor for your delivery.

If you are seeing a perinatologist, you may have to deliver your baby at a hospital other than the one you had chosen. This is usually because the hospital has specialized facilities or can administer specialized tests to you or your baby.

⌖ *Electric Blanket Use*

There has been controversy about use of electric blankets to keep you warm during pregnancy. There is still much disagreement and discussion about their safety. Some experts question whether they can cause health problems.

Electric blankets produce a low-level electromagnetic field. The developing fetus may be more sensitive than an adult to these electromagnetic fields.

Because researchers are uncertain about "acceptable levels" of exposure for a pregnant woman, the safest alternative at this time is not to use an electric blanket during pregnancy. There are many other ways to keep warm, such as down comforters and wool blankets. One of these is a better choice.

Week 20

Age of Fetus ∿ 18 Weeks

At this point in development, the crown-to-rump length is 5.6 to 6.4 inches (14 to 16cm). Your baby weighs about 9 ounces (260g).

How Big Are You?

Congratulations—20 weeks marks the midpoint. You're halfway through your pregnancy! Remember, the entire pregnancy is 40 weeks from the beginning of your last period if you go full term.

Your uterus is probably just about even with your bellybutton. Your doctor has been watching your growth and the enlargement of your uterus. Growth to this point may have been irregular but usually becomes more regular after the 20th week.

✿ **Measuring the Growth of Your Uterus**

Your uterus is measured often to keep track of your baby's growth. Your doctor may use his or her fingers and measure by finger breadth, or a measuring tape may be used.

Your doctor needs a point of reference against which to measure your growth. Some doctors measure from your bellybutton. Many measure from the pubic symphysis. The pubic symphysis is the place where the pubic bones meet in the middle-lower part of your abdomen. This bony area is just above your urethra (where urine comes out), 6 to 10 inches (15.2 to 25.4cm) below the bellybutton, depending on how tall you are. It may be felt 1 or 2 inches (2.5 to 5cm) below your pubic hairline.

Measurements are made from the pubic symphysis to the top of the uterus. After 20 weeks of pregnancy, you should grow about 0.4 inch (1cm) each week. If you are 8 inches (20cm) at 20 weeks, at your next visit (4 weeks later), you should measure about 9.6 inches (24cm).

If you measure 11.2 inches (28cm) at this point in pregnancy, you may require further evaluation with ultrasound to determine if you are carrying twins or to see if your due date is correct. If you measure 6 inches (15 to 16cm) at this point, it may be a reason to do further evaluation by ultrasound. Your due date could be wrong, or there may be a concern about intrauterine-growth retardation or some other problem.

Not every doctor measures the same way, and not every woman is the same size. Babies vary in size. If pregnant friends ask, "How much did you measure?" don't worry if their measurements are different. Measurements differ among women and may be different for a woman from one pregnancy to another.

If you see a doctor you don't normally see or if you see a new doctor, you'll probably measure differently. This does not indicate a problem or that someone is measuring incorrectly. It's just that everyone measures a little differently.

Having the same person measure you on a regular basis can be very helpful in following the growth of your baby. Within limits, changing measurements are a sign of fetal well-being and fetal growth. If they appear abnormal, it can be a warning sign.

If you're concerned about your size and the growth of your pregnancy, ask your doctor about it.

How Your Baby Is Growing and Developing

~ *Your Baby's Skin*

The skin covering your baby begins growing from two layers. These layers are the epidermis, which is on the surface, and the dermis, which is the deeper layer. By this point in your pregnancy, the epidermis is arranged in four layers. One of these layers contains epidermal ridges, which are responsible for patterns of surfaces on fingertips, palms and soles of the feet. They are genetically determined.

The dermis lies below the epidermis. It forms projections that push upward into the epidermis. Each projection contains a small blood vessel (capillary) or a nerve. This deeper layer also contains large amounts of fat.

When a baby is born, its skin is covered by a white substance that looks like paste. Called *vernix*, it is secreted by the glands in the skin beginning around 20 weeks of pregnancy. Vernix protects your growing baby's skin from amniotic fluid.

Hair appears at around 12 to 14 weeks of pregnancy. It grows from the epidermis; hair ends (hair papillae) push down into the dermis. Hair is first seen on the fetus on the upper lip and eyebrow. It is usually shed around the time of birth and is replaced by thicker hair from new follicles.

~ *Ultrasound Pictures*

The illustration on page 170 shows an ultrasound exam (and an interpretive illustration of the ultrasound) in a pregnant woman at about 20 weeks gestation. An ultrasound is often easier to understand when it is actually being done. The pictures you see are more like motion pictures.

If you look closely at the illustration, it may make sense to you. Read the labels and try to visualize the baby inside the uterus. An ultrasound picture is like looking at a slice of an object. The picture you see is 2-dimensional.

When Margaret had an ultrasound, she was disappointed—it didn't look like a baby to her. If you have an ultrasound exam and don't see everything or it doesn't make sense, don't feel bad. These images are difficult to interpret unless you've had extensive training and experience. Margaret was reassured to see the heart beat and to see her baby move.

An ultrasound done at this point in pregnancy is helpful for confirming or helping to establish your due date. If the ultrasound is done very early or very late (first or last 2 months), the accuracy of dating a pregnancy is not as good. If two or more fetuses are present, they can usually be seen. In many cases, fetal problems can also be seen at this time.

Tip for Week 20

An ultrasound test done at this point in pregnancy may make it possible to determine the sex of the baby, but the baby must cooperate. Sex is recognized by seeing the genitals. Even if the sex looks obvious, ultrasound operators have been known to be mistaken about a baby's sex.

∽ *Percutaneous Umbilical Blood Sampling*

Percutaneous umbilical blood sampling (PUBS), also called *cordocentesis,* is a test done on the fetus while it is still developing inside your uterus.

The advantage of the test is that results are available in a few days. The disadvantage is it carries a slightly higher risk of miscarriage than amniocentesis.

Guided by ultrasound, a fine needle is inserted through the mother's abdomen into a tiny vein in the umbilical cord. A small sample of the baby's blood is removed for analysis. PUBS detects blood disorders, infections and Rh-incompatability.

The baby's blood can be checked before birth, and the baby can be given a blood transfusion, if necessary. This procedure can help prevent life-threatening anemia that may develop if the mother is Rh-negative and has antibodies that are destroying her baby's blood.

Ultrasound of a baby at 20 weeks gestation (fetal age—18 weeks). The interpretive illustration may help you see more detail.

Changes in You

∿ *Increased Vaginal Discharge*

During pregnancy it is normal to have an increase in vaginal discharge or vaginal secretions called *leukorrhea*. This discharge is usually white or yellow and fairly thick. It is *not* an infection. We believe it is caused by the increased blood flow to the skin and muscles around the vagina, which causes a violet or blue coloration of the vagina. This symptom, visible to your doctor early in pregnancy, is called *Chadwick's sign.*

You may have to wear sanitary pads if you have a heavy discharge. Avoid wearing pantyhose and nylon underwear; choose underwear with a cotton crotch.

Vaginal infections can and do occur during pregnancy. The discharge that accompanies these infections is often foul-smelling, is yellow or green, and causes irritation or itching around or inside the vagina. If you suffer from any of these symptoms, call your doctor. Many creams and antibiotics that treat vaginal infections can be used safely during pregnancy.

↪ *Douching during Pregnancy*

Most doctors agree you should not douche during pregnancy. Bulb-syringe douches are definitely out!

Using a douche may cause you to bleed or may cause more serious problems, such as an air embolus. An air embolus results when air gets into your bloodstream from the pressure of the douche. It is rare, but it can cause very serious problems for you.

↪ *Abdominal Itching*

As your uterus has grown and filled your pelvis, your abdominal skin and muscles have stretched. Itchiness is a fairly natural consequence. Many women complain their abdomen itches with stretched skin. Lotions are OK to use to help reduce itching. Try not to scratch and irritate your skin—that can make it worse!

↪ *Stretching Abdominal Muscles*

Your abdominal muscles are also being stretched and pushed apart as your baby grows. Muscles are attached to the lower portion of your ribs and run vertically down to your pelvis. They may separate in the midline. These muscles are called the *rectus muscles;* when they separate, it is called a *diastasis recti.*

You will notice the separation most often when you are lying down and you raise your head, tightening abdominal muscles. It will look like there is a bulge in the middle of your abdomen. You might even feel the edge of the muscle on either side of the bulge. It isn't painful and doesn't harm you or your baby. What you feel in the gap between the muscles is the uterus. You may feel the baby's movement more easily here.

If this is your first baby, you may not notice the separation at all. With each pregnancy, separation may be more noticeable. Exercising can strengthen these muscles, but you may still have the bulge or gap.

Following pregnancy, these muscles fall back together. The separation won't be as noticeable, but it may still be present. A girdle probably won't help get rid of the bulge or gap.

How Your Actions Affect Your Baby's Development

ᕦ *Will You Get Varicose Veins?*

Varicose veins, also called *varicosities* or *varices*, occur to some degree in most pregnant women. There appears to be an inherited predisposition to varicose veins that can be made more severe by pregnancy, increased age and from pressure caused by standing for long periods of time.

Varicose veins are blood vessels that are engorged with blood. They occur primarily in the legs but may also be present in the vulva. The change in blood flow and pressure from the uterus make varices worse, which causes discomfort.

In most instances, varicose veins become more noticeable and more painful as pregnancy progresses. With increasing weight (especially if you spend a lot of time standing), they will get worse.

Symptoms vary. For some, the main symptom is a blemish or purple-blue spot on the legs with little or no discomfort except perhaps in the evening. Other women have bulging veins that require elevation at the end of the day.

ᕦ *Treating Varicose Veins*

Many women wear support hose; many types are available. They can be helpful. Wearing clothing that doesn't restrict circulation at the knee or the groin may also help. Spending only a little time on your feet and a lot of time lying on your side or elevating your legs can be beneficial. This enables the veins to drain more easily.

If you have varicose veins in your legs or vulva, stay off your feet as much as possible. Wear flat shoes when you can. When you're sitting down, don't cross your legs, which cuts off circulation and can make problems worse. Following these measures may help keep veins from swelling as much.

Following pregnancy, swelling in the veins should go down, but varicose veins probably won't disappear altogether. Surgery that can get rid of these veins is called *vein stripping*. It would be unusual to operate on varicose veins during pregnancy, although it is a treatment to consider when you are not pregnant.

You Should also Know

↪ *Hearing Your Baby's Heartbeat*

It may be possible to hear your baby's heartbeat with a stethoscope at 20 weeks. Before doctors had doppler equipment that enabled them to hear the heartbeat and ultrasound to see the heart beating, a stethoscope helped the listener hear the baby's heartbeat. This usually occurred after quickening for most women.

Listening with a stethoscope gives a different sound than you might be used to hearing at the doctor's office. The sound isn't loud. If you've never listened through a stethoscope, it may be difficult to hear at first. It does get easier as the baby gets larger and sounds are louder.

If you can't hear your baby's heartbeat with a stethoscope, don't worry. It's not always easy for a doctor who does this on a regular basis!

If you hear a swishing sound (baby's heartbeat), you have to differentiate it from a beating sound (mother's heartbeat). A baby's heart beats very rapidly, usually 120 to 160 beats every minute. Your heartbeat or pulse rate is slower, in the range of 60 to 80 beats a minute. Don't be afraid to ask your doctor to help you distinguish the sounds.

✋ *Lyme Disease*

Lyme disease refers to an infection transmitted to humans by ticks. I am often asked about it. There are several stages of the illness. In about 80% of those bitten, there is a skin lesion with a distinctive look, called a *bull's eye*. There may be flulike symptoms. After 4 to 6 weeks, symptoms may become more serious.

At the beginning of the illness, blood tests may not diagnose Lyme disease. A blood test done later in the illness can establish the diagnosis.

We know Lyme disease can cross the placenta. At this time, we don't know if it is dangerous to the baby. Researchers are studying it.

Treatment for Lyme disease requires long-term antibiotic therapy and sometimes intravenous antibiotic therapy. Many medications used to treat Lyme disease are safe to use during pregnancy.

Avoid exposure to Lyme disease, if possible. Stay out of areas known to have ticks, especially heavily wooded areas. If you can't avoid these areas, wear long-sleeved shirts, long pants, a hat or scarf, socks and boots or closed shoes. Be sure to check your hair when you come in; ticks often attach themselves there. Also, check your clothing to make sure no ticks remain in folds, cuffs or pockets.

Week 21

Age of Fetus ∼ 19 Weeks

How Big Is Your Baby?

Your baby is getting larger in this first week of the second half of your pregnancy! It now weighs about 10.5 ounces (300g), and its crown-to-rump length is about 7.2 inches (18cm). It is about the size of a large banana.

How Big Are You?

You can feel your uterus about half an inch (1cm) above your bellybutton. At the doctor's office, your uterus measures almost 8.5 inches (21cm) from the pubic symphysis. Your weight gain should be between 10 and 14 pounds (4.5 and 6.3kg).

By this week, your waistline is definitely gone. Your friends and relatives—and strangers, too—can tell you're pregnant. It would be hard to hide your condition!

How Your Baby Is Growing and Developing

The rapid growth rate of your baby has slowed. However, the baby continues to grow and to develop. Different organ systems within the baby are maturing.

✧ The Fetal Digestive System

The fetal digestive system is functioning in a simple way. By the 11th week of pregnancy, the small intestine begins to contract and relax, which pushes substances through it. The small intestine is capable of passing sugar from inside the small intestine into the baby's body.

By 21 weeks of pregnancy, development of the fetal digestive system enables the fetus to swallow amniotic fluid. After swallowing amniotic fluid, the fetus absorbs much of the water in it and passes unabsorbed matter as far as the large bowel.

✧ Fetal Swallowing

As mentioned above, your baby swallows before it is born. Swallowing by the baby at different stages of pregnancy can be observed by ultrasound. We have seen babies swallowing amniotic fluid as early as 21 weeks of pregnancy.

Why does a baby in the womb swallow? Researchers believe swallowing amniotic fluid may help growth and development of the fetal digestive system. It may condition the digestive system to function after birth.

Studies have determined how much fluid a fetus swallows and passes through its digestive system. Evidence indicates babies at full-term may swallow large amounts of amniotic fluid, as much as 17 ounces (500ml) of amniotic fluid in a 24-hour period.

Amniotic fluid swallowed by the baby contributes a small amount to its caloric needs. Researchers believe it may contribute essential nutrients to the developing baby.

✧ Meconium

During your pregnancy, you may hear the term *meconium* and wonder what it means. It refers to undigested debris from swallowed amniotic fluid in the fetal digestive system. Meconium is a greenish-black to light-brown substance that your baby passes from its bowels several days or weeks before delivery, during labor or after birth.

Passage of meconium into the amniotic fluid may be caused by distress in the fetus. Meconium seen during labor may be an indication of fetal distress.

If a baby has had a bowel movement before birth and meconium is present in the amniotic fluid, the fetus may swallow the fluid. If meconium is inhaled into the lungs, the baby could develop pneumonia or pneumonitis. For this reason, if meconium is seen at delivery, an attempt is made to remove it from the baby's mouth and throat with a small suction tube.

Changes in You

In addition to your growing uterus, other parts of your body continue to change and to grow. You may notice swelling in your lower legs and feet, particularly at the end of the day. If you're on your feet a lot, you may notice less swelling if you're able to get off of your feet and rest for a while during the day.

✍ *Blood Clots in the Legs*

A serious complication of pregnancy is a blood clot in the legs or groin. Symptoms of the problem are swelling of the legs accompanied by leg pain and redness or warmth over the affected area in the legs.

The problem has many names, including venous thrombosis, thromboembolic disease, thrombophlebitis and lower deep-vein thrombosis. The problem is not limited to pregnancy, but pregnancy is a time when it is more likely to occur. This is due to the slowing of blood flow in the legs because of uterine pressure and changes in the blood and its clotting mechanisms.

The most probable cause of blood clots in the legs during pregnancy is decreased blood flow, also called *stasis*. If you have had a previous blood clot—in your legs or any other part of your body—tell your doctor at the beginning of pregnancy. It's important information, and he or she needs to know it.

∽ *Deep-Vein Thrombosis*

A distinction is often made between superficial thrombosis and deep-vein thrombosis in the leg. A blood clot in the superficial veins of the leg is not as serious. This condition is usually noted in veins close to the surface of the skin that can often be felt on the surface. This type of clot is treated with a mild pain reliever such as acetaminophen (Tylenol), elevation of the leg, support of the leg with an ace bandage or support stockings and occasionally heat. If the condition doesn't improve rapidly, deep-vein thrombosis must be considered.

Deep-vein thrombosis is more serious; it requires diagnostic and treatment steps. Symptoms of deep-vein thrombosis in the lower leg can differ greatly, depending on the location of the clot and how bad it is. The onset of deep-vein thrombosis can be rapid, with severe pain and swelling of the leg and thigh.

With deep-vein thrombosis, the leg may occasionally appear pale and cool, but usually a portion of the leg is tender, hot and swollen. Often skin over the affected veins is red. There may even be streaks of red on the skin over veins where blood clots have occurred.

Squeezing the calf or leg may be extremely painful, and it may be equally painful to walk. One way to tell if you have deep-vein thrombosis is to lie down and flex your toes toward your knee. If the back of the leg is tender, it is a positive indication of this problem (Homan's sign). (This type of pain may also occur with a strained muscle or a bruise.) Check with your doctor if this occurs.

Diagnostic studies of deep-vein thrombosis may be different for a pregnant woman than for a nonpregnant woman. In the nonpregnant woman, an X-ray may be accompanied by an injection of dye into leg veins to look for blood clots. This test is not usually performed on a pregnant woman because of exposure to radiation and dye.

Ultrasound is used to diagnose this problem in pregnant women. Most major medical centers offer it, but the test is not available everywhere.

Treatment of deep-vein thrombosis usually consists of hospitalization and heparin therapy. Heparin (a blood thinner) must be given intravenously; it cannot be taken as a pill. It is safe during pregnancy and is not passed to the fetus. A woman may be required to take extra calcium during pregnancy if she receives heparin because it thins the blood to prevent the clot from enlarging. While heparin is being administered, the woman is required to stay in bed. The leg may be elevated and heat applied, and mild pain medicine is prescribed.

Recovery time, including hospitalization, may be 7 to 10 days. After this time, the woman continues taking heparin until delivery. Following pregnancy, she will need to continue taking a blood thinner for up to several weeks, depending on the severity of the clot.

If a woman has a blood clot during one pregnancy, she may need to use heparin during subsequent pregnancies. If so, heparin can be given by an in-dwelling I.V. catheter or by daily injections the woman administers to herself under her doctor's supervision.

Another medication used to treat deep-vein thrombosis is warfarin, an oral medication. Warfarin (Coumadin®) is not given during pregnancy because it crosses the placenta and can be harmful to the baby. Warfarin is usually given to the woman after pregnancy to prevent blood clots. It may be prescribed for a few weeks or a few months, depending on the severity of the clot.

If you have had a blood clot in the past for *any* reason, pregnancy-related or not, it's important to see your doctor early in pregnancy. Tell him or her about any problems you've had with blood clots at your first prenatal visit.

The greatest danger from deep-vein thrombosis is a pulmonary embolism, in which a piece of the blood clot breaks off and travels from the legs to the lungs. This is a rare problem during pregnancy and is reported in only 1 in every 3000 to 7000 deliveries. Although it is a serious complication in pregnancy, it can often be avoided with proper treatment.

How Your Actions Affect Your Baby's Development

∾ Safety of Ultrasound

On page 181 is an illustration of an ultrasound exam, accompanied by an interpretive illustration. These show a baby inside a uterus; the mother-to-be has a large cyst in her abdomen.

Many women wonder about the safety of ultrasound exams. Most medical researchers agree ultrasound exams do not pose any significant risk to you or your baby. Researchers have looked for potential problems many times without finding evidence the test causes any.

Ultrasound is an extremely valuable tool in diagnosing problems and answering some questions during pregnancy. Information that ultrasound testing provides can be reassuring to the doctor and the pregnant woman.

If your doctor has recommended ultrasound for you and you're concerned about it, discuss it with him or her. Your doctor may have an important reason for doing an ultrasound exam. It could affect the well-being of your developing baby.

You Should also Know

In the early weeks of pregnancy, your body did not change significantly. Now your body is changing rapidly. Your uterus is large enough to make it clear you are pregnant. Should you be making changes at this point in your pregnancy?

∾ Exercise

Everyone has heard stories of women who continued with strenuous exercise or strenuous activities until the day of delivery without problems. Stories are told of Olympic athletes who were pregnant at the time they won medals in the Olympic games. This kind of training and physical stress probably isn't a good idea for you.

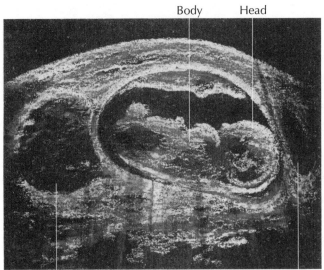

Body   Head

Cyst in abdomen   Mother's bladder

Ultrasound is also used to detect problems. In this ultrasound of a baby in utero, there is a cyst in the mother's-to-be abdomen. The interpretive illustration clarifies the ultrasound image.

As your uterus grows and your abdomen gets larger, you may find your sense of balance is affected. You may feel clumsy. This isn't the time for contact sports, such as basketball, or sports where you might fall easily, injure yourself or be struck in the abdomen.

Tip for Week 21
A good way to add calcium to your diet is to cook rice and oatmeal in skim milk instead of water.

Karen had been exercising since before pregnancy, and she wanted to know if she should continue. I reassured her that it would help her feel better and might help control her weight, but she needed to be wise about her choices.

I told her that she was going to have to ease up a little. This point in pregnancy—21 weeks—was a good time for her to begin decreasing the amount or intensity of exercise she was doing.

Listen to your body. It'll tell you when it's time to slow down.

‿ *Sexual Relations*

Pregnancy can be an important time of growing closer to your partner. As you get larger, sexual intercourse may become difficult because of discomfort for you. With some imagination and with different positions (ones in which you are not on your back and your partner is not directly on top of you), you can continue to enjoy sexual relations during this part of your pregnancy.

If you feel pressure from your partner—either his concern about the safety of intercourse or requests for frequent sexual relations—discuss it openly with him. Don't be afraid to invite your partner to visit your doctor with you to discuss these things.

If you're having problems with contractions, bleeding or complications, talk with your doctor about whether you should continue to have sexual relations with your partner.

Week 22

Age of Fetus ❧ 20 Weeks

Your baby now weighs about 12.25 ounces (350g). Crown-to-rump length at this time is about 7.6 inches (19cm).

Your uterus is now about 0.8 inch (2cm) above your bellybutton or almost 9 inches (22cm) from the pubic symphysis. You may feel "comfortably pregnant." Your enlarging abdomen is not too large and doesn't get in your way very much. You're still able to bend over and to sit comfortably. Walking shouldn't be an effort. Morning sickness has probably passed, and you're feeling pretty good. It's kind of fun being pregnant now!

How Your Baby Is Growing and Developing

Your baby continues to grow; its body is getting larger every day. As you can see by looking at the illustration on page 185, your baby's eyelids and even the eyebrows are developed. Fingernails can also be seen.

✢ Liver Function

Your baby's organ systems are becoming specialized for their particular functions. Consider the liver. The function of the fetal liver is different from that of an adult. Enzymes (chemicals) are made in an adult liver that are important in various body functions. In the fetus, these enzymes are present but in lower levels than those present after birth.

An important function of the liver is the breakdown and handling of bilirubin. Bilirubin is produced by blood cells. The life span of a fetal red blood cell is shorter than that of an adult. Because of this, more bilirubin is produced by the fetus than by an adult.

The fetal liver has a limited capacity to convert bilirubin and to remove it from the fetal bloodstream. Bilirubin passes from fetal blood through the placenta to your blood. Your liver helps get rid of fetal bilirubin. If a baby is born prematurely, it may have trouble processing bilirubin because the liver is too immature to get rid of bilirubin from the bloodstream by itself.

A newborn baby with high bilirubin may exhibit jaundice. A baby with jaundice has a yellow tint to the skin and eyes. Jaundice is usually treated with phototherapy. Phototherapy uses light that penetrates the skin and destroys the bilirubin.

Jaundice in a newborn is typically triggered by the transition from bilirubin being handled by the mother's system to the baby handling it on its own. The baby's liver can't keep up. Jaundice is more likely to occur in an immature infant when the liver is not ready to take over this function.

By the 22nd week of pregnancy (fetal age—20 weeks), your baby's eyelids and eyebrows are well developed. Fingernails have grown and now cover the fingertips.

Changes in You

↭ *Fetal Fibronectin*

In some cases, normal discomforts of pregnancy, such as lower-abdominal pain, dull backache, pelvic pressure, uterine contractions (with or without pain), cramping and a change in vaginal discharge may be confused with preterm labor. Until now, we have not had a reliable method of determining if a woman was truly at risk of delivering a preterm baby. A test is now available that can help doctors make this determination.

Fetal fibronectin (fFN) is a protein found in the amniotic sac and fetal membranes. However, after 22 weeks of pregnancy, fFN is not normally present until term.

When it is present in the cervical-vaginal secretions of a pregnant woman after 22 weeks, it indicates increased risk for preterm delivery. If it is absent, risk of premature labor is low and the woman probably won't deliver within the next 2 weeks.

The test is performed like a Pap smear. A swab of vaginal secretions is taken from the top of the vagina, behind the cervix. It is sent to the lab, and results are available within 24 hours.

჌ *Anemia in Pregnancy*

Anemia is a common problem during pregnancy. If you suffer from anemia, treatment is important to you and your baby. If you are anemic, you won't feel well during pregnancy. You'll tire easily. You may experience dizziness.

There is a fine balance in your body between the production of blood cells that carry oxygen to the rest of your body and destruction of these cells. Anemia is the condition in which the number of red blood cells is low. If you are anemic, you have an inadequate number of red blood cells.

During pregnancy, the number of red blood cells in your bloodstream increases. The amount of plasma (the liquid part of the blood) also increases but at a higher rate. Your doctor keeps track of these changes in your blood with a hematocrit reading. Your *hematocrit* is a measure of the percentage of the blood that is red blood cells. Your hemoglobin level is also tested. *Hemoglobin* is the protein component of red blood cells. If you are anemic, your hematocrit is lower than 37 and your hemoglobin is under 12.

A hematocrit determination is usually made at the first prenatal visit, along with other lab work. It may be repeated once or twice during pregnancy. It is done more often if you are anemic.

There is always some blood loss at delivery. If you're anemic when you go into labor, you are at higher risk of needing a blood transfusion after your baby is born. Follow your doctor's advice about diet and supplementation if you suffer from anemia.

⤳ *Iron-Deficiency Anemia*

The most common type of anemia seen in pregnancy is iron-deficiency anemia. During pregnancy, your baby uses some of the iron stores you have in your body. If you have iron-deficiency anemia, your body doesn't have enough iron left to make red blood cells because the baby has used some of your iron for its own blood cells.

Iron is contained in most prenatal vitamins and can also be taken as a supplement. If you are unable to take a prenatal vitamin, you may be given 300 to 350mg of ferrous sulphate or ferrous gluconate 2 or 3 times a day. Iron is the most important supplement to take. It is required in almost all pregnancies.

——— Looking Out for Iron Deficiency ———

Even with supplemental iron, some women develop iron-deficiency anemia during pregnancy. Several factors may make a woman more likely to have this condition in pregnancy, including:

- failure to take iron or failure to take a prenatal vitamin containing iron
- bleeding during pregnancy
- multiple fetuses
- previous surgery on the stomach or part of the small bowel (making it difficult to absorb an adequate amount of iron before pregnancy)
- antacid use that causes a decrease in absorption of iron
- poor dietary habits

The goal in treating iron-deficiency anemia is to increase the amount of iron you consume. Iron is poorly absorbed through the gastrointestinal tract and must be taken on a daily basis. It can be given as an injection, but it's painful and may stain the skin.

Side effects of taking iron supplements include nausea and vomiting, with stomach upset. If this occurs, you may have to take a lower dose. Taking iron may also cause constipation.

If you cannot take an oral iron supplement, an increase in dietary iron from foods, such as liver or spinach, may help prevent anemia.

✥ Sickle-Cell Anemia

For women who are dark-skinned, sickle-cell anemia can cause significant anemia during pregnancy. Anemia occurs in these cases because the bone marrow, which produces the body's red blood cells, cannot replace red blood cells as quickly as they are destroyed. In sickle-cell anemia, the red blood cells produced are also abnormal, which can cause anemia or severe pain.

You may carry the trait for sickle-cell anemia without having the disease. You could possibly pass the trait or the disease to your baby. Tell your doctor of any family history of the disease.

A blood test easily detects the sickle-cell trait. Sickle-cell anemia can be diagnosed in the fetus with amniocentesis (discussed in Week 16) or chorionic villus sampling (discussed in Week 10).

Women with sickle-cell trait are more likely to have pyelonephritis (see Week 23) and bacteria in the urine during pregnancy. They are also susceptible to developing sickle-cell anemia during pregnancy.

Women with sickle-cell anemia may have repeated episodes of pain (sickle crises) throughout their lifetime. Pain in the abdomen or limbs is caused by the blockage of blood vessels by abnormal red blood cells. Episodes of pain may be severe and may require hospitalization for treatment with fluids and pain medication.

Hydroxurea has proved effective as the treatment of the disease, but its use carries some risks. Because we do not have research data on long-term effects, pregnant women are advised not to use it.

Sickle-cell disease risks to a pregnant women are those of painful sickle crisis, infections and even congestive heart failure. Risks to the fetus include a high incidence of miscarriage and stillbirth, estimated to be as high as 50%. Even though the risks are greater, many women with sickle-cell anemia have successful pregnancies.

∽ *Thalassemia*

A type of anemia encountered less frequently is thalassemia, which occurs most often in Mediterranean populations. It is characterized by underproduction of part of the simple protein that makes up red blood cells, and anemia results. If you have a family history of thalassemia or know you have thalassemia, discuss it with your doctor.

How Your Actions Affect Your Baby's Development

∽ *Lower-Back Pain*

Lower-back pain is a common problem during pregnancy. Almost every pregnant woman experiences back pain at some point in her pregnancy, including mild to moderate pain that may increase as pregnancy progresses. However, as mentioned previously, pain may be an indication of more serious problems, such as pyelonephritis or a kidney stone. Check with your doctor if back pain is a chronic problem for you.

It's OK to take acetaminophen (Tylenol) for back pain. Use heat on the area that is painful. If pain becomes constant or more severe, talk to your doctor about it.

∽ *Driving a Car as Pregnancy Progresses*

I am often asked whether it's safe to drive a car during pregnancy. The answer is "Yes." I tell patients it may be more uncomfortable for them to get in and out of a car as their abdomens grow larger, but it shouldn't interfere with their ability to drive.

As discussed in Week 12, it's important for you to use a seat belt and shoulder harness during pregnancy, as well as all other times. There is no reason not to drive while you're pregnant if your pregnancy is normal and you feel OK.

Use a seat belt and shoulder harness throughout pregnancy.

✑ *Fluid Intake*

Kathleen was concerned because she heard she should drink more fluid during pregnancy. She wanted to know how much she needed to consume. What she heard is true: Fluid intake during pregnancy is important. I told Kathleen that she might feel better if she drank more fluid than she normally did. Many women who suffer with headaches and various other problems during pregnancy find increasing their water intake helps resolve some of their symptoms.

It's best to avoid fluids that contain a lot of calories, such as soda. Drink plain water or water with a little fruit juice added for flavor. You'll find it can be very refreshing and tasty.

Some women find it helps to have a glass of water at hand all day. Decrease your intake in the early evening—you don't want to be up all night going to the bathroom! However, even if you decrease your fluid intake at night, you may find you're going to the bathroom a lot anyway. This is a normal part of pregnancy.

Tip for Week 22

Drink extra fluids (water is best) throughout pregnancy to help your body keep up with the increases in your blood volume. You'll know you're drinking enough fluid when your urine looks like almost-clear water.

You Should also Know

✍ *Do You Have Hemorrhoids?*

Hemorrhoids are a common problem during or following pregnancy. Hemorrhoids are dilated blood vessels around the area of the anus or inside it. They are caused during pregnancy by the increased blood flow in the area around the uterus and the pelvis because of the weight of the uterus, causing congestion or blockage of circulation.

Hemorrhoids may worsen toward the end of pregnancy. They may also get worse with each succeeding pregnancy.

Hemorrhoid treatment includes avoiding constipation by eating adequate amounts of fiber and drinking lots of fluid. Hemorrhoids may also be avoided through the use of stool softeners. Other measures include sitz baths or suppository medications. These can be bought without a prescription. Very rarely, hemorrhoids are treated during pregnancy with surgery.

After pregnancy, hemorrhoids usually improve, but they may not go away completely. You can use the treatment methods mentioned above when pregnancy is over.

If hemorrhoids cause you a great deal of pain, discuss it with your doctor. He or she will know what treatment method is best for you.

—— Relieving the Discomfort of Hemorrhoids ——

If hemorrhoids are a problem, try any of the following suggestions for relief.

- Rest at least 1 hour every day with your feet and hips elevated.
- Lie with your legs elevated and knees slightly bent (*Sims position*) when you sleep at night.
- Eat adequate amounts of fiber, and drink lots of fluid.
- Take warm baths for relief.
- Suppository medications, available without a prescription, may help.
- Apply ice packs or cotton balls soaked in witch hazel to the affected area.
- Don't sit for long periods.

———— ✳ ————

Week 23

Age of Fetus ❧ 21 Weeks

By this week, your baby weighs almost 1 pound (455g)! Its crown-to-rump length is 8 inches (20cm). Your baby is about the size of a small doll.

Your uterus extends about 1.5 inches (3.75cm) above your belly-button or about 9.2 inches (23cm) from the pubic symphysis. The changes in your abdomen are progressing slowly, but you definitely have a round appearance now. Your weight gain should be between 12 and 15 pounds.

How Your Baby Is Growing and Developing

Your baby is continuing to grow. Its body is getting plumper, but its skin is still wrinkled because it will gain even more weight. See the illustration on page 194. Lanugo hair on the body occasionally turns darker at this time. The baby's face and body begin to assume more of the appearance of an infant at birth.

✂ *Pancreas Function*

Your baby's pancreas is developing. It is important in hormone production, particularly insulin production; insulin is necessary for the body to break down and use sugar.

When the fetus is exposed to high blood-sugar levels, the fetal pancreas responds by increasing the blood-insulin level. Insulin has been identified in a fetal pancreas as early as 9 weeks of pregnancy. Insulin in the blood has been detected as early as 12 weeks of pregnancy.

Insulin levels are generally high in the blood of babies born to diabetic mothers. That is one reason your doctor may monitor you for diabetes.

Changes in You

At this point, friends may comment on your size. They may say you must be carrying twins because you're so large. Or they may say you're too small for how far along you think you are. If these comments concern you, discuss them with your doctor.

Your doctor will measure you at every visit after this point. He or she is watching for changes in your weight gain and in the size of your uterus. Remember that women and babies are different sizes and grow at different rates. What's important for you is continual change and continual growth.

As your baby gets larger, the placenta gets larger. The amount of amniotic fluid also increases.

By the 23rd week of pregnancy (fetal age—21 weeks), your baby's eyelids and eyebrows are well developed.

∿ *Loss of Fluid*

As your pregnancy progresses, your uterus grows larger and gets heavier. In early pregnancy, it lies directly behind the bladder, in front of the rectum and the lower part of the colon, which is part of the bowel.

Later in pregnancy, the uterus sits on top of the bladder. As it increases in size, it can put a great deal of pressure on your bladder. You may notice times when your underwear is wet. You may be uncertain whether you have lost urine or if you are leaking amniotic fluid. It may be difficult to tell the difference between the two. However, when your membranes rupture, you usually experience a gush of fluid or a continual leaking from the vagina. If you experience this, call your doctor immediately!

✧ Urinary-Tract Infections

The possibility of a urinary-tract infection (UTI) increases during pregnancy because of changes in your urinary tract. As the uterus grows larger, it sits directly on top of the bladder and on the ureters, the tubes leading from the kidneys to the bladder.

Urinary-tract infections may cause you to lose urine more frequently while you're pregnant. A UTI is the most common problem involving your bladder or kidneys during pregnancy.

Your doctor may do a urinalysis and urine culture at your first prenatal visit. He or she may check your urine on subsequent visits to look for infection.

Symptoms of a urinary-tract infection include frequent urination, burning urination and a feeling that you need to urinate and nothing will come out. A severe urinary tract infection can cause blood to appear in the urine.

If you think you have a bladder infection, contact your doctor. He or she may order a urine culture to look for specific bacteria causing the infection.

✧ Pyelonephritis

A more serious problem resulting from a bladder infection is pyelonephritis (kidney infection). This type of infection occurs in 1% to 2% of all pregnant women. The right kidney is most often affected.

Symptoms include frequent urination, burning urination, the feeling you need to urinate and nothing will come out, high fever, chills and back pain. Pyelonephritis may require hospitalization and treatment with intravenous antibiotics.

If you have pyelonephritis or recurrent bladder infections during pregnancy, you may have to take antibiotics during your entire pregnancy to prevent reinfection.

✄ Kidney Stones

Another problem involving the kidneys and bladder is kidney stones or urinary calculi. They occur about once in every 1500 pregnancies. Kidney stones cause severe pain in the back or lower abdomen. They may also be associated with blood in the urine.

A kidney stone during pregnancy can usually be treated with pain medication and by drinking lots of fluid. In this way, the stone may be passed without having to be removed surgically or with lithotripsy (an ultrasound treatment).

✄ Emotional Changes Continue

Do you find your mood swings are worse? Are you still crying easily? Do you wonder if you'll ever be in control again?

Don't worry. These emotions are typical at this point in your pregnancy. Most authorities believe they occur from the hormonal changes that continue throughout pregnancy.

There is little you can do about periods of moodiness. If you think your partner or others are suffering from your emotional outbursts, talk about it with them. Explain that these feelings are common in pregnant women. Ask them to be understanding. Then relax; try not to get upset about it. Feeling emotional is a normal part of being pregnant.

How Your Actions Affect Your Baby's Development

✄ Diabetes in Pregnancy

Once a very serious problem during pregnancy, diabetes continues to be an important complication of pregnancy. Today, however, many diabetic women go through pregnancy safely with proper medical care, good nutrition and following their doctor's instructions.

Diabetes is a condition defined as a lack of insulin in the bloodstream. Insulin is important for breaking down sugar and transporting it to the cells. If you do not have insulin, you will have high blood sugar and a high sugar content in your urine.

The condition can cause several medical problems, including kidney problems, eye problems and other blood or vascular problems, such as atherosclerosis or myocardial infarction (heart attack). These can be serious for you and your baby.

Before insulin was available, it was unusual for a diabetic woman to get pregnant. With the discovery of insulin and the development of various ways to monitor a fetus, it is uncommon to have a severe problem today. Survival rate of babies is good.

Pregnancy is well known for its tendency to reveal women who are predisposed to diabetes. Women who have trouble with high blood-sugar levels during pregnancy are more likely to develop diabetes in later life. Symptoms of diabetes include:

- an increase in urination
- blurred vision
- weight loss
- dizziness
- increased hunger

It may be necessary to do blood tests to diagnose diabetes during pregnancy. In some areas, this testing is done routinely.

If you have diabetes or know members of your family have had diabetes in the past, tell your doctor. He or she will decide what course of action is best for you.

✒ *Gestational Diabetes*

Some women develop diabetes *only* during pregnancy, called *gestational diabetes.* Gestational diabetes affects about 10% of all pregnancies. After pregnancy is over, nearly all women who experience this problem return to normal, and the problem disappears. However, if gestational diabetes occurs with one pregnancy, there is almost a 90% chance it will recur in subsequent pregnancies.

We believe gestational diabetes occurs for two reasons. One is the mother's body produces less insulin during pregnancy. The second is the mother's body can't use insulin appropriately. Both situations result in high blood-sugar levels.

If left untreated, gestational diabetes can be very serious for you and your baby. You will both be exposed to a high concentration of sugar, which is not healthy for either of you. You might experience *polyhydramnios* (excessive amounts of amniotic fluid). This may cause premature labor because the uterus becomes overdistended.

A woman with gestational diabetes may have a very long labor because the baby is quite large. Sometimes a baby cannot fit through the birth canal, and a Cesarean is required.

If your blood-sugar level is high, you may experience more infections during pregnancy. The most common include those in the kidneys, the bladder, the cervix and the uterus.

Treatment of gestational diabetes includes regular exercise and increased fluid intake. Diet is essential in handling this problem. Your doctor will probably recommend a six-meal, 2000- to 2500-calorie/day eating plan. You may also be referred to a dietitian.

↭ Sodium Intake

Avoid foods that contain a large amount of salt, such as salted nuts, potato chips, pickles, and canned and processed foods. Sodium is the culprit; most salty foods contain large amounts of sodium. Consuming too much sodium may make you retain water. This can cause you to swell and to bloat.

To watch your sodium intake during pregnancy, read labels. Food labels list the amount of sodium in a serving. Some books contain sodium content of foods without labels, such as fast foods. Look at them. You'll be surprised how many milligrams of sodium a fast-food hamburger contains!

Tip for Week 23
Keep your consumption of sodium to 3 grams (3000mg) or less a day. This may help you reduce fluid retention.

Look at the following chart of some foods and their sodium content. You can see foods that contain sodium do not always taste salty. Read labels, and check other available information before you eat!

———— Sodium Content of Various Foods ————

Food	Serving Size	Sodium Content (mg)
American cheese	1 slice	322
Asparagus	14.5-oz. can	970
Big Mac hamburger	1 regular	963
Chicken a la king	1 cup	760
Cola	8 oz.	16
Cottage cheese	1 cup	580
Dill pickle	1 medium	928
Flounder	3 oz.	201
Gelatin, sweet	3 oz.	270
Ham, baked	3 oz.	770
Honeydew melon	1/2	90
Lima beans	8.5-oz. can	1070
Lobster	1 cup	305
Oatmeal	1 cup	523
Potato chips	20 regular	400
Salt	1 teaspoon	1938

———— ✳ ————

You Should also Know

↣ *Appendicitis*

Appendicitis can happen, even during pregnancy. Martha's husband called me from the emergency room; Martha was having pain in her abdomen. They had done an ultrasound, and the baby was fine. The ER doctor thought Martha might have appendicitis.

Pregnancy can make the diagnosis difficult because some of the symptoms are typical in a normal pregnancy, such as nausea and vomiting. Diagnosis is also difficult because as the uterus grows larger, the appendix moves upward and outward, so pain and tenderness are located in a different place than normal. See the illustration on page 200.

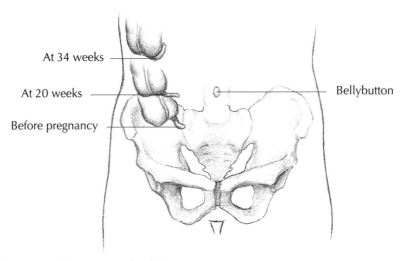

At 34 weeks

At 20 weeks

Before pregnancy

Bellybutton

Location of the appendix during pregnancy

Treatment for appendicitis is immediate surgery. This is major abdominal surgery, with a 3- or 4-inch incision, and requires a few days in the hospital. Laparoscopy, with smaller incisions, is used in some situations, but laparoscopy may be more difficult to perform during pregnancy because of the enlarged uterus.

Serious complications can arise when an infected appendix ruptures. Most physicians believe it's better to operate and remove a "normal" appendix than to risk infection of the abdominal cavity if the infected appendix ruptures. Antibiotics are administered; many antibiotics are safe to use during pregnancy.

ﾝ *Are Microwave Ovens Safe?*

Many women express concerns over the safety of microwave ovens. Is there exposure to radiation from a microwave oven? Microwave ovens are helpful to busy people who prepare meals. However, we don't know if there is danger to you if you use a microwave oven during pregnancy. More research is needed.

Initial research indicates tissues developing in the body, which would include the human fetus, may be particularly sensitive to the effects of microwaves. A microwave oven heats tissues from the inside.

Follow the directions provided with your microwave oven. It's not good to stand next to or directly in front of the microwave oven while it is in use.

Week 24

Age of Fetus ⤳ 22 Weeks

By this week, your baby weighs about 1.2 pounds (540g). Its crown-to-rump length is about 8.4 inches (21cm).

Your uterus is now about 1.5 to 2 inches (3.8 to 5.1cm) above the bellybutton. It measures almost 10 inches (24cm) above the pubic symphysis.

How Your Baby Is Growing and Developing

Your baby is filling out. Its face and body look more like that of an infant at the time of birth. Although it weighs a little over 1 pound at this point, it is still very small.

℘ Role of the Amniotic Sac and Amniotic Fluid

By about the 12th day after fertilization, there is an early beginning of the amniotic sac, where the fetus grows and develops during pregnancy. The baby rests inside the amniotic sac in the amniotic fluid. See the illustration on page 203. Amniotic fluid has several important functions.

- It provides an environment in which the baby can move easily.
- It cushions the fetus against injury.
- Amniotic fluid regulates temperature for the baby.
- It provides a way of assessing the health and maturity of the baby.

Amniotic fluid increases rapidly, from an average volume of 1.5 ounces (50ml) by 12 weeks of pregnancy to 12 ounces (400ml) at midpregnancy. Following the 24th week of pregnancy, the volume of amniotic fluid continues to increase as your due date approaches. There is a maximum of about 2 pints (1 liter) of fluid at 36 to 38 weeks gestation.

Composition of amniotic fluid changes during pregnancy. During the first half of pregnancy, amniotic fluid is similar to maternal plasma (the fluid in blood without blood cells), except it has a much lower protein content.

Amniotic fluid contains old fetal blood cells, lanugo hair and vernix. As pregnancy advances, fetal urine makes an increasingly important contribution to the amount of amniotic fluid present.

The fetus swallows amniotic fluid during much of pregnancy. If it can't swallow amniotic fluid, you will develop a condition of excess amniotic fluid, called *hydramnios* or *polyhydramnios*. If the fetus swallows but urination does not occur (for example, if the baby lacks kidneys), the volume of amniotic fluid surrounding the fetus may be very small. This is called *oligohydramnios*.

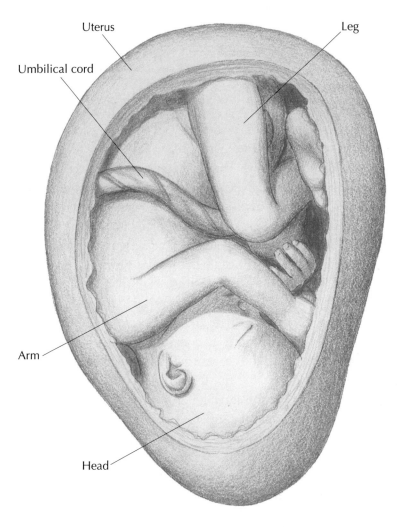

The fetus doesn't appear to have a great deal of room to move in the uterus by the 24th week. As the weeks pass, space gets even tighter!

Amniotic fluid is important. It provides the baby space to move and allows it to grow. If there is an inadequate amount of amniotic fluid, the baby usually shows decreased growth.

Changes in You

↗ An Incompetent Cervix

This term is applied to the painless, premature dilatation of the cervix, which usually results in delivery of a premature baby. It can be an important problem during pregnancy.

Dilatation or stretching of the cervix goes unnoticed by the woman until the baby is delivering; it often occurs without warning. Diagnosis is usually made after one or more deliveries of a premature infant without any pain before delivery.

The cause of cervical incompetence is usually unknown. Some medical researchers believe it occurs because of previous trauma to the cervix, such as dilatation and curettage (D&C) for an abortion or a miscarriage. It may also occur after cervical surgeries.

Usually the cervix doesn't dilate like this before the 16th week of pregnancy. Before this time, the products of conception are not large enough to cause the cervix to dilate and to thin out.

A pregnancy that is lost from an incompetent cervix is completely different from a miscarriage. A miscarriage during the first trimester is common. Incompetent cervix is a relatively rare complication early in pregnancy.

Treatment for an incompetent cervix is usually surgical. The weak cervix is reinforced with a suture that sews the cervix shut.

If this is your first pregnancy, there is no way you can know whether you have an incompetent cervix. If you have had problems in the past or have had premature deliveries and have been told you might have an incompetent cervix, share this important information with your doctor.

How Your Actions Affect Your Baby's Development

↗ Eating Out during Pregnancy

Many pregnant women share a common concern related to eating out. Trish called my office because she wanted to know if she should avoid certain types of food, such as Mexican, Vietnamese, Thai or Greek food, when dining out. She was concerned that spicy foods could be harmful to her baby or her pregnancy.

I told her it's OK to eat out, but she might find certain foods wouldn't agree with her. And of course, if you don't do well eating certain foods anyway, it doesn't make a lot of sense to go out and eat those foods frequently during pregnancy.

The best types of food to eat at restaurants are those you tolerate well at home. Fish, fresh vegetables and salads are usually good choices. Restaurants that feature spicy foods or unusual cuisine may cause you distress. You may even notice an increase in weight from water retention after visiting these restaurants.

During pregnancy, avoid restaurants that serve highly salted foods, foods high in sodium or foods loaded with calories and fat, such as gravies, fried foods, junk food and rich desserts. It is difficult to control your calorie intake at specialty restaurants.

You Should also Know

✺ *When You Feel "Under the Weather"*

It's possible you could have diarrhea during pregnancy as well as viral infections, such as the flu. These problems can raise concerns for you.

- What can I do when I feel ill?
- What medication or treatment is acceptable?
- If I'm sick, should I take my prenatal vitamins?
- If I'm sick and unable to eat my usual diet, what should I do?

If you become sick during pregnancy, don't hesitate to call your doctor's office. Get your doctor's advice about a plan of action. He or she will be able to advise you about what medications you may be able to take to help you feel better. Even if it's only a cold or the flu, your doctor wants to know you're feeling ill. If any further measures are needed, your doctor will recommend them.

Is there anything you can do to help yourself? Yes, there is. If you have diarrhea or a possible viral infection, increase your fluid intake. Drink a lot of water, juice and other clear fluids, such as broth. You may find a bland diet without solid food helps you feel a little better.

Going off your regular diet for a few days won't be harmful to you or your baby, but you do need to drink plenty of fluids. Solid foods may be difficult for you to handle and can make diarrhea a bigger problem. Milk products may also make diarrhea worse.

If diarrhea continues beyond 24 hours, call your doctor. Ask which medications you can take for diarrhea during pregnancy.

Don't take any medication without consulting your doctor first. Usually a viral illness with diarrhea is a short-term problem and won't last more than a few days. You may have to stay home from work or rest in bed until you feel better.

Tip for Week 24

Overeating and eating before going to bed at night are two major causes of heartburn. Eating five or six small, nutritious meals a day instead of three large ones may make you feel better.

Week 25

Age of Fetus — 23 Weeks

How Big Is Your Baby?

Your baby now weighs about 1.5 pounds (700g), and crown-to-rump length is about 8.8 inches (22cm). These are average lengths and weights and vary from one baby to another and from one pregnancy to another.

How Big Are You?

Look at the illustration on page 209. By this week of pregnancy, your uterus has grown quite a bit. When you look at a side view, you're obviously getting bigger.

The measurement from the pubic symphysis to the top of your uterus is about 10 inches (25cm). If you saw your doctor when you were 20 or 21 weeks pregnant, you have probably grown about 1.5 inches (4cm). At this point, your uterus is about the size of a soccer ball.

The top of the uterus is about halfway between your bellybutton and the lower part of your sternum. (The sternum is the bone between your breasts where the ribs come together.)

How Your Baby Is Growing and Developing

✌ *Survival of a Premature Baby*

It may be hard to believe, but if your baby were delivered at this time, it would have a chance of surviving. Some of the greatest advances in medicine have been in the care of the premature baby. No one wants a baby to deliver this early, but with new treatment methods, such as ventilators, monitors and medication, a baby does have a chance of living.

The baby weighs less than 2 pounds and is extremely small. Survival is very difficult for an infant delivered this early. The baby would probably spend several months in the hospital, with risks of infection and other possible complications.

✌ *Is It a Boy? Is It a Girl?*

One of the most common questions I'm asked is, "What is the sex of my baby?" Amniocentesis can reveal the sex of the baby by chromosome study. Ultrasound examination can also be used to determine the sex of the baby, but it may be inaccurate. Don't get your heart set on a particular sex if ultrasound is used.

Tammy wanted to know if I could tell her what sex her baby was. Without ordering certain tests, I told her I couldn't predict the sex of her baby. To me, not knowing is part of the fun of having a baby.

Some people believe a baby's heartbeat rate can indicate its sex. A normal heart rate for a baby ranges from 120 to 160 beats a minute. Some believe a fast heartbeat indicates a girl, and a slower heartbeat indicates a boy. Unfortunately, there is no scientific proof of this. Don't pressure your doctor to guess based on this method because it is *only* a guess.

Comparative size of the uterus at 25 weeks of pregnancy (fetal age—23 weeks). The uterus can be felt about 2 inches (5cm) above your umbilicus (bellybutton).

A more reliable source might be a mother, mother-in-law or someone who can look at you and tell by how you're carrying the baby if it is a boy or girl. Although I make this statement with my tongue placed firmly in my cheek, many people believe it's true. Some people claim they're never wrong about guessing or predicting the sex of a baby before birth. Again, there is no scientific basis for this.

Your doctor is more concerned about your health and well-being and that of your baby. He or she will concentrate on making sure you and your baby, whether it's a boy or girl, are progressing through pregnancy safely and that you both get through pregnancy, labor and delivery in good health.

Changes in You

◦ *Your Growing Abdomen*

Beginning around week 20 or 21, your doctor began measuring you. You will be measured at every visit from now until delivery. In addition to your uterus growing upward from your bellybutton, you may notice you are also getting bigger on the sides of your abdomen.

Your doctor does not measure you around your waist or around your sides. Many women carry their pregnancies on their sides or low in their abdomen. The appearance or the size of your abdomen may make you look different than a pregnant friend. Don't be concerned; it's just a normal variation from one woman to another.

◦ *Thyroid Disease*

Thyroid problems and thyroid disease can affect your pregnancy. Thyroid hormone is made in the thyroid gland; this hormone affects your entire body. It is very important in your metabolism.

Thyroid-hormone levels may be high or low. High levels of thyroid cause a condition called *hyperthyroidism;* low levels cause *hypothyroidism.* Women who have a history of miscarriage or premature delivery or who have problems around the time of delivery may have problems with their thyroid-hormone levels.

Symptoms of thyroid disease may be hidden by pregnancy. Or you may notice changes during pregnancy that cause you and your doctor to suspect the thyroid is not functioning properly. These changes could include an enlarged thyroid, changes in your pulse, redness of the palms and warm, moist palms. Because thyroid-hormone levels can change during pregnancy (because of pregnancy), your doctor must be careful interpreting lab results about this hormone while you're pregnant.

The thyroid is tested primarily by blood tests (a thyroid panel), which measure the amount of thyroid hormone produced. The tests also measure levels of another hormone, thyroid stimulating hormone (TSH), made at the base of the brain. Another test, an X-ray study of the thyroid (radioactive iodine scan), should not be done during pregnancy.

If you have hypothyroidism, thyroid replacement (thyroxin) is prescribed. It is believed to be safe during pregnancy. Your doctor may check the level during pregnancy with a blood test to make sure you are receiving enough of the hormone.

If you have hyperthyroidism, the medication propylthiouracil is used for treatment. It does pass through the placenta to the baby. Your doctor will prescribe the lowest possible amount to reduce risk to your baby. Blood testing during pregnancy is necessary to monitor the amount of medication needed. Iodide is another medication used for hyperthyroidism. Avoid iodide during pregnancy because of harmful effects to a developing baby.

After delivery, it's important to test the baby and to watch for signs of thyroid problems related to the medications prescribed during pregnancy. If you have a past history of problems with your thyroid, if you are now taking medication or if you have taken medication in the past for your thyroid, tell your doctor. Discuss treatment during pregnancy.

How Your Actions Affect Your Baby's Development

↗ *Treating Broken Bones*

Sometimes a fall or accident causes a broken bone, which may require X-rays and surgery. Treatment cannot be delayed until after pregnancy; the problem must be dealt with immediately. If you find yourself in such a situation, insist your OB/GYN be contacted before *any* test or treatment is done.

If X-rays are required, your pelvis and abdomen must be shielded. If they cannot be shielded, the need for the X-ray must be weighed against the risks it poses to the baby.

Anesthesia or pain medications may be necessary with a simple break that requires setting or pinning. It is best for you and the baby to avoid general anesthesia if possible. Pain medication may be needed for pain relief, but its use should be kept to a minimum.

If general anesthesia is required to repair a break, the baby should be monitored closely. You may not have a lot of choice in the matter. Your surgeon and OB/GYN will work together to provide the best care for you and your baby.

ᴖ *Systemic Lupus Erythematosus (SLE)*

Some women have conditions before pregnancy that require medication for the rest of their lives. They are often concerned about the effects medication may have on their developing babies. One such condition is systemic lupus erythematosus (SLE).

Many young women have lupus and take steroids to control the problem. They want to know if medication they take can harm their baby. Should they continue to take steroids during pregnancy?

Lupus is a disease of unknown cause that occurs most often in young or middle-aged women. (Women have lupus much more frequently than men—about nine women to every man.) Those who have lupus have a large number of antibodies in their bloodstream. These antibodies are directed toward the woman's own tissues, which causes problems.

The diagnosis of SLE is made through blood tests, which look for the suspect antibodies. Blood tests done for lupus are a lupus antibody test and/or an antinuclear antibody test.

Antibodies can be directed to various organs in the body and may actually damage them. Affected organs include joints, skin, kidneys, muscles, lungs, the brain and the central nervous system. The most common symptom of lupus is joint pain, which is often mistaken for arthritis. Other symptoms include lesions, rashes or sores on the skin, fever and hypertension.

We don't have a cure for lupus. Systemic lupus erythematosus is generally unaffected by pregnancy. However, miscarriage, premature delivery and complications around the time of delivery are slightly increased in a woman with lupus. If kidneys were involved and there was kidney damage during the flareups, you must be on the lookout for kidney problems during pregnancy.

Steroids, short for *corticosteroids,* are generally prescribed to treat lupus. The primary medication used is prednisone. It is usually prescribed on a daily basis. It may be unnecessary to take prednisone every day, unless complications from lupus occur during pregnancy.

The many studies that have been done on the safety of prednisone during pregnancy have found it to be safe. If you are taking prednisone when you become pregnant, don't stop. It's important to talk to your doctor early if you have lupus or if you have been treated for the problem in the past.

Other medications are used when a woman is not pregnant. These include many anti-inflammatory medications, such as aspirin. It is best to avoid anti-inflammatory medications during pregnancy.

Tip for Week 25

Pregnancy can be a time of communication and personal growth with your partner. Listen when he talks. Let him know he is a very important source of emotional support for you.

You Should also Know

☞ *Sugar in Your Urine*

It is common for normal, pregnant, nondiabetic women to have a small amount of sugar in their urine. This occurs because of changes in sugar levels and how sugar is handled in the kidneys, which control the amount of sugar in your system. If excess sugar is present, you will lose it through the urine. Sugar in the urine is called *glucosuria.* It is common during pregnancy, particularly in the second and third trimesters.

Many doctors test every pregnant woman for diabetes, usually around the end of the second trimester. Testing is particularly important if there is a family history of diabetes. Blood tests used to diagnose diabetes are a fasting blood sugar and a glucose-tolerance test (GTT).

For a fasting-blood-sugar test, you eat the evening before the test. In the morning, before eating anything, you go to the lab and have the blood test done. A normal result indicates that diabetes is unlikely. An abnormal result is a high level of sugar in the blood, which needs further study.

Further study involves taking the glucose-tolerance test. You have to fast the night before this test. In the morning at the lab, you are given a solution to drink that has a measured amount of sugar in it. It is similar to a bottle of soda pop but doesn't taste as good.

Before you drink the sugar solution, a fasting-blood-sugar test is done. After you drink the solution, blood is drawn at predetermined intervals; usually at 30 minutes, 1 hour and 2 hours and sometimes even 3 hours. Drawing the blood at intervals gives an indication of how your body handles sugar.

If you need treatment, your doctor will devise a plan for you.

Week 26

Age of Fetus ~ 24 Weeks

How Big Is Your Baby?

Your baby now weighs almost 2 pounds (910g). By this week, its crown-to-rump length is around 9.2 inches (23cm). See the illustration on page 217. Your baby is beginning to put on weight.

How Big Are You?

The measurement of your uterus is about 2.5 inches (6cm) above your bellybutton or nearly 10.5 inches (26cm) from your pubic symphysis. During this second half of pregnancy, you will grow about 0.4 inch (1cm) each week. If you have been following a nutritious, balanced meal plan, your weight gain is probably between 16 and 22 pounds (7.2 to 9.9kg).

How Your Baby Is Growing and Developing

By now you have heard your baby's heartbeat at several visits. Listening to your developing baby's heart beat is very reassuring.

๛ *Heart Arrhythmia*

When listening to your baby's heartbeat during pregnancy, you may be startled to hear a skipped beat. An irregular heartbeat is called an *arrhythmia*. This is best described by regular pulsing or pounding with an occasional skipped or missed heartbeat. Arrhythmias in a fetus are not unusual.

There are many causes of fetal arrhythmias. An arrhythmia may occur as the heart grows and develops. As the heart matures, the arrhythmia often disappears. It may occur in the fetus of a pregnant woman who has lupus.

If an arrhythmia is discovered before labor and delivery, you may require fetal heart-rate monitoring during labor. (This is discussed in Week 35.)

When an arrhythmia is detected during labor, it may be desirable to have a pediatrician present at the time of delivery. He or she will make sure the baby is all right and is treated right away if a problem exists.

Changes in You

You are getting bigger as your uterus, placenta and baby grow larger. Discomforts such as back pain, pressure in your pelvis, leg cramps and headaches may occur more frequently.

Time is passing quickly. You are approaching the end of the second trimester. Two-thirds of the pregnancy is behind you; it won't be long until your baby is born.

By this week, your baby weighs about 2 pounds (910g). It is now putting on some weight and filling out.

How Your Actions Affect Your Baby's Development

✂ *Seizures*

A history of seizures—before pregnancy, during a previous pregnancy or during this pregnancy—is information you must share with your doctor. Another term for seizure is *convulsion*.

Seizures can and usually do occur without warning. A seizure indicates an abnormal condition related to the nervous system, particularly the brain. During a seizure, a person often loses body control. The serious nature of this problem during pregnancy is compounded because of concern about the baby's safety.

Doctors describe different types of seizures. Seizures involving the entire body are called *grand mal* seizures. A grand mal seizure begins with the sudden loss of consciousness; the person usually falls to the ground. Arms and legs often move about, and sometimes bowel control is lost at the same time. Following a seizure, the person may be in a state of recovery that may last for several minutes. As it passes, there can be mental confusion, headache and drowsiness.

Another type of seizure is a *petit mal* seizure. This type also comes without warning. It is noted for its short duration and minimal movement of arms or legs. It usually involves a loss of consciousness that lasts only a few seconds. Other types of seizures can also occur. They are not within the scope of this book.

If you have never had a problem with seizures, know that a short episode of dizziness or lightheadedness is not usually a seizure. Seizures are usually diagnosed by someone observing the seizure and noting the symptoms previously mentioned. An electroencephalogram (EEG) may be needed to diagnose a seizure. (In Week 31, seizures as they relate to eclampsia are discussed.)

✒ *Medication to Control Seizures*

If you take medication for seizure control or prevention, share this important information with your doctor at the beginning of pregnancy. Medication can be taken during pregnancy to control seizures, but some medications are safer than others.

For example, Dilantin® can cause birth defects in a baby, which include facial problems, microcephaly (a small head) and developmental delay. Other medications are used during pregnancy for seizure prevention. One of the more common is phenobarbital, but there is some concern about the safety of this medication.

Seizures during pregnancy or at any other time require serious discussion with your doctor and increased monitoring during pregnancy. If you have questions or concerns about a history of possible seizures, talk to your doctor about them.

✧ *Feeling Your Baby Move*

The movement of your baby is usually very reassuring and a sensation most pregnant women enjoy. Your partner can experience and enjoy the baby's movements by feeling your abdomen when the baby is active.

Women often ask how often a baby should move. They want to know if they should be concerned if the baby moves too much or doesn't move enough. These are hard questions to answer because your sensation is different from that of another woman. The movement of each baby you carry may be different. It is usually more assuring to have a baby move frequently. But it isn't unusual for a baby to have quiet times when there is not as much activity.

If you've been on the go, you may not have noticed the baby move because you've been active and busy. It may help to lie on your side to notice if the baby is moving or is still. Many women report their baby is much more active at night, keeping them awake and making it hard to sleep.

If your baby is quiet and not as active as what seems normal or what you expected, discuss it with your doctor. You can always visit your doctor to hear the baby's heartbeat if the baby hasn't been moving in its usual pattern. In most instances, there is nothing to worry about.

✧ *Pain Under Your Ribs*

Some women complain of pain under their ribs and in their lower abdomen when their baby moves. Is this pain normal?

This type of pain isn't an unusual problem, but it may cause enough discomfort to concern you. The baby's movement has increased to a point where you will probably feel it every day, and movements are getting stronger and harder. At the same time, your uterus is getting larger and putting more pressure on all your organs. Your growing, expanding uterus presses on the small bowel, bladder and rectum.

Jane asked me at her office visit why she was having "sharp, stabbing pains" under her ribs. She wanted to know what she could do about them. I told her this was normal for some women. There wasn't much she could do about the pain or pressure she felt from the baby's movement. I advised her the best thing she could do was to lie on her side to relieve pressure in the area that was painful. If she felt pressure up under her right ribs, for example, she should lie on her left side.

If the pressure really is pain, don't ignore it. You need to discuss it with your doctor. In most cases, it isn't a serious problem.

> *Tip for Week 26*
>
> Lying on your side (your left side is best) when you rest provides the best circulation to your baby. You may not experience as much swelling if you rest on your left side during the day.

᧓ Avoid Retin-A during Pregnancy

Many women are waiting until they're older to have their first baby, as evidenced by the interest in my book *Your Pregnancy After 30*. More older women are having a first baby than ever before! This increase in age raises questions and concerns that wouldn't have applied a few years ago.

One of these concerns is the use of Retin-A® (tretinoin), not to be confused with Accutane (isotrentinoin). Retin-A is a substance in cream or lotion form used by many women to help them get rid of fine wrinkles on the face. The medicine is also used by dermatologists to treat people with acne.

What course of action should you follow if you are now using Retin-A? Stop using it. We don't have enough data to know if it's safe to use during pregnancy. But we do know any type of medication you use—whether taken internally, inhaled, injected or used topically (spread on the skin)—gets into your bloodstream. Any substance in your bloodstream can be passed to your baby. Some medications a mother-to-be uses become concentrated in the baby. Your body can handle it, but your baby's body may not be able to. If some substances build up in the baby, they can have significant effects on its development.

I recommend you avoid using Retin-A during pregnancy. In the future, we may know more about its effects on a growing baby. It's best to avoid using it for the sake of your baby.

✍ *Steroid Creams and Ointments*

Conditions sometimes arise during pregnancy that require treatment with creams or ointments. This treatment could include steroid preparations.

Consult your doctor. Any medication used on the skin can be absorbed into the body and passed on to the baby. Remember, don't use any medication, cream or ointment that you used before pregnancy without consulting your doctor first.

Week 27

Age of Fetus ✦ 25 Weeks

See the illustration on page 225.

How Big Is Your Baby?

This week marks the beginning of the third trimester. In addition to weight and crown-to-rump length, I'm adding total length of your baby's body from head to toe. This will give you an even better idea of how big your baby is during this last part of your pregnancy.

Your baby now weighs a little more than 2 pounds (1000g), and crown-to-rump length is about 9.6 inches (24cm) by this week. Total length is 15.3 inches (34cm). See the illustration on page 225.

How Big Are You?

Your uterus is about 2.8 inches (7cm) above your bellybutton. If measured from the pubic symphysis, it is more than 10.5 inches (27cm) from the pubic symphysis to the top of the uterus.

How Your Baby Is Growing and Developing

↷ *Eye Development*

Eyes first appear around day 22 of development in the embryo (about 5 weeks gestation). In the beginning, they look like a pair of shallow grooves on each side of the developing brain. These grooves continue to develop and eventually turn into pockets called *optical vesicles.* The lens of each eye develops from the ectoderm. (Ectoderm is discussed in Week 4.)

Early in development, eyes are on the side of the head. They move toward the middle of the face between 7 and 10 weeks of gestation.

At about 8 weeks gestation, blood vessels form that lead to the eye. During the 9th week of gestation, the pupil forms, which is the round opening in the eye.

By the 8th or 9th week of gestation, the nerve connection from the eyes to the brain begins to form. This nerve is called the *optic nerve.*

Eyelids that cover the eyes are fused (connected together) at around 11 to 12 weeks. They remain fused until about 27 to 28 weeks of pregnancy, when they open.

The retina, at the back of the eye, is light-sensitive. It is the part of the eye where light images come into focus. It develops its normal layers by about the 27th week of pregnancy. These layers receive light and light information, and transmit it to the brain for interpretation—what we know as sight.

↷ *Congenital Cataracts*

A congenital cataract is an eye problem that may occur at birth. Most people believe cataracts only occur in old age, but that's a misconception. They can appear in a newborn baby! Instead of being transparent or clear, the lens that focuses light onto the back of the eye is opaque or cloudy. This problem is usually caused by a genetic predisposition. However, it has been found in children born to mothers who had German measles (rubella) around the 6th or 7th week of pregnancy.

ও Microphthalmia

Another congenital eye problem is microphthalmia, in which the overall size of the eye is too small. The eyeball may be only two-thirds its normal size. This abnormality often occurs with other abnormalities of the eyes. It frequently results from maternal infections while the baby is developing inside the uterus, such as cytomegalovirus (CMV) or toxoplasmosis.

Changes in You

Your breasts have probably gone through many changes as your pregnancy has progressed. Your breasts were probably very tender or sore early in pregnancy. Discomfort may have continued as they have increased in size.

ও *Discovering a Breast Lump*

Discovering a breast lump at any time is important, during pregnancy or any other time. It's important for you to learn at an early age how to do a breast exam on yourself and to perform this on a regular basis (usually after every menstrual period). Nine out of 10 breast lumps are found by women examining themselves.

Your doctor will probably perform exams at regular intervals, usually when you have your annual Pap smear. If you have an exam every year and are lump-free, it helps assure you no lumps are present before beginning pregnancy.

Finding a breast lump may be delayed during pregnancy because of changes in your breasts. It may be more difficult to feel a lump. Enlargement of the breasts during pregnancy and nursing tends to hide lumps or masses in the tissue of the breast.

Usually a breast exam is done at some point during pregnancy, perhaps at your first prenatal visit. If your breasts are very tender, this exam may be postponed until later in pregnancy.

Examine your breasts during pregnancy as you do when you are not pregnant. Do it every 4 or 5 weeks—the first day of every month is a good time to do it.

Around this time, your baby's eyelids open. Your baby begins
opening and closing its eyes while still inside your uterus.

✥ *Tests for Breast Lumps*

The routine test for breast lumps is examination by yourself or
your doctor. Other tests include X-ray examination, called a
mammogram, and ultrasound examination of the breast.

If a lump is found, it may be necessary to have an ultrasound exam performed on the breast, or a mammogram. Because a mammogram utilizes X-rays, your pregnancy must be protected during the procedure, usually by shielding your abdomen with a lead apron.

It has not been shown that pregnancy accelerates the course or growth of a breast lump. But we do know it is difficult to find a breast lump because of breast changes.

❧ Treatment during Pregnancy

Often a lump in the breast can be drained or aspirated. Fluid removed from the cyst is sent to the lab for evaluation to ensure there are no abnormal cells in the fluid. If a lump or cyst cannot be drained by a needle, a biopsy of the cyst or lump may be necessary.

If fluid is clear, it's a good sign. Bloody fluid is of more concern and must be studied under a microscope in the laboratory.

If examination of a lump indicates breast cancer, treatment during pregnancy is not significantly different from treatment for nonpregnant women. Treatment complications include the need for medication, such as anesthesia for a biopsy. If a lump is cancerous, the need for radiation therapy and chemotherapy must be considered.

How Your Actions Affect Your Baby's Development

❧ Falling and Injuries from Falls

A fall is the most frequent cause of minor injury during pregnancy. Fortunately, a fall is usually without serious injury to the baby or to the mother. The uterus is well protected in the abdomen inside the bony pelvis. The baby is protected against injury by the cushion of amniotic fluid surrounding it. Your uterus and abdominal wall also offer some protection.

❧ If You Fall

If you fall, contact your doctor; he or she may want to examine you. You may feel reassured if you are monitored and your baby's heartbeat is checked. The baby's movement after a fall can be reassuring.

—————— **Signs to Watch for after a Fall** ——————

Some signs can alert you to a problem after a fall. Signs that indicate potentially serious problems after a fall include:

- bleeding
- a gush of fluid from the vagina, indicating rupture of membranes
- severe abdominal pain

Placental abruption (discussed in Week 33) is one of the most serious events that can occur because of a fall or injury. With placental abruption, the placenta prematurely separates from the uterus. Another significant injury is a broken bone or an injury that immobilizes you. (See the discussion of treating broken bones in Week 25.)

—————— ✳ ——————

Minor injuries to the abdomen are treated in the usual fashion, as though you were not pregnant. However, avoid X-rays if possible.

Ultrasound evaluation may be important after a fall. This is judged on an individual basis, depending on the severity of your symptoms and your injury.

⌇ *Take Care to Avoid Falls*

Remember your balance and mobility change as you grow larger during pregnancy. Be careful during the winter when parking lots and sidewalks may be wet or icy. Many pregnant women also fall on stairs. Always use the handrail.

Slow down a little as you get larger; you won't be able to get around as quickly as you normally do. With the change in your balance, plus any dizziness you may experience, it's important to be vigilant about this.

ᔐ *Prenatal Classes*

Wendy asked me when she should think about signing up for prenatal classes. Even though she was just beginning the third trimester, I told her it wasn't too early to think about and to register for these classes. It's a good idea to get signed up for classes so you can take them *before* you get to the end of your pregnancy. By doing this, you'll have time to practice what you learn. You won't be just beginning your classes when you deliver!

During pregnancy, you have probably been learning what's going to happen at delivery by talking with your doctor and by asking questions. You have also learned what lies ahead from reading materials given to you by your doctor, from other books, such as *Your Pregnancy Questions & Answers* and *Your Pregnancy After 30*, or from pamphlets. Childbirth classes offer yet another way to learn about this important part of pregnancy. They help you prepare for labor and delivery.

Classes are usually held for small groups of pregnant women and their partners or labor coaches. This is an excellent way to learn. You can also interact with other couples and ask questions. You'll discover other women are concerned about many of the same things you are, such as labor and pain management. It's good to know you aren't the only one thinking about what lies ahead.

Childbirth classes are offered in various settings. Most hospitals that deliver babies offer prenatal classes, often taught by the labor-and-delivery nurses or by a midwife. Other types of classes have different degrees of involvement. This means the time commitment or depth of the subject covered is different for each of the various classes that may be available.

Ask your doctor or your doctor's nurse about classes they recommend. They can help you decide which type of class would be best for you.

Classes are intended to inform you and your partner or labor coach about what to expect, what happens at the hospital and what happens during labor and delivery. Some couples find classes are a good opportunity to get their partner more involved and to help make him feel more comfortable with the pregnancy. This may give him the opportunity to take a more active part at the time of labor and delivery, as well as during the rest of your pregnancy.

By meeting in class on a regular basis, usually once a week for 4 to 6 weeks, you can learn about many things that concern you. Classes often cover a wide range of subjects, including the following areas.

- Will you need an episiotomy?
- Do you need an enema?
- When is a fetal monitor necessary?
- What's going to happen when you reach the hospital?
- Is an epidural or some other type of anesthesia right for you?

These are important questions. Discuss them with your doctor if they are not answered in your childbirth-education classes.

Prenatal classes are not only for first-time pregnant women. If you have a new partner, if it has been a few years since you've had a baby, if you have questions or if you would like a review of what lies ahead, a prenatal class can help you.

> *Tip for Week 27*
> Childbirth-education classes are not just for couples. Classes are often offered for single mothers or for pregnant women whose partners cannot come to classes. Ask your physician about classes for you.

These classes may reduce the worry and concern you and your partner may feel about labor and delivery. And they'll help you enjoy the birth of your baby even more.

∼ Home Uterine Monitoring

Home uterine monitoring is used to identify women with premature labor. Conditions associated with premature delivery include a previous preterm delivery, infections, premature rupture of membranes, pregnancy-induced hypertension and multiple fetuses.

Home uterine monitoring combines recording uterine contractions with daily telephone contact with the healthcare provider. A recording of contractions is transmitted from the woman's home by telephone to a center where contractions can be evaluated. Thanks to personal computers, your doctor may be able to view the recordings at his or her own home.

Cost for home monitoring varies but runs between $80 and $100 a day; some insurance companies cover it. The cost of home monitoring can often be justified if a premature delivery is prevented—it saves thousands of dollars in the care of a premature baby (sometimes more than $100,000).

Not everyone agrees that home monitoring is beneficial or cost-effective. It may be difficult to identify all the patients who need this type of monitoring. Need for home uterine monitoring should be considered on an individual basis. Discuss this option with your physician if you have experienced preterm labor in the past or have other risk factors for preterm labor.

Week 28

Age of Fetus ~ 26 Weeks

How Big Is Your Baby?

Your baby weighs about 2.4 pounds (1100g). Crown-to-rump length is close to 10 inches (25cm). Total length is 15.75 inches (35cm).

How Big Are You?

Your uterus is now well above your umbilicus. Sometimes this growth seems gradual. At other times, it may seem as though changes happen rapidly, as if overnight.

Your uterus is about 3.2 inches (8cm) above your bellybutton. If you measure from the pubic symphysis, it is about 11 inches (28cm) to the top of the uterus. Your weight gain by this time should be between 17 and 24 pounds (7.7 and 10.8kg).

How Your Baby Is Growing and Developing

Until this time, the surface of the baby's developing brain has appeared smooth. At around 28 weeks of pregnancy, the brain forms characteristic grooves and indentations on the surface. The amount of brain tissue also increases.

Your baby's eyebrows and eyelashes may be present. Hair on the baby's head is growing longer.

The baby's body is becoming plumper and rounder. It's beginning to fill out a little because of increased fat underneath the skin. Before this time, the baby had a thin appearance.

Your baby now weighs about 2.4 pounds (1100g). This is an amazing growth compared to just 11 weeks ago, when it weighed only about 3.5 ounces (100g) at 17 weeks of pregnancy. Your baby has increased its weight more than 10 times in 11 weeks. In the last 4 weeks, from the 24th week of your pregnancy to this week, its weight has doubled. Your baby is growing rapidly!

Changes in You

↝ The Placenta

The placenta plays a critical role in the growth, development and survival of the baby. The illustration on page 233 shows the fetus attached to the umbilical cord, which attaches to the placenta.

Two important cell layers, the amnion and the chorion, are involved in the development of the placenta and the amniotic sac. Development and function of the cell layers is complicated, and their description is beyond the scope of this book. However, the amnion is the layer around the amniotic fluid in which the fetus floats.

The placenta begins to form with trophoblastic cells. These cells grow through the walls of maternal blood vessels and establish contact with your bloodstream without your blood or fetal blood mixing. (Fetal circulation is separate from your circulation.) These cells grow into the blood vessels without making a

Placenta

Cord

The placenta, shown here with the fetus, carries oxygen and nutrients to the growing baby. It is a very important part of pregnancy.

vascular connection (or opening) between the blood vessels. But fetal blood flow in the placenta is very close to your blood flow in the placenta.

We have closely followed your baby's weight gain in this book. The placenta is also growing at a rapid rate. At 10 weeks gestation, the placenta weighed about 0.7 ounce (20g). Ten weeks later, at 20 weeks gestation, it weighs almost 6 ounces (170g). In another 10 weeks, the placenta will have increased to 15 ounces

(430g). At full term, 40 weeks, it will weigh almost 1.5 pounds (650g)!

Connections are made between fetal blood vessels and the developing placenta as early as the 2nd or 3rd week of development. During the 3rd week of gestation, projections (villi) at the base of the placenta become firmly attached to the underlying layer of the uterus.

Villi are important during pregnancy. The space around the villi (intervillus space) becomes honeycombed with maternal blood vessels. The villi absorb nutrients and oxygen from the maternal blood; these are transported to the growing baby through the umbilical vein in the umbilical cord. Waste products from the baby are brought through the umbilical arteries to the intervillus space, and are transferred to the maternal bloodstream. In this way, the baby gets rid of waste products.

✧ What Does the Placenta Do?

The placenta is involved in moving oxygen and carbon dioxide to and from the baby. It is also involved in nutrition and the excretion of waste products from the baby.

In addition to these functions, the placenta has a very important hormonal role. It produces human chorionic gonadotropin (HCG) (discussed in Week 5). This hormone is found in your bloodstream in measurable amounts within 10 days after fertilization. Pregnancy tests check HCG levels to determine if a woman is pregnant. The placenta also begins making the hormones estrogen and progesterone by the 7th or 8th week of pregnancy.

✧ What Does the Placenta Look Like?

At full term, a normal placenta is flat and has a cakelike, round or oval appearance. It is about 6 to 8 inches (15 to 20cm) in diameter and 0.8 to 1.2 inches (2 to 3cm) thick at its thickest part. It weighs between 17.5 and 24 ounces (500 to 650g) on average.

Placentas vary widely in size and shape. A placenta that is too large (placentamegaly) can be found when a woman is infected with syphilis or when a baby has erythroblastosis (Rh-sensitization of the baby). Sometimes it occurs without any obvious explanation. A small placenta may be found in normal pregnancies but may also be found with intrauterine-growth retardation.

The part of the placenta that attaches to the wall of the uterus has a beefy or spongy appearance. The fetal side of the placenta, the side closest to the baby inside the amniotic sac, is smooth. It is covered with amniotic and chorionic membranes.

The placenta is a red or reddish-brown color. Around the time of birth, the placenta may have white patches on it, which are calcium deposits.

In multiple pregnancies, there may be more than one placenta. Or there may be one placenta with more than one umbilical cord coming from it. Usually with twins, there are two amniotic sacs, with two umbilical cords running to the fetuses from one placenta.

The umbilical cord, which is the attachment from the placenta to the baby, contains two umbilical arteries and one umbilical vein, which carry blood to and from the baby. It is about 22 inches (55cm) long. The cord is usually white and contains large blood vessels.

A few women experience problems involving the placenta during pregnancy. These include placental abruption (see Week 33) and placenta previa (see Week 34). After delivery, a retained placenta is sometimes a problem (see Week 38).

Tip for Week 28
You will probably receive an injection of RhoGAM at this point in your pregnancy, if you are Rh-negative. This keeps you from becoming sensitized if your baby's blood mixes with yours. The RhoGAM protects against sensitization until the time of delivery.

How Your Actions Affect Your Baby's Development

∼ *Dealing with Maternal Asthma*

Asthma is a respiratory illness characterized by an increased responsiveness or sensitivity to stimulation of the trachea and the bronchi, both important to breathing. Problems with asthma are manifested by difficulty breathing, shortness of breath, coughing and wheezing. (Wheezing is a noise like a whistling or a hissing made as air moves through narrowed airways.)

Asthma comes and goes, with acute worsening of symptoms interspersed with symptom-free periods. It affects about 2% of the population in the United States and Canada. It is equally common in other countries.

It may occur at any age, but about 50% of all asthma cases occur before age 10. Another 33% of the cases occur by age 40. Pregnancy does not seem to cause any consistent, predictable problem with asthma. Some pregnant women appear to get better during pregnancy, while others remain about the same. A few get worse.

ᢌ *Treating Asthma Attacks*

Most pregnant women with asthma can have a safe pregnancy, labor and delivery. If a woman has severe asthma attacks when she isn't pregnant, she may have severe attacks during pregnancy.

In general, the treatment plan used before pregnancy will probably continue to be helpful. This includes medications prescribed for asthma before or during pregnancy.

During pregnancy, oxygen consumption increases by about 25%. Your baby needs oxygen to grow and to develop. That's why asthma treatment is so important while you're pregnant.

Asthma medication, such as terbutaline, and steroids, such as hydrocortisone or methylprednisolone, can be used during pregnancy. Aminophylline or theophyline may also be used.

Leeanne was concerned about her asthma and wanted to know what she could do for it that didn't require medication. I told her that many women have found they can help themselves with their asthma during pregnancy fairly easily. Maintaining good hydration with more-than-adequate fluid intake seems to help many women.

You Should also Know

↣ *Additional Testing*

Twenty-eight weeks of gestation is a time when many doctors initiate or repeat certain blood tests or procedures. Glucose-tolerance testing may also be done at this time.

↣ *How Is the Baby Lying?*

It is common at this point in pregnancy to ask your doctor which way the baby is lying. Is the baby head first? Is it bottom first (breech)? Is the baby lying sideways?

It's difficult—usually impossible—at this point in pregnancy to tell just by feeling your abdomen how the baby is lying and if it is coming bottom first, feet first or head first. The baby changes position during pregnancy and may continue to change its position for another month.

It doesn't hurt to try to feel the abdomen to see where the head is and where the abdomen is. In another 3 to 4 weeks, the baby's head will be harder, and it will be easier then for your doctor to determine how the baby is lying (called *presentation of the fetus*).

Week 29

Age of Fetus ∻ 27 Weeks

How Big Is Your Baby?

By this time, your baby weighs about 2.7 pounds (1250g). Crown-to-rump length is 10.4 inches (26cm). Total fetal length is 16.7 inches (37cm).

How Big Are You?

Measuring from your bellybutton, your uterus is about 3.5 to 4 inches (7.6 to 10.2cm) above it. Your uterus is about 11.5 inches (29cm) above the pubic symphysis. If you saw your doctor 4 weeks ago, around the 25th week of pregnancy, you probably measured about 10 inches (25cm) at that time. You've grown about 1.5 inches (4cm) in 4 weeks.

Your weight gain by this week should be between 19 and 25 pounds (8.55 and 11.25kg).

How Your Baby Is Growing and Developing

⌒ **Fetal Growth**

Week by week, I've noted the change in the baby's size as pregnancy progresses. I use average weights to give you an idea of about how large your baby is at a particular time. However, these are only averages; babies do vary greatly in size and weight.

Because growth is rapid during pregnancy, infants born prematurely may be very small. Even a few weeks' less time in the uterus can have a dramatic effect on the size of your baby. The baby continues to grow after 36 weeks of gestation but at a slower rate.

A couple of interesting factors have been identified with regards to the birth weight of your baby.

- Boys weigh more than girls.
- Birth weight of an infant increases with the increasing number of pregnancies you have or the number of babies you deliver.

These are general statements and don't apply to everyone, but they appear to apply in most cases. The average baby's birth weight at full term is 7 to 7.5 pounds (3280g to 3400g).

⌒ **How Mature Is Your Baby?**

A baby born between the 38th and 42nd weeks of pregnancy is a term baby or full-term infant. Before the 38th week, the term *preterm* can be applied to the baby. At 42 weeks of pregnancy, and after this time, *postterm* is used. *Postdate* is a newer term that some doctors use.

When a baby is born before the end of pregnancy, many people use the terms *premature* and *preterm* interchangeably. There is a difference. An infant that is 32 weeks gestational age but has mature pulmonary or lung function at the time of birth is more appropriately called a *preterm infant* than a *premature infant*. *Premature* best describes an infant that has immature lungs at the time of birth.

ᴖ *Premature Babies*

Premature birth increases the risk of problems in the baby. It also increases the risk of fetal death. Babies born prematurely usually weigh less than 5.5 pounds (2500g).

The illustration on page 243 shows a premature baby with several leads attached to monitor the baby's heart rate. Many other attachments are used, such as I.V.s, tubes and masks that provide oxygen.

In 1950, the neonatal death rate was about 20 per 1000 live births. Today, the rate is less than 10 per 1000 live births. More preterm infants survive today than did 40 years ago.

The decreasing death rate applies primarily to infants delivered during the third trimester (27 weeks or more of gestation) who weigh at least 2.2 pounds (1000g) and are without birth defects. When gestational age and birth weight are below these levels, the death rate increases.

Better methods of caring for premature babies have contributed to higher survival statistics. Today, infants born as early as 25 weeks of pregnancy can survive. However, the long-term survival and quality of life for these babies remains to be seen as they grow older.

What is the survival rate for premature babies? The most recent information indicates for infants who weighed 1.1 pound (500g) to 1.5 pounds (700g), the survival rate is about 43%. For babies weighing between 1.5 pounds and 2.2 pounds (1000g), the survival rate is about 72%. These rates vary from hospital to hospital.

The average hospital stay for premature babies ranges from 125 days for infants weighing between 1.3 and 1.5 pounds (600 and 700g) to 76 days for babies in the 2- to 2.2-pound (900 to 1000g) birth-weight range.

Any discussion of survival rates must include the frequency rate of disabilities these premature babies suffer. In the lower birth-weight range, many babies who survived had disabilities. Higher-weight babies also had disabilities, but statistics for this group were much lower.

It's usually best for the baby to remain in the uterus as long as possible, so it can grow and develop fully. Occasionally it is best for the baby to be delivered early; for example, when the fetus is not receiving adequate nutrition. This is a rare occurrence.

———— Causes of Premature Labor ————

In most cases, the cause of premature labor is unknown. Causes we do understand include:

- a uterus with an abnormal shape
- multiple fetuses
- polyhydramnios or hydramnios
- placental abruption or placenta previa
- premature rupture of membranes
- an incompetent cervix
- abnormalities of the fetus
- fetal death
- retained IUD
- abortion performed late in previous pregnancy
- serious maternal illness
- incorrect estimate of gestational age

Finding the cause of premature labor and delivery may be difficult. An attempt is always made to determine what causes preterm labor before active labor begins. In this way, treatment may be more effective.

Some difficult questions that must be answered when premature labor begins include those below.

- Is it better for the infant to be inside the uterus or to be delivered?
- Are the dates of the pregnancy correct?
- Is this really labor?

ꜱ *Intrauterine-Growth Retardation*

Intrauterine-growth retardation (IUGR) refers to a fetus that does not grow as fast as it should while in the uterus. A baby suffering from IUGR has a higher risk of serious problems. (IUGR is discussed in depth in Week 31.)

The word "retardation" may cause a mother-to-be some concern. Retardation in this sense doesn't apply to the development or function of the baby's brain. It means the total growth and overall size of the baby are inappropriately small; growth and size are considered to be retarded.

Changes in You

ᔧ *Treatment of Premature Labor*

Can anything be done about premature labor? Yes—we now can treat premature labor in several different ways.

The treatment most often used for premature labor is bed rest. A woman is advised to stay in bed and lie on her side. (Either side is OK.) Not everyone agrees on this treatment, but bed rest is often very successful in stopping contractions and premature labor. If this happens to you, it may mean you can't go to work or continue many activities. It's worth it to agree to bed rest if you can avoid premature delivery of your baby.

Beta-adrenergic agents, also called *tocolytic agents,* may be used to suppress labor. Beta-adrenergics are muscle relaxants. They relax the uterus and decrease contractions. (The uterus is mainly muscle, which is active in pushing the baby out through the cervix during labor.) At this time, only ritodrine (Yutopar®) is approved by the Food and Drug Administration (FDA) to treat premature labor.

Ritodrine is given in three different forms. It can be given intravenously, as an intramuscular injection and as a pill. It is usually initially given intravenously and may require a hospital stay of a couple of days or more.

When premature contractions stop, you can be switched to oral medications, which are taken every 2 to 4 hours. Ritodrine is approved for use in pregnancies over 20 weeks and under 36 weeks gestation. In some cases, medication is used without an I.V. first. This is done most often in women with a history of

Monitors on baby

Premature baby (born at 29 weeks of pregnancy) shown with fetal monitors attached to it. Note size of adult hand in comparison.

premature labor or for a woman with multiple pregnancies.

Side effects related to the use of ritodrine may be very uncomfortable. Side effects include tachycardia (rapid heartbeat), hypotension, the feeling of apprehension or fear, chest tightness or chest pain, changes in the electrocardiogram (record of the heart's electrical activity) and pulmonary edema (fluid in the lungs).

Ritodrine can cause maternal metabolic problems, including increased blood sugar, low blood potassium and even acidosis of the blood, similar to a diabetic reaction. Less serious complications include headaches, vomiting, shaking, fever and even hallucinations.

Similar problems probably occur in the baby. Low blood-sugar levels have been seen in babies after birth in some mothers who took ritodrine before delivery. Rapid heartbeat is also commonly seen in these babies.

Terbutaline is also frequently used as a muscle relaxant. Although it has been shown to be an effective medication, it has not been approved for this use by the FDA. Terbutaline side effects are similar to those of ritodrine.

Magnesium sulfate is used to treat pre-eclampsia (see Week 31 for information on pre-eclampsia). We have known for quite a while that magnesium sulfate can also be used to help stop labor. This medication is most often given through an I.V. and requires hospitalization. However, it is occasionally given as an oral preparation, without hospitalization. Your doctor must monitor you frequently if magnesium sulfate is prescribed.

Sedatives or narcotics may be used in early attempts to stop labor. This may consist of an injection of morphine or meperidine (Demerol). This is not a long-term solution but may be effective in initially stopping labor.

✑ Benefits of Stopping Premature Labor

Benefits of stopping premature labor include reducing the risks of fetal problems and problems related to premature delivery. If you experience premature labor, see your doctor frequently. Your doctor will probably monitor your pregnancy with ultrasound or nonstress tests.

How Your Actions Affect Your Baby's Development

Most of our discussion this week has been devoted to the premature infant and treatment of premature labor. If you are diagnosed as having premature labor and your doctor prescribes bed rest and medications to stop it, follow his or her advice!

If you're concerned about your doctor's instructions, discuss them with him or her. If you're told not to work or you are advised to reduce your activities and you ignore the advice, you're taking chances with your well-being and your unborn baby's. It isn't worth taking risks.

Don't be afraid to ask for another opinion or the opinion of a perinatologist if you experience premature labor.

✍ *Chlamydia Infections*

You may have heard about or read about chlamydia. It is a common sexually transmitted disease (STD); between 3- and 5-million people are infected every year. It may be difficult to determine if you have a chlamydial infection because you may not have symptoms.

Between 20% and 40% of all sexually active women have probably been exposed to chlamydia at some time. Chlamydia infection can cause serious problems if left untreated, but these problems can be avoided with treatment.

Infection is caused by a germ that invades certain types of healthy cells. Infection may be passed through sexual activity, including oral sex.

Chlamydia is most likely to occur in young people who have more than one sexual partner. It may also occur in women who have other sexually transmitted diseases. Some doctors believe chlamydia occurs more commonly in women who take oral contraceptives. Barrier methods of contraception, such as diaphragms and condoms used with spermicides, may offer protection from chlamydial infections.

One of the most significant complications of chlamydia is pelvic inflammatory disease (PID), a severe infection of the upper genital organs involving the uterus, the Fallopian tubes and even the ovaries. There may be pelvic pain, or there may be no symptoms at all. PID can result from an untreated infection that spreads throughout the pelvic area. Chlamydia is one of the main causes of PID.

If a PID infection is prolonged or recurrent, the reproductive organs, Fallopian tubes and uterus may be damaged, with formation of adhesions. Surgery may be required to repair them. If tubes are damaged, scar tissue can increase the risk of ectopic or tubal pregnancy.

✑ *Chlamydia in Pregnancy*

During pregnancy, a mother-to-be can pass a chlamydial infection to her baby as it comes through the birth canal and vagina. The baby has a 20% to 50% chance of getting chlamydia if the mother has it. It may cause an eye infection, but that is easily treated. Complications that are more serious include pneumonia, which may require the baby's hospitalization.

✑ *Testing for Chlamydia*

Chlamydia can be detected by a cell culture, but as I've said, more than half of those infected with chlamydia have no symptoms. Symptoms that may appear include burning or itching in the genital area, discharge from the vagina, painful or frequent urination, or pain in the pelvic area. Men may also experience symptoms.

Rapid diagnostic tests can be done in the doctor's office. They can provide a result quickly, possibly even before you go home.

Chlamydia is usually treated with tetracycline, but this drug should not be given to a pregnant woman. During pregnancy, erythromycin may be the drug of choice. After treatment, your doctor may want to do another culture to make sure the infection is gone.

If you're concerned about a possible chlamydial infection, discuss it with your doctor.

Tip for Week 29
Most women find their shoe size increases by half a size in the third trimester. You may need larger shoes for your comfort.

Week 30

Age of Fetus ⸙ 28 Weeks

At this point in your pregnancy, your baby weighs about 3 pounds (1360g). Its crown-to-rump length is a little over 10.8 inches (27cm), and total length is 17 inches (38cm).

Measuring from your bellybutton, your uterus is about 4 inches (10cm) above it. From the pubic symphysis, the top of your uterus measures about 12 inches (30cm).

It may be hard to believe you still have 10 weeks to go! You may feel like you're running out of room as your uterus grows up under your ribs. However, your fetus, placenta and uterus, along with the amniotic fluid, will continue to get larger.

The average weight gain during pregnancy is 25 to 35 pounds (11.4 to 15.9kg). About half of this weight is concentrated in the growth of the uterus, the baby and the placenta, and in the volume of amniotic fluid. This growth is mostly in the front of your abdomen and in your pelvis, where it is very noticeable to you. You may experience increasing discomfort in your pelvis and abdomen as pregnancy progresses. At this point, you should be gaining about a pound a week.

How Your Baby Is Growing and Developing

✎ Umbilical-Cord Knots

The illustration this week (opposite) shows a fetus and its umbilical cord. Can you see the knot in the cord? You may wonder how a knot like this can occur. We do not believe the cord grows in a knot.

A baby is usually quite active during pregnancy. We believe these knots occur as the baby moves around in early pregnancy. A loop forms in the umbilical cord; the baby moves through the loop, and a knot results. Your actions do not cause or prevent this kind of complication, which is very serious. A knot in the umbilical cord does not occur often. (Also see Week 35.)

✎ Your Baby's Movements before Birth

Feeling your baby move (quickening) is one of the more precious parts of pregnancy. Before you feel the baby move, you probably had a positive pregnancy test and heard the baby's heartbeat at your doctor's office.

Feeling life inside you can be the beginning of your bonding with your baby. Many women feel they begin to relate to the baby and its personality before delivery through feeling the baby's movements. Share this miraculous time with your partner by having him feel your abdomen when the baby moves.

Movement of your baby can vary in intensity. It can range from a faint flutter, sometimes described as a feeling of a butterfly or a gas bubble in early pregnancy, to brisk motions or even painful kicks and pressure as your baby gets larger.

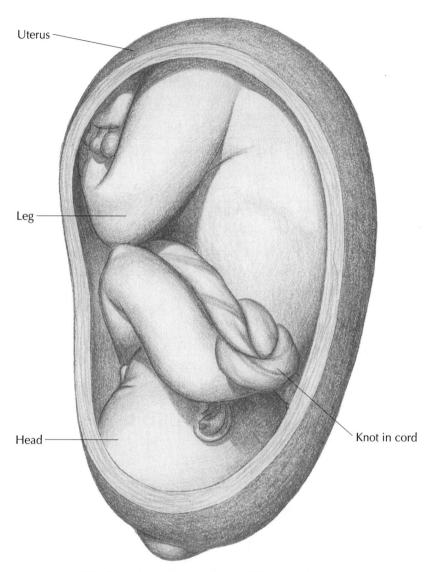

Uterus

Leg

Head

Knot in cord

This fetus has a knot in its umbilical cord.

Changes in You

Pregnancy is a happy time for most women, filled with anticipation and excitement. Very occasionally, however, serious problems can occur. Cancer in pregnancy is one serious complication that very rarely occurs.

This discussion is included not to scare you but to provide you with information. It is not a pleasant subject to discuss, especially at this time. However, I believe every woman should have this information available. Its inclusion in this book is twofold:

- to increase your awareness of this serious problem
- to provide you with a resource to help you formulate questions for a dialogue with your healthcare provider if you wish to discuss it

᧤ Cancer before Pregnancy

If you are now pregnant and you have had cancer in the past, tell your doctor as soon as you discover you are pregnant. He or she may need to make decisions about individualized care for you during pregnancy.

᧤ Cancer in Pregnancy

The occurrence of cancer at any time is very stressful. When cancer occurs during pregnancy, it is even more stressful. The doctor must consider how to treat the cancer, but he or she is also concerned about the developing baby.

How many issues are handled depends on when cancer is discovered. A woman's concerns may include the following.

- Will the pregnancy have to be terminated so the cancer can be treated?
- Will medications used for treatment harm the baby?
- Will the malignancy or therapy used to treat the malignancy affect the baby or be passed to the baby?
- Should therapy be delayed until after delivery or after termination of the pregnancy?

Fortunately, many cancers in women occur after the reproductive years, which lowers the likelihood of cancer during pregnancy. Cancer during pregnancy is a rare occurrence and must be treated on an individual basis.

᧤ Cancers Found during Pregnancy

Some cancers found during pregnancy include breast tumors, leukemia and lymphomas, melanomas, gynecologic cancers (cancer of the female organs, such as the cervix, uterus and ovaries) and bone tumors.

Tremendous changes affect your body during pregnancy. Researchers suggest that these changes can affect the possible discovery of cancer during pregnancy.

- Some believe cancers influenced by the increased hormone levels during pregnancy may increase in frequency during pregnancy.
- Increased blood flow, with accompanying changes in the lymphatic system, may contribute to the transfer of cancer to other parts of the body.
- Anatomical and physiological changes of pregnancy (growth of the abdomen and changes in the breast) can make it difficult to find or to diagnose an early cancer.

These three beliefs about cancer during pregnancy appear to have some validity but vary widely depending on the cancer and the organ involved.

♍ *Breast Cancer*

Breast cancer is rare in women younger than 35. Fortunately, it is an uncommon complication of pregnancy.

During pregnancy, it may be harder to find breast cancer because of changes in the breasts, such as tenderness, increased size and even lumpiness. Of all women who have breast cancer, about 2% are pregnant at the time of diagnosis. Most evidence indicates pregnancy does not increase the rate of growth or spread of a breast cancer.

Treatment of breast cancer during pregnancy varies and must be individualized. It may require surgery, chemotherapy or radiation; a combination of all these treatments may be used.

♍ *Pelvic Cancers*

Cervical cancer is believed to occur about once in every 10,000 pregnancies. However, about 1% of the women who have cancer of the cervix are pregnant when it is diagnosed. Cancer of the cervix is curable, particularly if it is found and treated in its early stages.

Malignancies of the vulva, the tissue surrounding the opening to the vagina, have been also reported during pregnancy. But only a few cases have occurred.

⋰ *Other Cancers in Pregnancy*

Hodgkin's disease (a form of cancer) commonly affects young people. It is now being controlled for long periods with radiation and chemotherapy. The disease occurs in about 1 of every 6000 pregnancies. Pregnancy does not appear to have a negative effect on the course of Hodgkin's disease.

Pregnant women who have leukemia have demonstrated an increased chance of premature labor. They may also experience an increase in bleeding after pregnancy. Leukemia is usually treated with chemotherapy or radiation therapy.

Melanoma may occur during pregnancy. A melanoma is a cancer derived from skin cells that produce melanin (pigment). A malignant melanoma spreads through the body. Pregnancy may cause symptoms or problems to worsen. A melanoma can spread to the placenta and to the baby.

Bone tumors are rare during pregnancy. However, two types of benign (noncancerous) bone tumors can affect pregnancy and delivery. These cancers, endochondromas and benign exostosis, can involve the pelvis; tumors may interfere with labor. The possibility of having a Cesarean delivery is more likely with these tumors.

How Your Actions Affect Your Baby's Development

⋰ *Bathing during Pregnancy*

Nicole asked me about the safety of bathing toward the end of her pregnancy. She was concerned that taking a bath would in some way harm her baby. Most doctors believe it's safe to bathe throughout pregnancy. They may caution you to be careful as you get in or out of the bathtub, as I cautioned Nicole. Most will not tell you to avoid a bath while you're pregnant. However, if you think your water has broken, avoid a tub bath.

Women also ask me how they would know if their water breaks, if it happens while they are in the tub. When your water breaks, you'll usually notice a gush of water followed by slow leakage. If your water breaks while you're in the tub, you may not notice the initial gush of fluid. However, you'll probably notice the leakage of fluid, which can last for quite a while.

> *Tip for Week 30*
> Good posture can help relieve lower-back stress and eliminate some backache discomfort.

You Should also Know

∾ *Rupture of Membranes*

The membranes around the baby that contain the amniotic fluid are called the *bag of waters*. They usually do not break until just before labor begins, when labor begins or during labor. But that isn't always the case.

Once your water breaks, take certain precautions. The membranes of pregnancy help protect your baby from infection. When your water breaks and you leak fluid, your risk of infection increases. An infection could be harmful to your baby. Call your doctor immediately when your water breaks.

Week 31

Age of Fetus ∞ 29 Weeks

How Big Is Your Baby?

Your baby continues to grow. It weighs about 3.5 pounds (1600g), and crown-to-rump length is 11.2 inches (28cm). Its total length is 18 inches (40cm).

How Big Are You?

Measuring from the pubic symphysis, it is now a little more than 12 inches (31cm) to the top of the uterus. From your bellybutton, it is about 4.4 inches (11cm).

At 12 weeks gestation, the uterus was just filling the pelvis. As you can see in the illustration on page 257, by this week the uterus fills a large part of your abdomen.

Your total pregnancy weight gain by this time should be between 21 and 27 pounds (9.45 and 12.15kg).

How Your Baby Is Growing and Developing

᠕ *Intrauterine-Growth Retardation*

Intrauterine-growth retardation (IUGR) indicates a newborn infant is small for its gestational age. By definition, its birth weight is below the 10th percentile for the baby's gestational age (the lowest 10%). This means 9 out of 10 babies of normal growth are larger.

When gestational age is appropriate—meaning dates are correct and the pregnancy is as far along as expected—and weight falls below the 10th percentile, there is reason for concern. Growth-retarded infants have a higher rate of death and injury than infants in the normal-weight range.

᠕ *Causes of IUGR*

What causes intrauterine-growth retardation? Below are some conditions that increase the chance of intrauterine-growth retardation or a small fetus.

Smoking and other tobacco use inhibits the baby's growth. The more cigarettes smoked, the greater the impairment.

Poor weight gain in the mother-to-be can cause problems in the baby. If a woman is average size or smaller and doesn't gain enough weight, it may result in a growth-retarded baby. This is one of the reasons that good nutrition and a healthful diet are so important during pregnancy. Do not attempt to restrict normal weight gain during pregnancy. Research indicates that when calories are restricted to under 1500 calories a day for an extended time, IUGR may result.

Maternal blood-flow problems, particularly pre-eclampsia, may cause IUGR. A more common problem is high blood pressure (hypertension), which can have a marked effect on fetal growth.

Kidney disease in a pregnant woman can cause retardation of fetal growth. Women who live at high altitudes are also more likely to have babies that weigh less than those born to women who live at lower altitudes.

Alcoholism can cause intrauterine-growth retardation. Drug use and abuse can also cause IUGR. Multiple fetuses may result in smaller fetal growth. Infections in the fetus, such as cytomegalovirus, rubella or other infections, may also restrict fetal growth.

Maternal anemia may be another cause of IUGR. (Anemia is discussed in depth in Week 22.) However, not every authority accepts maternal anemia as a cause of intrauterine-growth retardation.

Abnormalities of the umbilical cord or placenta may cause inhibited growth because the baby has received less nutrition during pregnancy. A woman who has delivered a growth-retarded infant may be more likely to do so again in subsequent pregnancies.

Other reasons for a small baby, unrelated to IUGR, include the fact that that a woman who is small might have a small baby. Prolonged pregnancy can lead to an undernourished, smaller baby. A malformed or abnormal fetus may also be smaller, especially when chromosomal abnormalities are present.

⚭ Diagnosing and Treating Intrauterine-Growth Retardation

Diagnosing IUGR can be difficult. One reason your doctor measures you at each visit is to see how your uterus is growing. A problem is usually found by measuring the uterus over a period of time and finding no change. If you measured 10.8 inches (27cm) at 27 weeks gestation and at 31 weeks you measure only 11 inches (28cm), your doctor might become concerned about IUGR and order tests.

Diagnosis of this type of problem is one important reason to keep all your prenatal appointments. You may not like being weighed at every appointment, but it helps your doctor see that your pregnancy is growing and the baby is getting bigger.

Intrauterine-growth retardation can be diagnosed or confirmed by ultrasound. Ultrasound may also be used to assure that the baby is healthy and no malformations exist that must be taken care of at birth.

When IUGR is diagnosed, avoid doing anything that could make it worse. Stop smoking. Improve your nutrition. Stop using drugs and alcohol.

Bed rest is another treatment. Resting enables the baby to receive the best blood flow, and better blood flow is the best

Comparative size of the uterus at 31 weeks of pregnancy (fetal age—29 weeks). The uterus can be felt about 4.4 inches (11 cm) above the bellybutton.

chance it has to improve growth. If IUGR is caused by maternal disease, attempts are made to improve the mother's general health.

An infant with intrauterine-growth retardation is at risk of dying before delivery. To avoid this, it may require delivering the baby before it is full term. Infants with IUGR may not tolerate labor well; a C-section is more likely because of fetal distress. The baby may be safer outside the uterus than inside in some cases.

Changes in You

⁓ *What Is Pre-eclampsia during Pregnancy?*

Pre-eclampsia, once called *toxemia of pregnancy*, describes a variety of conditions that occur only during pregnancy or shortly after delivery. For our discussion, I will use the term *pre-eclampsia* to simplify matters. Pre-eclampsia problems are characterized by a collection of symptoms, including:

- swelling (edema)
- protein in the urine (proteinuria)
- hypertension (high blood pressure)
- a change in reflexes (hyperreflexia)

Other nonspecific, important symptoms of pre-eclampsia include pain under the ribs on the right side, headache, seeing spots or changes in vision. These are all warning signs. Report them to your doctor immediately, particularly if you've had blood-pressure problems during pregnancy!

Pre-eclampsia can progress to eclampsia. *Eclampsia* refers to seizures or convulsions in a woman with pre-eclampsia. Seizures are not caused by a previous history of epilepsy or a seizure disorder.

Most pregnant women have some swelling during pregnancy; swelling in the legs does *not* mean you have pre-eclampsia. You must have some other symptoms of pre-eclampsia as well. It is also possible to have hypertension during pregnancy without having pre-eclampsia.

⁓ *What Causes Pre-eclampsia?*

No one knows what causes pre-eclampsia or eclampsia. It occurs most often during a woman's first pregnancy. Women over 30 years old who are having their first baby are more likely to develop high blood pressure and pre-eclampsia.

✌ *Treating Pre-eclampsia*

The goal in treating pre-eclampsia is to avoid eclampsia (seizures). That means keeping a close watch on you throughout pregnancy, and checking your blood pressure and weight at every prenatal visit.

Weight gain can be a sign of pre-eclampsia or worsening pre-eclampsia. Pre-eclampsia affects weight gain because it increases water retention. If you notice any symptoms, call your doctor's office.

Treatment of pre-eclampsia begins with bed rest at home. You may not be able to work or to spend much time on your feet. Bed rest allows for the most efficient functioning of your kidneys and blood flow to the uterus.

Lie on your side, not on your back. Drink lots of water. Avoid salt, salty foods and foods that contain sodium, which may make you retain fluid. Diuretics, which were used in the past, are not prescribed to treat pre-eclampsia today. They are not recommended.

If you can't rest at home in bed or if symptoms do not improve, your doctor may have to admit you to the hospital or deliver your baby. A baby is delivered for the following reasons:

- for your well-being
- to avoid seizures in you
- for the baby's well-being

During labor, pre-eclampsia may be treated with magnesium sulfate. It is given in an I.V. to prevent seizures during and after delivery. High blood pressure may be treated with antihypertensive medication.

If you think you've had a seizure, call your doctor immediately! Diagnosis may be difficult. It may be helpful to have someone who observed the possible seizure describe it to your doctor. Eclampsia (seizure) is treated with medications similar to those prescribed for seizure disorders (see Week 26).

How Your Actions Affect Your Baby's Development

♾ *Sleeping Positions*

I've already described the importance of resting on a regular basis and lying on your side when you sleep. (See Week 16.) Now is when it will pay off. You may notice you begin to retain water if you don't lie on your side when sleeping or resting. Lying on your side could help you feel better quickly.

Use extra pillows to support your abdomen or your legs as your pregnancy progresses.

♾ *Visiting Your Doctor*

It's important to keep appointments with your doctor. It may seem to you that not much happens at these visits, especially when everything is normal and going well. But the information your healthcare provider collects tells him or her a lot about your condition and your baby's.

Your doctor is watching for signs that tell him or her you might have a problem, such as changes in your blood pressure, changes in your weight or the inadequate growth of the baby. If these problems are not discovered early, they may have serious consequences for you and your baby.

You Should also Know

ᔓ *Pregnancy-induced Hypertension*

Pregnancy-induced hypertension occurs only during pregnancy. With hypertension of pregnancy, the systolic pressure (the first number) increases to higher than 140ml of mercury or a rise of 30ml of mercury over your beginning blood pressure. A diastolic reading (the second number) of over 90 or a rise of 15ml of mercury also indicates a problem. An example is a woman whose blood pressure at the beginning of pregnancy is 100/60. Later in pregnancy, it is 130/90. This indicates she may be developing hypertension or pre-eclampsia.

Your doctor will be able to determine if your blood pressure is rising to a serious level by checking it at every prenatal appointment.

ᔓ *You Can Affect Blood Flow to Your Legs and Arms*

Margo couldn't get her shoes on after she'd been up for a couple of hours, and her rings were getting tight. She thought something might be wrong. I told her that some swelling is normal in most pregnancies and that wearing tight-fitting clothing that restricts blood flow can produce a problem in blood return from the arms and legs. Sure enough, she said she had been wearing regular pantyhose. Clothing that is tight at the waist, knees, ankles, shoulders, elbows or wrists can all cause problems.

You may notice, especially as you near the end of pregnancy, that when you take your shoes off you may not be able to put them back on if you leave them off for a while. This problem is related to swelling.

You may also notice that wearing nylon stockings that are tight at the knee (or tight socks) leaves an indentation in your legs. It may look like you still have clothing on.

The way you sit can also affect circulation. Crossing your legs, either at the knee or at the ankle, restricts blood flow to your legs. To improve circulation, don't cross your legs.

∞ *Does Every Woman Need an Enema?*

Many women want to know if their doctor performs routine procedures at the time of delivery. One such procedure is an enema.

In the past, many doctors and many hospitals gave enemas routinely, without giving you much choice in the matter. Having an enema early in labor has its benefits. It decreases the amount of contamination by bowel movement or feces at the time of delivery and during labor, resulting in infection. It may also help after delivery, if you have an episiotomy. You may be happy not to have a bowel movement for a while.

Ask your doctor if an enema is routine or considered helpful. Tell him or her you'd like to know about the benefits of an enema and the reason for giving an enema in early labor. It isn't required by all doctors or all hospitals.

Week 32

Age of Fetus ⁓ 30 Weeks

By this week, your baby weighs almost 4 pounds (1800g). Crown-to-rump length is over 11.6 inches (29cm), and total length is 18.9 inches (42cm).

Measurement to the top of the uterus from the pubic symphysis is about 12.8 inches (32cm). Measuring from your bellybutton, the top of the uterus now measures almost 5 inches (12cm).

How Your Baby Is Growing and Developing

✤ Twins? Triplets? More?

When talking about pregnancies of more than one baby, in most cases we refer to twins. The chance of a twin pregnancy is more likely than pregnancy with triplets, quadruplets or quintuplets.

You and your partner may be in shock if you learn you have more than one baby on the way! It's a normal reaction. Eventually the joy of expecting two babies may help offset the fear and responsibility you may feel.

If you are expecting two or more babies, you will visit your doctor more often. You will need to plan carefully for delivery and care of the babies after you go home.

✤ Identical Twins and Fraternal Twins

Twin fetuses most commonly result from the fertilization of two separate eggs. These are called *dizygotic twins* or *fraternal twins*. With fraternal twins, you can have a boy and a girl.

About 33% of the time, twins come from a single egg that divides into two similar structures. Each has the potential of developing into a separate individual. These are known as *monozygotic twins* or *identical twins*. The two babies are almost always the same sex. Identical twins are not always identical. It is possible for fraternal twins to appear more alike than identical twins!

Either or both processes may be involved when more than two fetuses are formed. For example, quadruplets may result from fertilization of one, two, three or four eggs.

Division of the fertilized egg occurs between the first few days and about day 8. In this book, I refer to it as the third week of pregnancy. If division of the egg occurs after 8 days, the result can be twins that are connected, called *conjoined twins*. (Conjoined twins used to be called *Siamese twins*.) These babies may share important internal organs, such as the heart, lungs or liver. Fortunately this is a rare occurrence.

Placenta · Mother's abdomen

Babies' heads

Ultrasound of twins shows two babies in the uterus. If you look closely, you can see the two heads. The interpretive illustration shows how the babies are lying.

✍ *Frequency of Twin Births*

The frequency of twins depends on the type of twins. Identical twins occur about once in every 250 births around the world. This type of twin formation appears to be uninfluenced by age, race, heredity, number of pregnancies or medications taken for infertility (fertility drugs). The incidence of fraternal twins is influenced by race, heredity, maternal age, the number of previous pregnancies and the use of fertility drugs.

The frequency of multiple fetuses varies significantly among different races. Twins occur in 1 out of every 100 pregnancies in white women compared to 1 out of every 79 pregnancies in black women. Certain areas of Africa have an incredibly high frequency of twins. In some places, twins occur once in every 20 births! The occurrence of twins among Asians is less common: about 1 in every 150 births.

Heredity also plays a part in the occurrence of twins. In one study of fraternal twins, the chance of a female twin giving birth to a set of twins herself was about 1 in 58 births.

The occurrence of twins is probably more common than we know. Early ultrasound exams often reveal two sacs or two pregnancies. Later ultrasounds of the same woman may show one sac or one pregnancy has disappeared, while the other pregnancy continues to grow and to develop normally. Some researchers believe ultrasound should not be done in the first 8 to 10 weeks of pregnancy. Parents who are informed of twins at this point may be distraught to learn later that one of the babies will not be born.

Triplets occur once in every 8000 deliveries. Many doctors never deliver or participate in the delivery of triplets in their medical careers. I have been fortunate in my medical practice to deliver two sets of triplets.

Some families are more blessed than others. In one case I know of, a woman had three single births. Her fourth pregnancy was twins, and her fifth pregnancy was triplets! She and her husband decided on another pregnancy—they were surprised (and probably very relieved) when the sixth pregnancy resulted in only one baby.

✢ Fertility Medication, In-Vitro Fertilization and Multiple Pregnancies

We have known for a long time that fertility drugs increase the chance of multiple pregnancies. Several different medications are used to treat infertility. Each one affects your chances of conceiving more than one fetus to a different degree. One of the more common medications is clomiphene (Clomid®). It increases the chance of multiple fetuses somewhat less than other medications. But an increased chance is still there.

Twins are more common in pregnancies that result from the use of fertility drugs or with the implantation of more than one embryo with in-vitro fertilization. The percentage of male fetuses decreases as the number of fetuses per pregnancy increases. This means more females are born in these multiple pregnancies.

➳ *Discovering You're Carrying More than One Baby*

Diagnosis of twins was more difficult before ultrasound was available. The illustration on page 265 shows an ultrasound of twins. You can see parts of both fetuses.

It is uncommon to discover twin pregnancies just by hearing two heartbeats. Many people believe when only one heartbeat is heard, there could be no possibility of twins. This may not be the case. Two very rapid heartbeats may have a similar or almost-identical rate. That could make it difficult to tell there are two babies.

Measuring and examining your abdomen during pregnancy is important. Usually a twin pregnancy is noted during the second trimester because you are too big and growth seems too fast for a single pregnancy.

Ultrasound examination is the best way to tell if you are carrying more than one baby. Diagnosis can also be made by X-ray after 16 to 18 weeks of pregnancy, when fetal skeletons are visible. However, this method is used very infrequently today.

➳ *Do Multiple Pregnancies Have More Problems?*

With a multiple pregnancy, the possibility of problems goes up. Possible problems include:

- increased miscarriage
- fetal death or mortality
- fetal malformations
- low birth weight or growth retardation
- pre-eclampsia
- maternal anemia

- problems with the placenta, including placental abruption and placenta previa
- maternal bleeding or hemorrhage
- problems with the umbilical cord, including entwinement or tangling of the umbilical cords with the babies
- hydramnios or polyhydramnios
- labor complicated by abnormal fetal presentation, such as breech or transverse lie
- premature labor

One of the biggest problems with multiple pregnancies is premature delivery. As the number of fetuses increases, the length of gestation and the birth weight decreases, although this is not true in every case. When I was a resident, I delivered a set of triplets, and each baby weighed over 6 pounds at birth!

The average pregnancy for twins is about 37 weeks. For triplets it is about 35 weeks. For every week the babies remain in the uterus, their birth weights increase, along with the maturity of organs and systems.

Major malformations in multiple pregnancies are more common than they are in single pregnancies. The incidence of minor malformation is twice as high as it is in a single pregnancy. Malformations are more common among identical twins than fraternal twins.

One of the main goals in dealing with multiple fetuses is to continue the pregnancy as long as possible to avoid premature delivery. This may best be accomplished by bed rest. You may not be able to carry on with regular activities during your entire pregnancy. If your doctor recommends bed rest, follow his or her advice.

Weight gain is very important with a multiple pregnancy. You will gain more than the normal 25 to 35 pounds, depending on the number of fetuses you are carrying. Supplementation with iron is essential.

Some researchers believe use of a tocolytic agent (medication to stop labor), such as ritodrine, is critical in preventing premature delivery. (See Week 29.) These agents are used to relax the uterus to keep you from going into premature labor.

Follow your doctor's instruction very closely. Every day and every week you're able to keep the babies inside you are days or weeks you won't have to visit them in an intensive-care nursery while they grow, develop and finish maturing.

↷ Delivering More than One Baby

How multiple fetuses are delivered often depends on how the babies are lying in your uterus. Possible complications of labor and delivery, in addition to prematurity, include:

- abnormal presentations (breech or transverse)
- prolapse of the umbilical cord (the umbilical cord comes out ahead of the babies)
- placental abruption
- fetal distress
- bleeding after delivery

These problems occur more often with multiple fetuses. Because there is higher risk during labor and delivery, precautions are taken before delivery and during labor. These include the need for an I.V., the presence of an anesthesiologist and the availability and possible presence of pediatricians or other medical personnel to take care of the babies.

With twins, all possible combinations of fetal positions can occur. Both babies may come head first (vertex). They may come *breech,* meaning bottom or feet first. They may come sideways or *oblique*, meaning at an angle that is neither breech nor vertex. Or they may come in any combination of the above. (See discussion of birth presentation in Week 38.)

When both twins are head first, a vaginal delivery may be attempted and may be accomplished safely. It may be possible for one baby to deliver normally. The second one could require a C-section if it turns, the cord comes out ahead of the baby or the baby is distressed following delivery of the first fetus. Some doctors believe delivery of two or more babies requires a C-section.

After delivery of two or more babies, doctors pay strict attention to maternal bleeding because of the rapid change in the size of the uterus. It is greatly overdistended with more than one baby. Medication, usually oxytocin (Pitocin®), is given by I.V. to contract the uterus to stop bleeding so the mother doesn't lose too much blood. A heavy blood loss could produce anemia and make a blood transfusion or long-term treatment with iron supplementation necessary.

> *Tip for Week 32*
> Your requirements for calories, protein, vitamins and minerals increase if you carry more than one baby. You'll need to eat about 300 calories a day *more* per baby than for a normal pregnancy.

Changes in You

Until this week, your visits to the doctor have probably been on a monthly basis, unless you've had complications or problems. At week 32, most doctors begin seeing a pregnant woman every 2 weeks. This will continue until you reach your last month of pregnancy; at that time, you'll probably switch to weekly visits.

By this time, you probably know your doctor fairly well and feel comfortable talking about your concerns. Now is a good time to ask questions and to discuss concerns about labor and delivery. If there are complications or problems later in pregnancy or at delivery, you'll be able to communicate better with your doctor and know what is going on. You'll feel comfortable with the care you're receiving.

Your doctor may plan on talking to you about many things in the weeks to come, but you can't always assume this. You may be taking prenatal classes and hearing different things about labor and delivery, such as stories about enemas, I.V.s and complications. Don't be afraid to ask your doctor any questions you have. Most doctors and nurses are receptive to your queries. They want you to discuss things you're concerned about instead of having you worry about them unnecessarily.

❧ Taking Prenatal Vitamins

Jackie admitted to me that she wasn't taking her prenatal vitamins as regularly as she had early in pregnancy. She said she was tired of taking them and asked if it was OK to skip them now that she was in the third trimester. I told her it was a mistake not to take her prenatal vitamin every day.

The vitamins and iron in prenatal vitamins are essential to your well-being and the well-being of your baby. If you're anemic at the time of delivery, a low blood count could have a negative effect on you and your baby. Your chance of needing a blood transfusion could be higher. After I explained these things, Jackie realized that taking her prenatal vitamin every day until delivery was good for her and her baby.

❧ Postpartum Bleeding and Hemorrhage

It's not unusual to lose blood during labor and delivery. However, a heavy postpartum hemorrhage is different and significant. *Postpartum hemorrhage* is a loss of blood in excess of 17 ounces (500ml) in the first 24 hours after your baby's birth.

There can be many reasons for postpartum hemorrhage. The most common causes include a uterus that will not contract and lacerations or tearing of the vagina or cervix during the birth process.

Other causes include trauma to the genital tract, such as a large or bleeding episiotomy, or a rupture, hole or tear in the uterus. Blood loss may be related to the failure of blood vessels inside the uterus (where the placenta was attached) to compress to stop bleeding. This may occur if the uterus fails to contract because of very rapid labor, a long labor, several previous deliveries, a uterine infection, an overdistended uterus (with multiple fetuses) or certain agents used for general anesthesia.

Heavy bleeding may also result from retained placental tissue. In this situation, most of the placenta delivers, but part of it remains inside the uterus. Retained placental tissue may cause bleeding immediately, or bleeding may occur weeks or even months later.

Problems with blood clotting can cause hemorrhaging. This may be related to pregnancy, or it may be a congenital medical problem. Bleeding following delivery requires constant attention from your doctor and the nurses caring for you.

Week 33

Age of Fetus ❧ 31 Weeks

How Big Is Your Baby?

Your baby weighs about 4.4 pounds (2000g) by this week. Its crown-to-rump length is about 12 inches (30cm) and total length is 19.4 inches (43cm).

How Big Are You?

Measuring from the pubic symphysis, it is now about 13.2 inches (33cm) to the top of the uterus. Measurement from your belly-button to the top of your uterus is about 5.2 inches (13cm). Your weight gain should be between 22 and 28 pounds (9.9 and 12.6kg).

How Your Baby Is Growing and Developing

∞ *Placental Abruption*

The illustration on page 275 shows placental abruption, which is separation of the placenta from the wall of the uterus. Normally, the placenta does not separate from the uterus until after the baby is delivered. Separation before delivery can be very serious.

The frequency of placental abruption is estimated to be about 1 in every 80 deliveries. We do not have a more-exact statistic because time of separation varies, altering risk to the fetus. If the placenta separates at the time of delivery and the infant is delivered without incident, it is not as significant as a placenta separating during pregnancy.

The cause of placental abruption is unknown. Certain conditions may increase its chance of occurring. Factors include:

- physical injury to the mother, as from a car accident
- a short umbilical cord
- very sudden change in the size of the uterus (from delivery or rupture of membranes)
- hypertension
- dietary deficiency
- a uterine abnormality, such as a band of tissue in the uterus where the placenta cannot attach properly

Separation of the placenta may involve partial or total separation from the uterine wall. The situation is most severe when the placenta totally separates from the uterine wall. The fetus relies entirely on circulation from the placenta. With separation, it cannot receive blood from the umbilical cord, which is attached to the placenta.

Studies indicate that folic-acid deficiency can play a role in causing placental abruption. Others suggest maternal smoking and alcohol consumption may make a woman more likely to have placental abruption.

A woman who has had placental abruption in the past is at increased risk of having it recur. Rate of recurrence has been

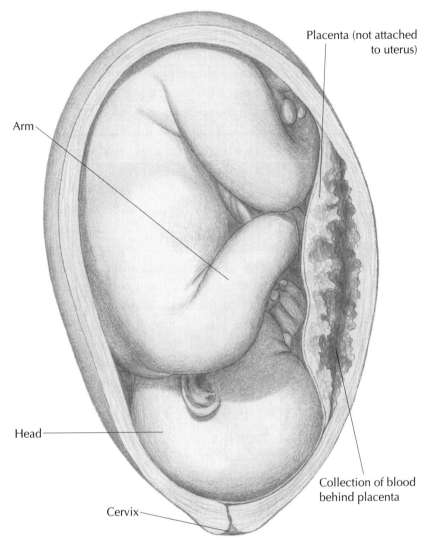

Placenta (not attached to uterus)

Arm

Head

Cervix

Collection of blood behind placenta

This illustration of placental abruption shows the placenta has separated from the wall of the uterus.

estimated to be as high as 10%. This can make a pregnancy following placental abruption a high-risk pregnancy.

ᲙᲔ Symptoms of Placental Abruption

Symptoms of placental abruption can vary a great deal. There may be heavy bleeding from the vagina, or you may experience no bleeding at all. The illustration above shows bleeding behind the placenta with complete separation. There is no apparent bleeding from the cervix and vagina. Other symptoms can include lower-back pain, tenderness of the uterus or abdomen, and contractions or tightening of the uterus.

Ultrasound may be helpful in diagnosing this problem, although it does not always provide an exact diagnosis. This is particularly true if the placenta is located on the back surface of the uterus where it cannot be seen easily with ultrasound examination.

Serious problems, such as shock, may occur with separation of the placenta. Shock occurs because of the rapid loss of large quantities of blood. Intravascular coagulation, in which a large blood clot develops, can also be a problem. Factors that clot the blood may be used up, which can make bleeding a problem.

Of the various symptoms associated with placental abruption, vaginal bleeding occurs in about 75% of all cases. Tenderness of the uterus occurs about 60% of the time, as does fetal distress or problems with the fetal heart rate. Tightening or contraction of the uterus occurs about 34% of the time. Premature labor occurs in about 20% of the cases. Fetal death, while uncommon, occurs about 15% of the time.

✍ Can Placental Abruption Be Treated?

Treatment of placental abruption varies, based on the ability to diagnose the problem and the status of the mother and baby. With very heavy bleeding, delivery of the baby may be necessary.

When bleeding is not heavy, the problem may be treated with a more conservative approach. This depends on whether the fetus is in distress and if it appears to be in immediate danger.

Placental abruption is one of the most serious problems related to the second and third trimesters of pregnancy. If you have any symptoms, call your doctor immediately!

Changes in You

✷ *How Will You Know Your Membranes Have Ruptured?*

Caroline was unsure of how she would know when her water broke, so she asked me what she needed to look for. I told her, "When your bag of waters breaks, it isn't usually just one gush of water, with no further leakage. There is often a gush of amniotic fluid, usually followed by a leaking of small amounts of fluid. Women describe it as a constant wetness or water running down their leg when they stand. Continual leakage of water is a good clue your water has broken."

Amniotic fluid is usually clear and watery. Occasionally it may have a bloody appearance, or it may be yellow or green.

It isn't uncommon to have an increase in vaginal discharge or to lose urine in small amounts as your baby puts pressure on your bladder. But there are ways for your doctor to tell if your water has broken. Two tests can be done on the amniotic fluid.

One is a nitrazine test. When amniotic fluid is placed on a small strip of paper, it changes the color of the paper. This test is based on the acidity or pH of the amniotic fluid. However, blood can also change the color of nitrazine paper, even if your water hasn't broken.

Another test that may be done is a ferning test. Amniotic fluid or fluid from the back of the vagina is taken with a swab and placed on a slide for examination under a microscope. Dried amniotic fluid has the appearance of a fern or branches of a pine tree. Ferning is often more helpful in diagnosing ruptured membranes than looking at color changes on nitrazine paper.

✷ *What Do You Do When Your Water Breaks?*

Your membranes may rupture at any point in pregnancy. Don't assume it will only happen around the time of labor.

If you think your water has broken, notify your doctor. Avoid sexual intercourse at this time. Intercourse increases the possibility of introducing an infection into your uterus and thus to your baby.

How Your Actions Affect Your Baby's Development

❧ *Weight Gain*

You are continuing to gain weight as your pregnancy progresses. You may be gaining weight faster than at any other time during pregnancy. This is because your baby is going through a period of increased growth. It may be gaining as much as 8 ounces (224g) or more every week!

Continue to eat the right foods for you. Heartburn may be more of a problem now because your growing baby may not allow your stomach much room. You may find eating several small meals, rather than three large meals, makes you feel more comfortable. Follow the guidelines in Week 7, and listen to your doctor's advice.

Tip for Week 33
Don't stop eating or start skipping meals as your weight increases. Both you and your baby need the calories and nutrition you receive from a healthy diet.

You Should also Know

❧ *Will Your Doctor Perform an Episiotomy?*

You may be wondering whether you will need an episiotomy. An episiotomy is an incision made from the vagina toward the rectum during delivery to avoid undue tearing as the baby's head passes through the birth canal. It may be a cut directly in the midline toward the rectum, or it may be a cut to the side.

There is little you can do if you *need* an episiotomy. Some people practice, teach and believe in stretching the birth canal during labor and at the time of delivery to try to avoid an episiotomy. It may work for some, but it doesn't work for every woman. Others suggest an episiotomy to avoid stretching the vagina, bladder and rectum. Stretching the vagina can change sensations experienced during sexual intercourse.

The reason for an episiotomy usually becomes clear at delivery when the baby's head is in the vagina. The episiotomy substitutes a controlled, straight, clean cut for a tear or rip that could go in many directions. This may include tearing or ripping into the bladder, into large blood vessels or into the rectum. An episiotomy heals better than a ragged tear.

Ask your doctor if he or she thinks you may need an episiotomy. Discuss why an episiotomy is necessary. Find out whether it might be a cut in the middle or to the side of the vagina. You might also ask if there is anything you can do to prepare for the possibility of an episiotomy, such as an enema or stretching the vagina.

If a vacuum extractor or forceps are used for delivery, an episiotomy may be done before the device is placed on the baby's head.

Description of an episiotomy also includes a description of the depth of the incision:

- a *first-degree episiotomy* cuts only the skin
- a *second-degree episiotomy* cuts the skin and underlying tissue
- a *third-degree episiotomy* cuts the skin, underlying tissue and rectal sphincter, which is the muscle that goes around the anus
- a *fourth-degree episiotomy* goes through the three layers and through the rectal mucosa

After the baby is delivered, layers are closed separately with absorbable sutures that do not require removal after they heal.

After your baby is born, the most painful part of the entire birth experience might be the episiotomy. It may continue to cause some discomfort as it heals. Don't be afraid to ask for medication to ease any pain. You can take many safe medications, even if you are breastfeeding your baby, including acetaminophen (Tylenol). Tylenol with Codeine® or other medications may also be prescribed for pain.

ᴖ *Delivery of the Placenta*

In most instances, the placenta is delivered within 30 minutes after the birth of your baby and is a routine part of the delivery. However, complications can arise if the placenta adheres to the lining of the uterus. With a retained placenta, the placenta does not deliver spontaneously. (See Week 38 for further information.) Women who have had a previous retained placenta, Cesarean delivery or a D&C for miscarriage or heavy bleeding are more likely to have a retained placenta.

Week 34

Age of Fetus ⌁ 32 Weeks

Your baby weighs almost 5 pounds (2275g) by this week. Its crown-to-rump length is about 12.8 inches (32cm). Total length is 19.8 inches (44cm).

Measuring up from your bellybutton, it's about 5.6 inches (14cm) to the top of your uterus. From the pubic symphysis, you will measure about 13.6 inches (34cm).

It's not important that your measurements match any of your friends' at similar points in their pregnancies. What's important is that you're growing appropriately and that your uterus grows and gets larger at an appropriate rate. These are signs of normal growth of your baby inside your uterus.

How Your Baby Is Growing and Developing

↳ **Testing Your Baby Before Birth?**

An ideal test done before delivery would determine if the fetus is healthy. It would be able to detect major fetal malformations or fetal stress, which could indicate an impending problem. Ultrasound accomplishes some of these goals by enabling doctors to observe the baby inside the uterus, as well as to evaluate the brain, heart and other organs of the fetal body. Along with ultrasound examinations, fetal monitoring has been done in the form of a nonstress test or a contraction stress test to indicate fetal well-being or problems. (This is described in Week 35.)

↳ *Biophysical Profile*

A comprehensive test, called a *biophysical profile*, is used to examine the fetus while it is still in the uterus. The test helps determine fetal health and is done when there is concern about fetal well-being. It may also be done when a pregnancy passes the expected due date.

A biophysical profile uses a particular scoring system. The first four of the five tests listed below are made with ultrasound; the fifth is done with external fetal monitors. A score is given to each area. The five areas of evaluation include:

- fetal breathing movements
- fetal body movements
- fetal tone
- amount of amniotic fluid
- reactive fetal heart rate

During the test, doctors evaluate fetal "breathing"—the movement or expansion of the baby's chest inside the uterus. This score is based on the amount of fetal breathing that occurs.

Movement of the baby's body is noted. A normal score indicates normal body movements. An abnormal score is applied when there are few or no body movements during the allotted time period.

Fetal tone is evaluated similarly. Movement, or lack of movement, of the arms and legs of the baby is noted.

Amniotic-fluid volume evaluation requires experience in ultrasound examination. A normal pregnancy has adequate fluid around the baby. An abnormal test indicates no amniotic fluid or decreased amniotic fluid around the baby.

Fetal heart-rate monitoring is done with external monitors. It evaluates changes in the fetal heart rate associated with movement of the baby. The amount of change and number of changes in the fetal heart rate differ, depending on who is doing the test and their definition of normal.

A normal score is 2; an abnormal score is 0 for any of these tests. A score of 1 in any of the tests is a middle score. From these five scores, a total score is obtained by adding all the values together. Evaluation may vary depending on the sophistication of the equipment used and the expertise of the person doing the test. The higher the score, the better the baby's condition. A lower score may cause concern about the well-being of the fetus.

If the score is low, a recommendation may be made to deliver the baby immediately. If the score is reassuring, the test may be repeated at weekly or twice-weekly intervals. If results fall between these two values, the test may be repeated the following day. It depends on the circumstances of your pregnancy and the biophysical-profile findings. Your doctor will evaluate all the information before making any decision.

A biophysical profile may be valuable in evaluating an infant with IUGR, pregnancy of a diabetic mother, a pregnancy in which the baby doesn't move very much, high-risk pregnancies or overdue pregnancies. Because ultrasound is an important part of a biophysical profile, it may be useful in finding major congenital problems and evaluating the well-being of the infant inside the uterus.

Changes in You

↬ *How Much Does Your Baby Weigh?*

By this time, you have probably asked your doctor several times how big your baby is or how much your baby will weigh when it's born. Next to asking about the sex of a baby, this is the most frequently asked question I hear.

Estimating the weight of the baby is extremely difficult. Many doctors will guess and give a range of 1 to 2 pounds in either direction. It's very difficult to determine how much a baby, placenta and amniotic fluid will weigh. A few of my estimates have been really off! Claudia asked me to tell her how much her baby would weigh at birth. I guessed over 8 pounds and was surprised when she delivered an 6-pound, 10-ounce baby!

As you can see by the illustration on page 285, you're getting larger. The baby is growing, the placenta is growing and the amount of fluid around the baby is increasing. All these factors make estimating fetal weight more difficult.

✣ *Using Ultrasound to Estimate Fetal Weight*

Ultrasound can be used to estimate fetal weight, but errors in weight estimates can and do occur. The accuracy of predicting fetal weight using ultrasound is improving. Making an accurate estimate can be valuable.

Several measurements are used in a formula to estimate a baby's weight. These include diameter of the baby's head, circumference of the baby's head, circumference of the baby's abdomen, length of the femur of the baby's leg and, in some instances, other fetal measurements.

Ultrasound is the method of choice to estimate fetal weight. But even with ultrasound, estimates may vary as much as half a pound (225g) in either direction.

✣ *Will Your Baby Fit through the Birth Canal?*

Even with a fetal-weight estimate, whether by your doctor or by ultrasound, your doctor can't tell if the baby is too big for you or whether you'll need a C-section. Usually, it's necessary for you to labor to be able to see how the baby fits into your pelvis and if there is room for it to pass through the birth canal.

In some women who appear to be average or better-than-average size, a 6- or 6.5-pound (2.7 to 2.9kg) baby won't fit through the pelvis. Experience has also shown women who may appear to be petite are sometimes able to deliver 7.5-pound

Comparative size of the uterus at 34 weeks of pregnancy (fetal age—32 weeks). The uterus can be felt about 5.6 inches (14cm) above your bellybutton.

(3.4kg) or larger babies without much difficulty. The best test or method of evaluating whether your baby will deliver through your pelvis is labor.

How Your Actions Affect Your Baby's Development

The end of your pregnancy begins with labor. One of the end results of labor is the birth of your baby.

Some women are concerned (or hope!) that their actions can cause labor to begin. The old wives' tales about going for a ride over a bumpy road or taking a long walk to start labor aren't true. We do know intercourse and stimulation of the nipples may cause labor to start in some cases, but this isn't true for every woman.

Going about your daily activities (unless your doctor has advised bed rest) will not cause labor to start before your baby is ready to be born.

‿ Understanding Labor

It's important to know what to expect when labor occurs and what to do when it begins. What causes labor? Why does it happen?

We don't have a good answer to this question. The factors that cause labor to begin are unknown. There are many theories; one is that hormones made by the mother and fetus trigger labor. It could be that a hormone produced by the fetus makes the uterus contract.

Labor is the dilatation (stretching, expanding) of the cervix. This occurs because the uterus, which is a muscle, tightens to squeeze out its contents (the baby). As it pushes the baby out, the cervix stretches. It may be possible to feel tightening, contractions or cramps, but in the purest sense, it isn't labor until there is a change in the cervix.

‿ Three Stages of Labor

Labor is divided into three stages. The first stage of labor begins with uterine contractions of great enough intensity, duration and frequency to cause thinning (effacement) and dilatation of the cervix. The first stage of labor ends when the cervix is fully dilated (usually 10cm) and sufficiently open to allow the baby's head to come through it.

The second stage of labor begins when the cervix is completely dilated at 10cm. This stage ends with the delivery of the baby.

The third stage of labor begins after delivery of the baby. It ends with delivery of the placenta and the membranes that have surrounded the fetus.

Some doctors have even described a fourth stage of labor, referring to a time period after delivery of the placenta during which the uterus contracts. Contraction of the uterus is important in controlling bleeding that can occur after delivery of the baby and the placenta.

↬ *Braxton-Hicks Contractions and False Labor*

Braxton-Hicks contractions are painless, nonrhythmical contractions you may be able to feel when you place your hand on your abdomen. These contractions often begin early in pregnancy and are felt at irregular intervals. They may increase in number and strength when the uterus is massaged. Like false labor, they are not positive signs of true labor.

False labor often occurs before true labor begins. False labor contractions can be very painful and may appear to be real labor to you.

In most instances, false-labor contractions are irregular. They are usually of short duration (less than 45 seconds). The discomfort of the contraction may occur in various parts of your body, such as the groin, lower abdomen or back. With true labor, uterine contractions produce pain that starts at the top of the uterus and radiates over the entire uterus, through the lower back into the pelvis.

False labor is usually seen in late pregnancy. It seems to occur more often in women who have been pregnant and delivered more babies. It usually stops as quickly as it begins. There doesn't appear to be any danger to your baby.

↬ *What Is a "Bloody Show"?*

Often following a vaginal examination or with the beginning of early labor and early contractions, you may bleed a small amount. This is called a *bloody show;* it can occur as the cervix stretches and dilates. You shouldn't lose a large amount of blood. If it causes you concern or appears to be a large amount of blood, call your doctor immediately.

Along with a bloody show, you may pass a mucus plug at the beginning of labor. This is different from your bag of waters breaking (ruptured membranes). Passing this mucus plug doesn't necessarily mean you'll have your baby soon or even that you'll go into labor in the next few hours. It poses no danger to you or your baby.

✌ How Long Will Labor Last?

The length of the first and second stages of labor, from the beginning of cervical dilatation to delivery of the baby, can last 14 to 15 hours or more in a first pregnancy. Women have had faster labors than this, but don't count on it.

A woman who has already had one or two children will probably have a shorter labor, but don't count on that either! The average time for labor is usually decreased by a few hours for a second or third delivery.

Everyone's heard of women who barely make it to the hospital or had labor lasting only 1 hour. For every one of those patients, there are many women who have labored 18, 20, 24 hours or longer.

It's almost impossible to predict the amount of time that will be required for labor. You may ask your doctor about it, but his or her answer is only a guess.

✌ Timing Contractions

Most women are instructed in prenatal classes or by their health-care provider about how to time contractions during labor. To time how long a contraction lasts, begin timing when the contraction starts and end timing when the contraction lets up and goes away.

It's also important to know how often contractions occur. There is much confusion about this. You can choose from two methods. With the first, the interval between contractions is noted as the time period between when a contraction starts to the time the next contraction starts. This is the most commonly used method and the most reliable.

With the second method, the interval between contractions is noted by the time period from when a contraction ends to the time the next contraction starts. Ask your doctor which method he or she prefers.

It's helpful for you and your partner or labor coach to time your contractions before calling your doctor or the hospital. Your doctor will probably want to know how often contractions occur and how long each contraction lasts. With this information, your doctor can decide when you should to go to the hospital.

You Should also Know

~ *Will My Baby Drop?*

A few weeks before labor begins or at the beginning of labor, you may notice a change in your abdomen. When examined by your doctor, measurement from your bellybutton or the pubic symphysis to the top of the uterus may be smaller than what you noticed on a previous visit. This phenomenon occurs as the head of the baby enters the birth canal. It can also be a part of the decrease in amniotic fluid that may occur without rupture of membranes or loss of fluid. This change is often called *lightening*.

Don't be concerned if you don't notice lightening or a drop of the fetus. This doesn't occur with every woman or with every pregnancy. It's very common for your baby to drop during labor or just before labor begins.

With lightening, you may experience benefits and problems. One benefit may be more room in your upper abdomen. This gives you more room to breathe because there's more room for your lungs to expand. However, with the descent of the baby, you may notice more pressure in your pelvis, bladder and rectum, which can make you more uncomfortable.

In some instances, your doctor may examine you and tell you your baby is "not in the pelvis" or "is high up." He or she is saying the baby has not yet descended into the birth canal. However, this situation can change very quickly.

If your doctor says your baby is "floating" or "ballotable," it means part of the baby is felt high in the birth canal. But the baby is not engaged (fixed) in the birth canal at this point. The baby may even bounce or move away from your doctor's fingers when you are examined.

Uncomfortable Feelings You May Experience

At this point in their pregnancies, some women have the uncomfortable feeling the baby is going to "fall out." This feeling is related to pressure the baby exerts because it has moved lower in the birth canal. Some women describe the feeling as an increase in pressure.

If you're concerned or worried about it, consult your doctor. It may be a reason to perform a pelvic exam to see how low the baby's head is. In almost all cases, the baby will not be coming out. But because it is at a lower position than what you're used to, the baby will exert more pressure than you noticed during recent weeks.

Another feeling associated with increased pressure may occur around this week. Some pregnant women have described it as a "pins-and-needles" sensation. The feeling is tingling, pressure or numbness in the pelvis or pelvic region from the pressure of the baby. It is a common symptom and shouldn't concern you.

These feelings may not be relieved until delivery occurs. You can lie on your side to help decrease pressure in your pelvis and on the nerves, vessels and arteries in the pelvic area. If the problem is severe, talk to your doctor about it. Don't try to move the baby or push the baby out of the way. It could be dangerous for both of you.

Tip for Week 34
A strip of paper, tape or a bandage can help cover a sensitive bellybutton.

Week 35

Age of Fetus ～ 33 Weeks

How Big Is Your Baby?

Your baby now weighs over 5.5 pounds (2550g). Crown-to-rump length by this week of pregnancy is about 13.2 inches (33cm). Its total length is 20.25 inches (45cm).

How Big Are You?

Measuring from the bellybutton, it is now about 6 inches (15cm) to the top of the uterus. Measuring from the pubic symphysis, the distance is about 14 inches (35cm).

By this week, your weight gain should be between 24 and 29 pounds (10.8 and 13kg).

How Your Baby Is Growing and Developing

ᐁ What Is Placenta Previa?

With placenta previa, the placenta lies close to the cervix or covers the cervix. The illustration on page 293 shows placenta previa.

Placenta previa is serious because of the chance of heavy bleeding. Bleeding may occur during pregnancy or during labor. This problem is not common; it happens about once in every 170 pregnancies.

The cause of placenta previa is not completely known. Risk factors for an increased chance of placenta previa include previous Cesarean delivery, many pregnancies and increased maternal age.

ᐁ Symptoms of Placenta Previa

The most characteristic symptom of placenta previa is painless bleeding without any contractions of the uterus. This doesn't usually occur until close to the end of your second trimester or later when the cervix thins out, stretches and tears the placenta loose.

Bleeding with placenta previa may occur without warning and may be extremely heavy. It occurs when the cervix begins to dilate with early labor, and blood escapes.

Placenta previa should be suspected when a woman experiences vaginal bleeding during the latter half of pregnancy. The problem cannot be diagnosed with a physical exam because a pelvic examination may cause heavier bleeding. Doctors use ultrasound to identify placenta previa. Ultrasound is particularly accurate in the second half of pregnancy as the uterus and placenta get bigger.

If you know you have placenta previa, your doctor may tell you not to have a pelvic exam. This is important to remember if you see another doctor or when you go to the hospital.

The baby is more likely to be in a breech position with placenta previa. For this reason, and to control bleeding, a Cesarean delivery is almost always performed. Cesarean delivery with placenta previa offers the doctor the advantage of delivering the baby, then removing the placenta so the uterus can contract. Bleeding can be kept to a minimum.

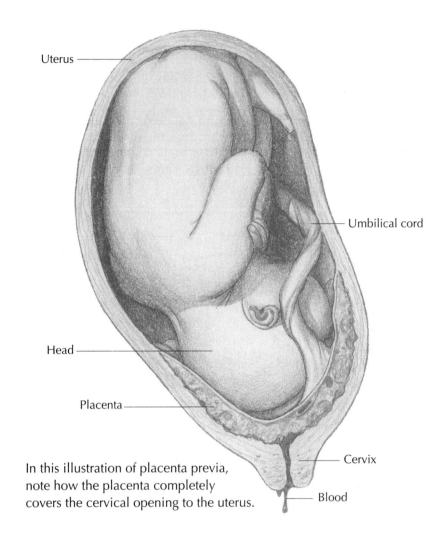

Uterus

Umbilical cord

Head

Placenta

Cervix

In this illustration of placenta previa, note how the placenta completely covers the cervical opening to the uterus.

Blood

Changes in You

✼ *Emotional Changes in Late Pregnancy*

As you reach the last trimester and come closer to delivery, you and your partner may become more anxious about the events to come. You may even have more mood swings, which seem to occur for no reason. Many women and their partners report a woman may become more irritable, which can place a significant strain on a relationship.

You may be concerned about insignificant or unimportant things. Your concern about the health and well-being of the baby may also increase during the last weeks of your pregnancy. This can include concern about how well you tolerate labor and how you will get through delivery. You may be concerned about whether you'll be a good mother or be able to raise a baby properly.

While these emotions rage inside you, you'll notice you're getting bigger and aren't able to do things you used to do. You may feel more uncomfortable, and you may not be sleeping well. These things can work together to make your emotions swing wildly from highs to lows.

↴ *How Can You Deal with These Changes?*

Changes are normal; don't feel as though you're the "Lone Ranger." Other pregnant women and their partners have the same concerns.

Talk with your partner about your concerns. Tell him how you feel and what's going on. You may be surprised to find out the concerns your partner has about you, the baby and his role during labor and delivery. By talking about these things, your partner may find it easier to understand what you're experiencing, including mood swings and crying spells.

Discuss emotional problems with your doctor. He or she may be able to reassure you that what you're going through is normal. Take advantage of prenatal classes and information available about pregnancy and delivery.

Emotional changes can occur, so be ready for them. Ask your partner, the nurse in the doctor's office and your doctor to help you understand what is normal and what can be done about mood swings.

⌇ Can Your Baby Get Tangled in the Cord?

You may have been told by friends not to raise your arms over your head or reach high to get things because it can cause the cord to wrap around the baby's neck. There doesn't seem to be any truth to this theory.

Some babies do get tangled in their umbilical cord and can get the cord tied in a knot or wrapped around their neck. However, nothing you do during pregnancy causes or prevents this from happening.

A tangled umbilical cord isn't necessarily a problem during labor. It only becomes a problem if the cord is stretched tight around the baby's neck or is in a knot. (Also see Week 30.)

⌇ Will Working at a Computer Terminal Hurt Your Baby?

Lots of my patients are concerned about working in front of a computer screen (at a computer terminal). Currently nothing suggests that working at a computer terminal is likely to harm your unborn baby.

If you work at a computer terminal (or at a typewriter), you probably should be concerned about the way you sit and how long you sit. Sit in a chair that offers good support for your back and legs. Don't slouch or cross your legs when sitting. Be sure to get up and walk around at least once every 15 minutes—you need to keep good circulation in your legs.

You Should also Know

⌇ Fetal Monitoring before Labor Begins

The biophysical profile (discussed in Week 34) evaluates the well-being of your baby inside your uterus. One part of the biophysical profile is fetal monitoring, commonly called a *nonstress test*.

A nonstress test is performed in your doctor's office or in the labor and delivery department of a hospital. While you are lying down, a technician attaches a fetal monitor to your abdomen. Every time your baby moves, you push a button to make a mark on a strip of monitor paper. At the same time, the monitor records the baby's heartbeat.

When the baby moves, its heart rate usually goes up. Doctors use the findings from fetal monitors to help them evaluate how well a baby is tolerating life inside the uterus. Your doctor will decide if further action is necessary.

~ Getting Ready for the Birth

At this point, you may be feeling a little nervous about the birth. You might be afraid you won't know when it's time to call the doctor or go to the hospital. Don't hesitate to talk to your doctor about it at one of your visits. He or she will tell you what signs to watch for. Prenatal classes teach you the signs of labor and when you should call your doctor or go to the hospital.

Ask your doctor what the signs of labor contractions are. Labor contractions are usually regular. They increase in duration and strength over time. You'll notice a regular rhythm to real labor contractions. You'll want to time them so you know how frequently they occur and how long they last. (See Week 33.) When you go to the hospital depends in part on your contractions.

Your bag of waters may rupture before you go into labor. In most cases, you'll notice this as a gush of water followed by a steady leaking. (See Week 33.)

During the last few weeks of pregnancy, have your suitcase packed and ready to go. That way, you'll have the things you wanted with you in the hospital ready to go.

If you can, tour the hospital facilities a few weeks ahead of your scheduled due date. Find out where to go and what to do when you get there.

Talk with your partner about the best ways to reach him if you think you've gone into labor. You might have him check with you periodically. It's common for a partner to wear a pager if he is often away from a phone, especially during the last few weeks of pregnancy.

Ask your doctor what you should do if you think you're in labor. Is it best to call the office? Should you go directly to the hospital? Should you call the answering service?

By knowing what to do, and when, you'll be able to relax a little and not worry about the beginning of labor and delivery.

> *Tip for Week 35*
>
> Maternity bras are designed to provide extra support to your growing breasts. You may feel more comfortable wearing one during the day and at night while you sleep.

Week 36

Age of Fetus ஃ 34 Weeks

How Big Is Your Baby?

By this week, your baby weighs about 6 pounds (2750g). Its crown-to-rump length is over 13.5 inches (34cm), and total length is 20.7 inches (46cm).

How Big Are You?

Measuring from the pubic symphysis, it's about 14.5 inches (36cm) to the top of your uterus. If you measure from your belly-button, it's more than 5.5 inches (14cm) to the top of your uterus.

You may feel as though you've run out of room! Your uterus has grown bigger in the past few weeks as the baby has grown inside of it. Now the uterus is probably up under your ribs.

~w Your Baby Is Growing and Developing

hat Is a Cesarean Delivery?

women plan on a normal vaginal birth, but a Cesarean ry is always a possibility. With a Cesarean, the baby is red through an incision made in the mother's abdominal .nd uterus. The illustration on page 301 shows a Cesarean :ry. Common names for this type of surgery are *C-section, rean section* and *Cesarean delivery.* C-sections are done for many reasons.

The most common reason for having a C-section is a previous Cesarean delivery. However, some women who have had C-sections can have a vaginal delivery with later pregnancies; this is called *vaginal birth after Cesarean (VBAC).* See the discussion on page 303. Discuss the matter with your doctor if you've had a C-section and would like to attempt a vaginal delivery this time.

There is some risk that the surgical scar from an earlier C-section could stretch and pull apart during subsequent labor and delivery, with serious consequences. In this case, a repeat C-section may be advised to avoid rupture of the uterus. However, if pregnancy and labor are closely monitored, a woman may be able to have a normal vaginal delivery (VBAC).

A Cesarean delivery may be necessary if your baby is too big to fit through the birth canal. This condition is called *cephalo-pelvic disproportion (CPD).* CPD may be suspected during pregnancy but usually labor must begin before it can be confirmed.

Fetal distress is another reason for a Cesarean section. Doctors use fetal monitors during labor to watch the fetal heartbeat and its response to labor. If the heartbeat indicates the baby is having trouble with labor contractions, a C-section may be necessary for the baby's well-being.

If the umbilical cord is compressed, a C-section may be necessary. The cord may come into the vagina ahead of the baby's head or the baby can press on part of the cord. This is a dangerous situation because a compressed umbilical cord can cut off the blood supply to the baby.

A C-section is necessary if the baby is in a breech presentation, which means the baby's feet or buttocks enter the birth canal first. Delivering the shoulders and the head after the baby's body may damage the baby's head or neck, especially with a first baby.

Placental abruption or placenta previa are also reasons to have a Cesarean delivery. If the placenta separates from the uterus before delivery (placental abruption), the baby loses its supply of oxygen and nutrients. This is usually diagnosed when a woman has heavy vaginal bleeding. If the placenta blocks the birth canal (placenta previa), the baby cannot be delivered any other way.

↜ Rising Rate of Cesarean Deliveries

In 1965, only 4% of all deliveries were by C-section. Today, in the United States, Cesarean deliveries account for 20% of all deliveries. In some areas this percentage is even higher. In Canada, Cesarean deliveries account for almost 18% of all deliveries. This increase is related in part to more stringent monitoring during labor and safer procedures for C-sections. Another reason for more Cesarean deliveries is bigger babies. With bigger babies, a C-section is sometimes the only way to deliver. (Researchers believe this increase in the size of babies is due to pregnant women eating a better diet and not smoking during pregnancy.) The rising rate may also be related to the pressure on doctors to deliver a baby safely.

↜ How Is a C-Section Performed?

You may be awake when a C-section is done. An anesthesiologist usually gives you an epidural or spinal anesthetic. (Types of anesthesia are discussed in Week 39.) If you're awake for the procedure, you may be able to see your baby immediately after delivery!

With a C-section, an incision is made through the skin of the abdominal wall to the uterus. The wall of the uterus is cut, then the amniotic sac containing the baby and placenta is cut. The baby is removed through the incision. Next, the placenta is removed. The uterus is closed in layers with sutures that absorb and do not have to be removed. The remainder of the abdomen is sewn together with absorbable sutures.

Most Cesarean deliveries done today are low-cervical Cesareans or low-transverse Cesareans. This means the incision is made low in the uterus.

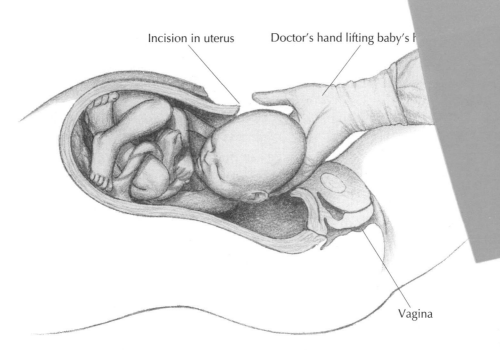

Incision in uterus   Doctor's hand lifting baby's F

Vagina

Delivery of a baby by Cesarean section.

In the past, a Cesarean was often done with a classical incision, in which the uterus is cut down the midline. This incision doesn't heal as well as a low-cervical incision. Because the incision is made in the muscular part of the uterus, it is more likely to pull apart with contractions (as in a vaginal birth after Cesarean). This can cause heavy bleeding and injure the baby. If you have had a classical Cesarean section in the past, you must have a C-section every time you have a baby.

A T-incision is another type of C-section incision. This incision goes across and up the uterus in the shape of an inverted T. It provides more room to get the baby out. If you have had this type of incision, you will need to have a Cesarean delivery with all subsequent pregnancies. It too is more likely to rupture than other types of incisions.

☙ *Advantages and Disadvantages of Having a C-Section*

There are advantages to having a C-section. The most important advantage is delivery of a healthy infant. The baby you are carrying may be too large to fit through your pelvis. The only safe method of delivery might be a C-section. Usually a woman needs to experience labor before her doctor will know if the baby will fit. It may be impossible to predict ahead of time.

The disadvantage is that a Cesarean section is a major operation and carries with it all the risks of surgery. Risks include infection, bleeding, shock due to blood loss, the possibility of blood clots and injury to other organs, such as the bladder or rectum. You will probably stay in the hospital an extra couple of days.

Recovery at home from a Cesarean section takes longer than recovery from a regular delivery. The normal time for full recovery from a C-section is usually 4 to 6 weeks.

In most areas, an obstetrician performs a C-section. In small communities, C-sections may be performed by a general surgeon or a general practitioner.

↣ Will You Need a Cesarean?

It would be nice to know you're going to need a C-section before delivery so you wouldn't have to go through labor. Unfortunately, it's usually necessary to wait for labor contractions for a couple of reasons. You won't know ahead of time if your baby is stressed by labor contractions. And it is often hard to predict if the baby will fit through your birth canal.

I've had women tell me that if they have a Cesarean, "it won't be like having a baby." They falsely believe they won't experience the entire birth process. That's not true. If you deliver by C-section, try not to feel this way. You haven't failed in any way!

Remember, having a baby has taken 9 long months. Even with a C-section, you have accomplished an amazing thing. After a C-section, you can hold the baby and perhaps even nurse.

Changes in You

You only have 4 to 5 weeks to go until your due date. It's easy to get anxious for your baby to be delivered. However, don't ask your doctor to induce labor at this point.

You may have gained 25 to 30 pounds (11.25 to 13.5kg), and

you still have a month to go. It isn't unusual for your weight to stay the same at each of your weekly visits after this point.

The maximum amount of amniotic fluid surrounds the baby now. In the weeks to come, the baby continues to grow. However, some amniotic fluid is reabsorbed by your body, which decreases the amount of fluid around the baby and decreases the amount of room in which the baby has to move. You may notice a difference in sensation of fetal movements. For some women, it feels as if the baby is not moving as much as it had been.

How Your Actions Affect Your Baby's Development

ᗒ *Vaginal Birth after Cesarean*

Should you attempt a vaginal delivery after having had a previous C-section? Vaginal birth after Cesarean (VBAC) is becoming more common. Medically speaking, the method of delivery is not as important as the well-being of you and your baby!

Before you and your doctor make a final decision, you need to weigh the risks and the benefits to you and your baby with both types of delivery. In some cases, you won't have any choice in the matter. In other cases, you and your doctor may decide to let you labor for a while to see if you can deliver vaginally.

Some women like having a repeat Cesarean section. They request one because they don't want to go through labor only to end up with a Cesarean delivery anyway.

ᗒ *Advantages and Risks of VBAC*

Advantages of a vaginal delivery include a decreased risk of problems associated with major surgery, which Cesarean birth is. Recovery after a vaginal delivery is shorter. You can be up and about in the hospital and at home in a much shorter amount of time.

The type of incision previously performed on the uterus dictates if labor can be attempted. One of my new patients, Carol, wanted a VBAC but didn't know what kind of uterine incision she'd had previously. When I got her records from Rhode Island,

I discovered she'd had a classical incision. Labor is not permitted after a classical incision that goes high up on the uterus. (You can't see this incision; your doctor can provide you with this information.) Carol was disappointed she couldn't try a vaginal birth, but she understood the reason for another C-section.

If you are small and the baby is large, you may need a C-section. Multiple fetuses may also make vaginal delivery difficult or impossible without danger to the babies. Medical complications, such as high blood pressure or diabetes, may require a repeat Cesarean section.

If you want to attempt VBAC, discuss it with your doctor in advance so plans can be made. During labor, you will probably be monitored more closely with fetal monitors. You may be attached to I.V.s in case a Cesarean section becomes necessary.

Consider the benefits and risks in deciding whether to attempt a vaginal delivery after a previous Cesarean section. Discuss advantages and disadvantages at length with your doctor and your partner before making a final decision. Don't be afraid to ask your doctor his or her opinion of your chances of a successful vaginal delivery. He or she knows your health and pregnancy history.

Tip for Week 36
Be prepared for delivery with bags packed, insurance papers filled out and available, and other important details taken care of.

You Should also Know

❧ *Group-B Streptococcus Infection*

Group-B streptococcus (GBS) infection in a mother-to-be can cause problems for her baby. GBS rarely causes problems in adults but can cause life-threatening infections in newborns.

GBS is often transmitted from person to person by sexual contact. In women, GBS is most often found in the vagina or rectum. It is possible to have GBS in your system and not be sick or have any symptoms.

The Centers for Disease Control, the American College of Obstetricians and Gynecologists and the American Academy of Pediatrics have developed recommendations aimed at preventing this infection in newborns. One recommendation is that all women who have risk factors be treated for GBS. Risk factors include a previous infant with GBS infection, preterm labor, ruptured membranes for more than 18 hours or a temperature of 100.4 (38C) immediately before or during childbirth.

The second recommendation is a GBS culture should be taken from the rectal and vaginal areas of all pregnant women at 35 to 37 weeks gestation. Penicillin is then used to treat women with positive results.

⌇ *Your Baby's Apgar Score*

After a baby is born, it is examined and evaluated at 1 minute and 5 minutes after delivery. The system of evaluation is called the *Apgar score*. This scoring system is a method of evaluating the overall well-being of the newborn infant.

In general, the higher the score, the better the infant's condition. The baby is scored in five areas. Each area is scored 0, 1 or 2; 2 points is the highest score for each category. The top total score is 10. Areas scored include:

Heart rate of the baby. If the heart rate is absent, a score of 0 is given. If it is slow, less than 100 beats per minute (bpm), a score of 1 is given. If it's over 100 bpm, 2 points are scored.

Respiratory effort of the baby. Respiratory effort indicates the newborn's attempts at breathing. If the baby isn't breathing, the score is 0. If breathing is slow and irregular, the score is 1. If the baby is crying and breathing well, the score is 2.

Baby's muscle tone. Muscle tone evaluates how well the baby moves. If arms and legs are limp and flabby, the score is 0. If some movement is observed and the arms and legs bend a little, the score is 1. If the baby is active and moving, the score is 2.

Reflex irritability of the baby. Reflex irritability is scored 0 if the baby doesn't respond to stimulus, such as rubbing his or her back or arms. If there is a small movement or a grimace when the baby is stimulated, the score is 1. A baby who responds vigorously is scored with 2 points.

Baby's color. The baby's color is rated 0 if the baby is blue or pale. A score of 1 is given if the baby's body is pink, and arms and legs are blue. A completely pink baby is scored at 2.

A perfect score of 10 is unusual. Most babies receive scores of 7, 8 or 9 in a normal, healthy delivery. A baby with a low 1-minute Apgar may need to be resuscitated. This means a pediatrician or nurse must help stimulate the baby to breathe and to recover from the delivery. In most cases, the 5-minute Apgar is higher than the 1-minute score because the baby becomes more active and more accustomed to being outside the uterus.

Week 37

Age of Fetus ⁓ 35 Weeks

How Big Is Your Baby?

Your baby weighs almost 6.5 pounds (2950g). Crown-to-rump length is 14 inches (35cm). Its total length is 21 inches (47cm).

How Big Are You?

Your uterus may stay the same size as measured in the last week or two. Measuring from the pubic symphysis, the top of the uterus is about 14.8 inches (37cm). From the bellybutton, it is 6.4 to 6.8 inches (16 to 17cm). Your weight gain by this time should be about as high as it will go at 25 to 35 pounds (11.2 to 13.5kg).

How Your Baby Is Growing and Developing

﹁ **Is My Baby's Head Down in the Pelvis?**

Your baby is continuing to grow and to gain weight, even during these last few weeks of pregnancy. As the illustration on page 309 shows, the baby's head is usually directed down into the pelvis around this time. However, in about 3% of all pregnancies, the baby's bottom or legs come into the pelvis first. Called a *breech presentation,* it is discussed in Week 38.

﹁ **Maturation of Your Baby's Lungs and Respiratory System**

A very important part of your baby's development is maturation of the lungs and respiratory system. When a baby is born prematurely, a common problem is development of respiratory-distress syndrome in the newborn fetus. This problem is also called *hyaline membrane disease.* In this situation, lungs are not completely mature, and the baby can't breathe on its own without help. Oxygen is necessary. The baby may require a machine, such as a ventilator, to breathe for it.

In the early 1970s, scientists developed a couple of methods for evaluating the maturity of fetal lungs. An amniocentesis test must be done at this point in pregnancy for either test. The first method, the *L/S ratio,* enables doctors to determine in advance if a baby can breathe on its own after delivery.

The L/S-ratio test doesn't usually indicate a baby's lungs are mature until at least 34 weeks of pregnancy. At that time, the relationship between two blood factors in the amniotic fluid changes. Levels of lecithin go up and levels of sphingomyelin go down. The ratio between these two levels indicates if a baby's lungs are mature.

The phosphatidyl glycerol (PG) test is another way doctors can evaluate the maturity of the baby's lungs. This test is either positive or negative. If phosphatidyl glycerol is present in the amniotic fluid (positive result), doctors are reassured; the infant will probably not suffer respiratory distress upon delivery.

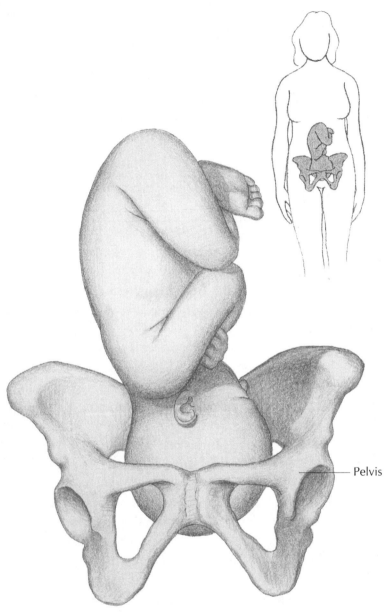

Alignment of baby with head in pelvis before delivery.
This is the preferable presentation.

Specific cells in the lungs produce chemicals that are essential for respiration immediately after birth. An important part of a newborn baby's breathing is determined by the chemical *surfactant.* A baby born prematurely may not have surfactant in its lungs. Surfactant can be introduced directly into the lungs of the newborn to prevent respiratory-distress syndrome. The chemical is available for immediate use by the baby. Many premature babies who receive surfactant do not have to be put on respirators—they can breathe on their own!

Changes in You

∽ Pelvic Exam in Late Pregnancy

About this time in your pregnancy, your doctor may do a pelvic exam. This pelvic exam helps your doctor evaluate the progress of your pregnancy. One of the first things he or she will observe is whether you are leaking amniotic fluid. If you think you are, it's important to tell your doctor.

Your doctor will examine your cervix at the pelvic exam. During labor, the cervix usually becomes softer and thins out. This process is called *effacement.* Your doctor will evaluate the cervix for its softness or firmness and the amount of thinning.

Before labor begins, the cervix is thick and is "0% effaced." When you're in active labor, the cervix thins out; when it is half-thinned, it is "50% effaced." Immediately before delivery, the cervix is "100% effaced" or "completely effaced."

The dilatation (amount of opening) of the cervix is also important. This is usually measured in centimeters. The cervix is fully open when the diameter of the cervical opening measures 10cm. The goal is to be a 10! Before labor begins, the cervix may be closed. Or it may be open a little way, such as 1cm (0.4 inch). The goal of labor is the stretching and opening of the cervix so the baby fits through it and can pass out of the uterus.

Your doctor also evaluates whether the baby's head, bottom or legs are coming first. (He or she may refer to a "presenting part.") The shape of your pelvic bones is also noted.

The station is also determined. *Station* describes the degree to which the presenting part of the baby has descended into the

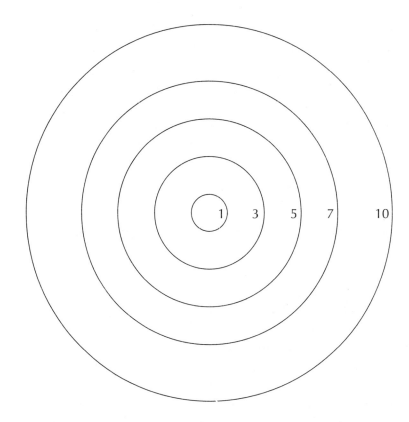

Cervical dilatation in centimeters (shown actual size).

birth canal. If the baby's head is at a -2 station, it means the head is higher inside you than if it were at a +2 station. The 0 point is a bony landmark in the pelvis, the starting place of the birth canal.

Think of the birth canal as a tube going from the pelvic girdle down through the pelvis and out the vagina. The baby travels through this tube from the uterus. It's possible that you may dilate during labor but the baby doesn't move down through the pelvis. In this case, a C-section may be called for because the baby's head doesn't fit through the pelvic girdle.

❧ What Can Your Doctor Tell from a Pelvic Exam?

When your doctor examines you, he or she may describe your situation in medical terms. You might hear you are "2cm, 50%

and a -2 station." This means the cervix is open 2cm (about 1 inch), it is halfway thinned out (50% effaced) and the presenting part (baby's head, feet or buttocks) is at a -2 station.

Try to remember this information. It's helpful information when you go to the hospital and are checked there by a nurse or doctor. You can tell the medical personnel in labor and delivery what your dilatation and effacement were at your last checkup so they can know if your situation has changed.

How Your Actions Affect Your Baby's Development

✣ Choosing Your Baby's Doctor

At this point in your pregnancy, it's time to choose a doctor for your baby. You might choose a pediatrician—a doctor who specializes in treating children. Or you might choose a family practitioner. If the doctor you are seeing during pregnancy is a family practitioner, and you want him or her to care for your baby, you probably don't need to consider this at all.

It's good to meet this doctor before the birth of your baby. Many pediatricians welcome it. This gives you the opportunity to discuss matters that are important to you with this new caregiver. You might want to talk to him or her about a circumcision for your baby if it's a boy. You may want to ask questions about breastfeeding, exams, inoculations and vaccinations, emergencies and other things that concern you. It's also good to find out whether a particular doctor shares your views on child rearing.

By choosing someone to care for your baby before it's born, you have a chance to take part in deciding who will have that important task. If you don't, the doctor who delivers your baby or hospital personnel will select someone. Another good reason for choosing someone ahead of time is if your baby has complications.

After your baby is born, the pediatrician will visit him or her in the hospital and give the baby a physical exam within 24 hours

Tip for Week 37
Now is the time to find a pediatrician for your baby. Ask for referrals; your healthcare provider can give you a reference. Or ask family, friends or people in your childbirth-education classes for names of doctors they like.

after birth. Then he or she will visit you in the hospital, let you know how things are going for the baby and arrange for follow-up care after you leave the hospital.

ᵔ Preregistering at the Hospital

During pregnancy, your doctor has recorded various things that have occurred during your pregnancy. A copy of this record is usually kept in the labor-and-delivery area.

It may be very helpful and save you time if you register at the hospital a few weeks before your due date. You will be able to do this with forms that you get at your doctor's office or by getting forms from the hospital. It's wise to do this before you go to the hospital in labor because by then you may be in a hurry or concerned with other things.

You should know certain facts that may not be included in your chart. It's helpful to know your blood type and Rh-factor. You should be able to say when your last period was and when your due date is. Be able to describe other pregnancies or complications with other pregnancies. Know your doctor's name and your pediatrician's name.

ᵔ Will You Have an Enema?

Will you be required to have an enema when you arrive at labor and delivery? Most hospitals offer an enema at the beginning of labor, but it is not usually mandatory.

Paige didn't want an enema, but she decided to follow her friends' advice and have one. She told me after her delivery she was glad she did. There are certain advantages to having an enema before labor. You may not want to have a bowel movement soon after your baby's delivery because of discomfort with an episiotomy. Having an enema before labor can prevent this discomfort.

An enema before labor can also make the birth of your baby a more pleasant experience. When the baby's head comes out through the birth canal, anything in the rectum comes out, too.

Discuss it with your doctor. Ask his or her opinion, and find out about the policy at the hospital you're going to.

You Should also Know

↣ What Is Back Labor?

Some women experience back labor. *Back labor* refers to a baby that is coming out through the birth canal looking straight up. With this type of labor, you will probably experience lower-back pain.

The mechanics of labor work better if the baby is looking down at the ground so it can extend its head as it comes out through the birth canal. If the baby can't extend its head, its chin points toward its chest. This can cause pain in your lower back during labor.

This type of labor can last longer. Your doctor may need to rotate the baby's head so it comes out looking down at the ground rather than up at the sky.

↣ How Is Your Baby Presenting?

At what point in your pregnancy can your doctor tell how baby is presenting for delivery—for example, if the baby's head is down or if you are carrying the baby breech? At what point will the baby stay in the position it is in?

Usually between 32 and 34 weeks of pregnancy, you can feel the baby's head in the lower abdomen below your umbilicus. Some women can feel different parts of the baby earlier than this. But the baby's head may not be hard enough yet to identify as the head.

The head gradually becomes harder as calcium is deposited in the fetal skull. Your baby's head has a distinct feeling. It is different from the feeling your doctor gets with a breech. A breech position has a soft, round feeling.

Beginning at 32 to 34 weeks, your doctor will probably feel your abdomen to determine how the baby is lying inside you. This position may have changed many times during pregnancy.

At 34 to 36 weeks of pregnancy, the baby usually gets into the position it's going to stay in. If you have a breech at 37 weeks, it's possible the baby can still turn to be head-down. But it becomes less likely the closer you get to the end of your pregnancy.

It may be difficult at times to tell the exact location of different parts of the baby. You may have a good idea according to where you feel kicks and punches. Ask your doctor to show you on your tummy how the baby is lying. Some doctors even take a pen and draw on your stomach to show you. You can leave it so you can show your partner how your baby was lying when you were seen in the office that day.

✣ *Will My Doctor Have to Use Forceps?*

The use of forceps—metal instruments used in the delivery of babies—has decreased in recent years for a couple of reasons. One is the more frequent use of Cesarean delivery to deliver a baby that might be very high up in the pelvis. A C-section may be much safer for the baby if it's not very close to delivering on its own.

Another reason for the decrease in the use of forceps is the use of a vacuum extractor. There are two types of vacuum extractors. One has a plastic cup that fits on the baby's head by suction. The other has a metal cup. The doctor is able to pull on the vacuum cup to deliver the baby's head. The vacuum easily releases from the baby's head, so the baby can't be pulled as hard through the birth canal as with forceps.

The goal with every birth is to deliver the baby as safely as possible. If a large amount of traction with forceps is needed to deliver the baby, a Cesarean section might be a better choice.

If the possible use of a vacuum extractor or forceps causes you concern, discuss it with your physician. It's important to establish good communication with your doctor so you can communicate before and during labor about these concerns.

Week 38

Age of Fetus ⚭ 36 Weeks

At this time, your baby weighs about 6.8 pounds (3100g). Crown-to-rump length hasn't changed much; it's still about 14 inches (35cm). Total length is 21 inches (47cm).

Many women don't grow larger during the last several weeks of pregnancy, but they feel very uncomfortable. The distance between your uterus and the pubic symphysis is 14.4 to 15.2 inches (36 to 38cm). From your bellybutton to the top of your uterus is about 6.4 to 7.2 inches (16 to 18cm).

How Your Baby Is Growing and Developing

‍ Fetal Monitoring during Labor

You may wonder how your doctor can tell your baby is all right, especially during labor. In many hospitals, the baby's heart rate is monitored throughout labor. Being able to detect problems early is important so they can be resolved.

Every time the uterus contracts during labor, less oxygenated blood flows from you to the placenta. Most babies are able to handle this stress without any problem. However, some are affected, and this is called *fetal distress.*

There are two ways to monitor the baby's heartbeat during labor. External fetal monitoring can be used before your membranes rupture. A belt with a receiver is strapped to your abdomen. It uses a principle similar to ultrasound to detect the baby's heartbeat.

An internal fetal monitor is able to monitor the baby's heartbeat more precisely. This type of monitoring can be very helpful in determining the well-being of your baby. An electrode is placed on the baby's scalp and is connected by wires to a machine that records the fetal heart rate. Only women whose membranes are broken and who are dilated at least 1cm can be attached to an internal fetal monitor.

‍ Evaluating the Results of Fetal Monitoring

In evaluating a fetal heart rate, a doctor looks at a large portion of the fetal monitoring strip, not just a small section. He or she also looks for other information. For example, if you are having contractions, it's important to know how your baby is affected. Fetal monitoring can help determine this.

A contraction stress test (CST) gives an indication of how well the baby will tolerate contractions and labor. If the baby doesn't respond well to contractions, it can be a sign of fetal distress. Some believe this test is more accurate than the nonstress test (discussed in Week 35) in evaluating the baby's well-being. A monitor is placed on your abdomen to monitor the baby. An I.V. is started, and the hormone oxytocin is given in small amounts to make your uterus contract. This test gives an indication of how well the baby will tolerate contractions and labor. If the baby doesn't respond well to the contractions, it can be a sign of fetal distress.

If you've had problem pregnancies before, such as a stillbirth, or medical problems during pregnancy, such as diabetes, your doctor may have you tested as you go through pregnancy. You may be tested weekly or biweekly to determine if the baby is doing well inside your uterus.

∾ Fetal Blood Sampling

Doctors can also test your baby's blood pH to see how well your baby is tolerating the stress of labor. Before this test can be done, your membranes must be ruptured, and you must be dilated at least 2cm.

An instrument is applied to the scalp of the baby to make a small nick in the skin. The baby's blood is collected in a small tube or pipette, and its pH (acidity) is checked. If the baby is having trouble with labor and is under stress, the pH level can help determine this. This test may be useful in making a decision as to whether labor can continue or if a C-section needs to be done.

Changes in You

∾ Depression during Pregnancy

Antidepressant medication is not generally given during pregnancy because it is not considered safe. If medication is necessary, most physicians prefer to use those that have been in use for a while, such as tricyclic antidepressants (amitriptyline, desipramine, Sinequan®, Amoxopine®). Recent studies indicate Prozac® is safe to use during pregnancy.

Most evidence indicates there is no rate of increased malformations if these medications must be used during pregnancy. There is little information about the use or safety in pregnancy of some of the newer medications for depression. Without some evidence they are safe, physicians hesitate to prescribe them.

All antidepressant medications pass through the placenta to the baby. There have been isolated case reports of damage to the embryo from these substances (see Week 9). If these medications must be used during pregnancy, it's best to use the lowest dosage possible.

Treating depression during pregnancy can be a difficult problem and must be done on an individualized basis. Your doctor and possibly a psychologist or psychiatrist may be involved in your treatment. Discuss medications you take for depression with your doctor. An infant born to a mother who takes antidepressants during pregnancy may have withdrawal symptoms.

~ *Postpartum Distress*

After your baby is born, you may feel very emotional. You may even wonder if having a baby was a good idea. This is called *postpartum distress*. Many women experience some degree of postpartum distress; in fact, up to 80% of all women have "baby blues." It usually appears between 2 days and 2 weeks after the baby is born. It is a temporary situation and usually leaves as quickly as it comes.

Many experts consider some degree of postpartum distress to be normal. Symptoms include:

- anxiety
- crying for no reason
- exhaustion
- impatience
- irritability
- lack of confidence
- lack of feeling for the baby
- low self-esteem
- oversensitivity
- restlessness

If you believe you may be suffering from some form of postpartum distress, contact your healthcare provider. Every postpartum reaction, whether mild or severe, is usually temporary and treatable.

The mildest form of postpartum distress is baby blues. This situation lasts only a couple of weeks, and symptoms do not worsen.

A more serious version of postpartum distress is called *postpartum depression (PPD)*. It affects about 10% of all new mothers. The difference between baby blues and postpartum depression lies in the frequency, intensity and duration of the symptoms.

PPD can occur from 2 weeks to 1 year after the birth. A mother may have feelings of anger, confusion, panic and hopelessness. She may experience changes in her eating and sleeping patterns. She may fear she will hurt her baby or feel as if she is going crazy. Anxiety is one of the major symptoms of PPD.

The most serious form of postpartum distress is *postpartum psychosis*. The woman may have hallucinations, think about suicide or try to harm the baby.

We don't really know what causes postpartum distress; not all women experience it. We believe a woman's individual sensitivity to hormonal changes may be the cause, but hormones are only part of it.

One of the most important ways you can help yourself is to have a good support system. Ask family members and friends to help. Have your mother or mother-in-law stay for a while. Ask your husband to take some work leave, or hire someone to come in and help each day.

There is no particular treatment for baby blues, but there are ways you can help relieve the symptoms. Ask for help. Rest when the baby sleeps. Find other mothers who are in the same situation; it helps to share your feelings and experiences. Don't try to be perfect. Pamper yourself. Do some form of moderate exercise every day. Eat nutritiously, and drink plenty of fluids. Go out every day.

With postpartum depression, follow the suggestions above. In addition, you may need medication. About 85% of all women who suffer from postpartum depression require medication for up to 1 year.

How Your Actions Affect Your Baby's Development

✌ Breech Presentation

As I've mentioned already, it's common for your baby to be in the breech presentation early in pregnancy. However, when labor starts, only 3% to 5% of all babies, not including multiple pregnancies, present as a breech. Do your actions determine how your baby presents?

Certain factors make a breech presentation more likely. One of the main causes is the baby's prematurity. Near the end of the second trimester, a baby may be in a breech presentation. By taking care of yourself, you can more easily avoid going into premature labor. That gives your baby the best opportunity to change its position naturally.

Other factors that may result in a breech presentation include relaxation of the uterus because of previous pregnancies and multiple fetuses. Conditions such as polyhydramnios, hydrocephalus and uterine abnormalities or tumors may also increase the chance of a breech presentation.

There are different kinds of breech presentations. A frank breech occurs when the lower legs are flexed at the hips and extended at the knees. This is the most common type of breech found at term or the end of pregnancy; feet are up by the face or head.

With a complete breech presentation, one or both knees are flexed, not extended. See the illustration on page 323.

✌ Delivering a Breech Baby

There is some controversy in obstetrics over the best method of delivering a breech baby. For many years, breech deliveries were performed vaginally. Then it was believed the safest method was to deliver the breech by C-section, especially if it was a first baby.

Many doctors believe a Cesarean section is still the safest method of delivering a breech baby. However, some doctors believe a woman can deliver a breech without difficulty if the situation is right. This usually includes a frank breech in a mature fetus of a woman who has had previous normal deliveries. Most agree a footling breech presentation (one leg extended, one knee flexed) should be delivered by Cesarean section.

Most doctors believe a baby in the breech position can probably be delivered more safely by a Cesarean section performed during early labor or before labor begins. Ask your doctor what he or she normally does in this situation.

Attempts may be made to turn the baby from a breech to a head-down (vertex) presentation. It is more difficult to do this after your water breaks or when you are in labor.

If your baby is breech, it's important to discuss it with your doctor. When you get to the hospital, tell the nurses and hospital personnel you have a breech presentation. If you call with a question about labor and you have a breech presentation, mention this information to the person you talk with.

Tip for Week 38

If your healthcare provider suspects your baby is in a breech position, he or she may order an ultrasound to confirm it. It helps identify how the baby is lying in your uterus.

✃ *Other Types of Presentations*

Another unusual presentation is a face presentation. The baby's head is hyperextended so the face comes into the birth canal first. This type of presentation is most often delivered by C-section if it does not convert to a regular presentation during labor.

In a shoulder presentation, the shoulder presents first. In a transverse lie, the baby is lying almost as if in a cradle in the pelvis. The baby's head is on one side of your abdomen, and its bottom is on the other side. There is only one way to deliver this type of presentation, and that is by Cesarean section.

Baby aligned in the pelvis bottom-first, with knees flexed, is called a *complete breech presentation*.

Pelvis

✏ *What Is a Retained Placenta?*

In most cases, the placenta separates on its own from the implantation site on the uterus in the first few minutes after delivery. It is delivered after the baby. In some cases, a piece of placenta remains inside the uterus. When this happens, the uterus cannot contract adequately, resulting in vaginal bleeding, which can be heavy.

In other cases, the placenta does not separate because it's still attached to the wall of the uterus. This can be a very serious situation. However, this complication is rare.

Bleeding is usually severe after delivery, and surgery may be necessary to stop it. An attempt may be made to remove the placenta by D&C.

Reasons for an abnormally adherent placenta are many. It is believed a placenta may attach over a previous Cesarean-section scar or other previous incisions on the uterus. The placenta may attach over an area that has been scraped, such as with a D&C, or over an area of the uterus that was infected at one time.

Your doctor will pay attention to the delivery of your placenta while you are paying attention to your baby. Some people ask to see the placenta after delivery; you may wish to have your doctor show it to you.

Week 39

Age of Fetus ~ 37 Weeks

How Big Is Your Baby?

Your baby weighs a little more than 7 pounds (3250g). By this point in your pregnancy, crown-to-rump length is about 14.4 inches (36cm). The baby's total length is 21.5 inches (48cm).

How Big Are You?

The illustration on page 327 shows a side view of a woman with a very large uterus and her baby inside it. As you can see, she's about as big as she can get. You probably are, too!

If you measure from the pubic symphysis to the top of the uterus, the distance is 14.4 to 16 inches (36 to 40cm). Measuring from the bellybutton, the distance is 6.4 to 8 inches (16 to 20cm).

You're almost at the end of your pregnancy. Your weight should not increase much from this point. It should remain between 25 and 35 pounds (11.4 and 15.9kg) until delivery.

How Your Baby Is Growing and Developing

The baby continues to gain weight, even up to the last week or two of pregnancy. It doesn't have much room to move inside your uterus.

At this point, all the organ systems are developed and in place. The last organ to mature is the lungs.

Changes in You

It would be unusual for you *not* to be uncomfortable and feel huge at this time. Your uterus has filled your pelvis and most of your abdomen. It has pushed everything else out of the way.

At this point in pregnancy, you may think you'll never want to be pregnant again because you're so uncomfortable. Or you may be sure your family is complete. At this point, some women consider permanent sterilization, such as tubal ligation.

~ Tubal Ligation after Delivery?

Some women choose to have a tubal ligation done while they are in the hospital after having their baby. Now is not the time to make the decision about having a tubal ligation if you haven't seriously considered it before.

Being sterilized following delivery of a baby has some advantages. You're in the hospital and won't need another hospitalization. However, there are disadvantages to having a sterilization at this time. Consider the procedure permanent and not reversible. If you have your tubes tied within a few hours or a day after having your baby, then change your mind, you may regret the tubal ligation.

If you have an epidural, it's possible to use the epidural as anesthesia for a tubal ligation. If you didn't have an epidural, it's

Comparative size of the uterus at 39 weeks of pregnancy (fetal age—37 weeks) with a baby that is close to full term.

necessary to put you to sleep. This is often done the morning after you've had your baby. This procedure does not usually lengthen the time you're in the hospital.

Different kinds of procedures are performed for permanent sterilization. Most common is a small incision underneath your bellybutton. The Fallopian tubes can be seen through this incision.

A piece of the tube can be removed, or a ring or clip can be placed on the tube to block it. This type of surgery usually requires about 30 to 45 minutes to perform.

If you have second thoughts or are unsure about having it done, don't have the surgery performed. Consider the procedure permanent. Tubal ligations can be reversed, but it's very expensive and requires a longer hospital stay—3 to 4 days. Reversals are about 50% effective, but pregnancy cannot be guaranteed.

How Your Actions Affect Your Baby's Development

This discussion of how your actions affect your baby's growth and development actually concerns *your* actions after your baby is born! I'm talking about your decision about breastfeeding your baby.

↜ Is Breastfeeding Right for You and Your Baby?

Your decision about breastfeeding is a personal one. One of the more compelling reasons to breastfeed is the bonding that occurs between mother and baby. This close relationship can begin as soon as the baby is born—some women breastfeed on the delivery table. It helps stimulate uterine contractions, which can prevent hemorrhage.

Breastfeeding encourages the natural intimacy of a newborn baby with its mother and the mother with her baby. The opportunity to breastfeed may be a relaxing time for you. It may give you a chance to spend some wonderful time with your new baby. However, if it doesn't work out, it's all right to stop and switch to formula.

Benefits of Breastfeeding

Both you and your baby benefit if you breastfeed. Mother's milk is good for your baby because it contains all the nutrients your baby needs during the first months of life. Commercial formulas have good mixtures of vitamins, protein, sugar, fat and minerals, but none can match your breast milk.

Another advantage of breastfeeding is you pass protection against infection (through antibodies) to your baby in your breast milk. Many people believe a breastfed baby is less likely to get colds and infections than a bottlefed baby.

Breastfeeding is also good for the baby because the baby will probably have to nurse more vigorously than is necessary with some bottle nipples. This encourages good tooth and jaw development.

Advantages for you include decreased cost as compared to buying formula. It's convenient to breastfeed; you don't have to carry bottles and formula with you for the baby. Some women find breastfeeding makes it easier for them to regain their figure.

You may have noticed during pregnancy that your breasts got larger and were probably tender at times. This happens because increased hormonal activity makes the alveoli in the breasts get larger. Milk in the breast is stored in small sacs of these alveoli.

Laura called the office because she was concerned about a discharge from her nipples—was it an infection? I explained to her that late in pregnancy, a woman's breasts may begin to secrete colostrum. Colostrum is rich in antibodies that provide the baby with protection against various infections. I told her colostrum is normal and should not cause her concern.

The first milk that comes from the breasts usually arrives 2 or 3 days after delivery. Its arrival is initiated by stimulation from the baby suckling at your breast. The sucking sends a message to your brain to produce prolactin; this hormone stimulates milk production in the alveoli.

——— Find Out about Breastfeeding ———

Talk with your doctor during pregnancy about breastfeeding. Ask friends about their experiences and how much they enjoyed it. You may also want to contact the local La Leche League, an organization that encourages and promotes breastfeeding. It offers help to women who may be having trouble getting started with breastfeeding. Give them a call if you need information or support.

——— ✳ ———

Some women have trouble breastfeeding because of inverted nipples. This happens when the nipple retracts inward instead of pointing outward. If you have inverted nipples, it is possible to breastfeed. Plastic breast shields are available to wear under clothing to help bring out an inverted nipple. Some doctors also recommend pulling on the nipple and rolling it between the thumb and index finger.

Some women find wearing a support bra very helpful in the last few weeks of pregnancy. A nursing bra is useful while nursing. Many doctors suggest wearing a nursing bra all the time, even when you sleep. You may be more comfortable.

There may be times when you are away from the baby, but you want to continue to breastfeed. You can do this by using a pump. You can pump your breasts with battery-operated pumps, electrical pumps, or manual pumps.

᧠ Learning to Breastfeed

You may want to learn how to breastfeed while you're in the hospital. Ask the nurses to show you some of the tricks they've learned to help your baby catch on to breastfeeding. Ask them any questions you have. What you learn may make the difference in keeping your baby happy with breastfeeding.

Breastfeeding requires a healthful nutrition plan for you, just as you consumed during pregnancy. You'll need at least 500 extra calories each day. Some doctors recommend you continue taking your prenatal vitamins after pregnancy while you are nursing.

Be careful about what you eat and drink because things you eat can pass into your breast milk. Certain foods may not "sit" well with you or your baby. Spicy foods you eat may cause an upset stomach in your baby! Caffeine can also pass to your baby. Any alcohol you drink passes to your baby through your breast milk, so be careful about your consumption of alcoholic beverages. The longer you breastfeed, the more you'll realize what you can and cannot eat and drink.

᧠ Breastfeeding Problems

A common breastfeeding problem for some women is breast engorgement. The breasts become swollen, tender and filled with breast milk. The best cure is to drain the breasts, if possible, as by breastfeeding. Some women take a hot shower and empty their breasts in the warm water. Ice packs may also help.

Mild pain medicines, such as acetaminophen (Tylenol), are often useful in relieving the pain of engorgement. Acetaminophen is recommended by the American Academy of Pediatrics as safe to use while you're breastfeeding. You might need to use stronger medications, such as Tylenol with Codeine, a prescription medication. Call your doctor if engorgement is especially painful. He or she will decide on treatment.

One way to prevent breast engorgement is to feed your baby from both breasts each time you feed. Don't feed on only one side. When you're away from your baby, try to express some breast milk to keep your milk flowing and breast ducts open. You'll feel more comfortable.

Most nursing mothers have sore nipples at some point, partic-ularly at first. Keep your breasts dry and clean. It may be helpful to use a lanolin lotion on the breasts to keep nipples from getting too dry. Before too long—a few days to a few weeks—your breasts will become accustomed to breastfeeding.

It is possible to get an infection in your breast while breast-feeding. If you think you have an infection, call your doctor. An infection may cause pain in the breast, and the breast may turn red and become swollen. You may have streaks of red discoloration on the breast; you may also feel as though you have the flu.

You Should also Know

∞ *Pain Relief during Labor*

Pain relief during labor is approached in many ways. When you take pain medication, remember there are two patients to consid-er—you and your unborn baby. It is best to find out in advance what is available for pain control. Then see how labor goes for you before making a final decision.

A valuable part of your experience in labor and delivery is your preparation for it. This includes being aware of things that are happening to you, and why, and not being frightened by the pain you feel. You should have confidence in those taking care of you, including the staff at the hospital and your doctor.

When contractions are regular and the cervix is beginning to dilate, uterine contractions may be very uncomfortable. For pain in this early stage of labor, many hospitals use a mixture of a narcotic analgesic drug, such as meperidine (Demerol), and a tranquilizer, such as promethazine (Phenergen®). This decreases pain and causes some sleepiness or sedation. Medication may be given through an I.V. or by injection into a muscle.

Narcotic analgesics pass to your baby through the placenta and may decrease respiratory function in the newborn infant. It can also affect your baby's Apgar scores. These medications should not be given close to the time of delivery.

In many places, anesthesia for delivery is given by an injection of a particular medication to affect a particular area of the body. This is called a *block,* such as a pudendal block, an epidural block or a cervical block. Medication is similar to the type used to block pain when you have a tooth filled. The agents are xylocaine or xylocaine-like medications.

Very occasionally, it is necessary to use general anesthesia for delivery of a baby, usually for an emergency Cesarean section. A pediatrician attends the birth because it is possible the baby will be asleep following delivery.

✒ What Is an Epidural Block?

The epidural block is a frequently used regional block. It provides relief from the pain of uterine contractions and delivery.

It should be administered only by someone trained and experienced in this type of anesthesia. Some obstetricians have this experience, but in most areas an anesthesiologist must administer it.

A continuous epidural block can be started when you are sitting up or lying on your side. An area of skin over your lower back in the middle of your spinal cord is numbed. A needle is introduced through the numbed area of the skin; anesthetic is placed around the spinal cord but not into the spinal canal. A plastic catheter is left in place.

Epidural pain medication may be given during labor with a pump. The anesthesiologist uses the pump to inject a small amount of medication at regular intervals or as needed. An epidural provides excellent relief from labor pain.

A problem with an epidural block is that it can make your blood pressure drop. Low blood pressure may affect blood flow to the baby. Fortunately, I.V. fluids administered with the epidural help reduce the risk of hypotension (low blood pressure). You may also have problems pushing during delivery.

✐ *Other Pain Blocks*

Spinal anesthesia may be used for a Cesarean section. With this anesthesia, pain relief lasts long enough for the Cesarean section to be performed. Epidural anesthesia is used more often than spinal anesthesia for labor.

Other types of blocks used occasionally include a pudendal block. It is given through the vaginal canal and decreases pain in the birth canal itself. You still feel the contraction and tightening with pain in the uterus. Some hospitals use a paracervical block. It provides pain relief for the dilating cervix, but doesn't relieve the pain of contractions.

There is no perfect method for pain relief during labor and delivery. Discuss the possibilities with your doctor, and mention your concerns. Find out what types of anesthesia are available and the risks and benefits of each.

✐ *Anesthesia Complications*

There are other possible complications from use of anesthesia. These include increased sedation of the baby with use of narcotics, such as Demerol. The newborn may have lower Apgar scores and depressed breathing. The baby may require resuscitation or it may need to receive another drug, such as naloxone (Narcan®), to reverse the effects of the first drug.

Increased sedation, slower respiration and a slower heartbeat may also be observed in a baby whose mother is given general anesthesia. The mother is usually "out" for more than an hour and is unable to see her newborn infant until later.

It may be impossible to determine before you go into labor which anesthesia will be best for you. But it's helpful to know what's available and what types of pain relief you might be able to count on during your labor and delivery.

⁊ Contraction of the Uterus after Delivery

After you deliver your baby, your uterus shrinks from about the size of a watermelon to the size of a volleyball. When this happens, the placenta detaches from the uterine wall. At this time, there may be a gush of blood from inside the uterus signaling delivery of the placenta.

After the placenta is delivered, you may be given oxytocin (Pitocin). This helps the uterus contract and clamp down so it won't bleed. Extremely heavy bleeding after vaginal delivery is called *postpartum hemorrhage,* which is bleeding more than 17 ounces (500ml). It can often be prevented by massaging the uterus and using medications to help the uterus contract.

The main reason a woman experiences heavy bleeding after delivering a baby is her uterus does not contract, called an *atonic uterus.* Your doctor or the nurse attending you may massage your uterus after delivery. They may tell you how to do it so your uterus will stay firm and contracted. This is important so you won't lose more blood and become anemic.

⁊ Cord-Blood Banking

Cord blood is blood left in the umbilical cord and placenta after a baby is born. In the past, the placenta and the umbilical cord were usually discarded following delivery. There is a great deal of interest now about saving cord blood after delivery. Cord-blood banking was called one of the top-10 medical advances of 1996 by the *Harvard Health Letter.*

Umbilical-cord blood can be used to treat cancer and genetic diseases that are now treated by bone-marrow transplants. Cord blood has been used successfully to treat childhood leukemia, some immune diseases and other blood diseases. At present research is being conducted in the United States and Europe to use cord blood for gene therapy in a number of diseases, including sickle-cell anemia, diabetes and AIDS.

Cord blood contains the same valuable cells that are found in bone marrow. These "stem cells" are the building blocks of the blood and immune systems. These special cells are undeveloped in cord blood. Because they are undeveloped, cord blood does not need to be matched as closely for a transplant as bone-marrow blood does. This feature can be especially important for members of ethnic minority groups or people with rare blood types. These groups traditionally have had more difficulty finding acceptable donor "matches."

Before their baby's birth, parents may request that the baby's cord blood be collected and "banked" for future use. The blood can be used by the child from whom it was collected, his siblings and parents. You also may donate your baby's cord blood at no cost to you, similar to blood banking.

Blood is collected directly from the umbilical cord immediately after delivery. There is no risk or pain to the mother or baby. The blood is transported to a banking facility where it is frozen and cryogenically stored.

The cost of cord-blood banking includes an initial fee of about $1,000, with about a $100-a-year storage fee. As more is learned about blood banking and its use becomes more common, the cost may go down. Some health-insurance companies pay the fees for families at high risk of cancer or genetically based diseases. Also, cord-blood banking services themselves may waive fees for at-risk families who are unable to afford them.

For more information about cord-blood banking services, contact the International Cord Blood Foundation at (415) 635-1456.

Tip for Week 39

Don't take tags off shower gifts and other gifts until after your baby is born. You may need to exchange the gift if its size, color or "sex" isn't correct.

Week 40

Age of Fetus ⁓ 38 Weeks

How Big Is Your Baby?

Your baby weighs about 7.5 pounds (3400g). Its crown-to-rump length is about 14.8 to 15.2 inches (37 to 38cm). Total length is 21.5 inches (48cm).

Your baby fills your uterus and has very little room to move. See the illustration on page 339.

How Big Are You?

From the pubic symphysis to the top of the uterus, you probably measure 14.4 to 16 inches (36 to 40cm). From your bellybutton to the top of your uterus is 6.4 to 8 inches (16 to 20cm).

By this time, you probably don't care an awful lot about how much you measure. You feel you're as big as you could ever be, and you're ready to have your baby. You may continue to grow and even to get a little bit bigger until you have your baby. But don't be discouraged—you'll have your baby soon.

How Your Baby Is Growing and Developing

Bilirubin is a breakdown product from red blood cells. Before your baby is born, bilirubin is transferred easily across the placenta from the fetus to the maternal circulation. Through this process, your body is able to get rid of the bilirubin from the baby. Once your baby is delivered and the umbilical cord is clamped, the baby is on its own to handle the bilirubin produced in its own body.

Jaundice in a Newborn

After birth, if your baby has problems dealing with bilirubin, it may develop high levels of it in the blood. Your baby may develop jaundice—yellowing of the skin and the whites of the eyes. Bilirubin levels typically increase for 3 or 4 days after the baby's delivery, then decrease.

Your pediatrician and the nurses in the nursery check for jaundice by observing your baby's color. Your baby may have a blood test to measure his or her bilirubin levels at the hospital or at your pediatrician's office.

A baby is treated for jaundice with phototherapy. The baby is placed under special lights; the light penetrates the skin and destroys the bilirubin. If very high levels of bilirubin are present, the baby may undergo an exchange blood transfusion.

Kernicterus in a Newborn

Extremely high levels of bilirubin (hyperbilirubinemia) in a newborn infant cause doctors concern because a very serious condition called *kernicterus* can develop. Kernicterus is seen more frequently in premature infants than in babies delivered at full term. If the baby survives the kernicterus, it may have neurologic problems—spasticity, lack of muscle coordination and varying degrees of mental retardation. However, kernicterus in a newborn is a rare occurrence.

Changes in You

∿ What Happens When You're Overdue?

By now you're anticipating the delivery of your baby. You're probably counting the days to your due date. As I've mentioned, not every woman delivers by her due date. A pregnancy is considered to be overdue (postdate) when it exceeds 42 weeks or 294 days from the first day of the last menstrual period.

While the fetus is growing and developing inside your uterus, it depends on two important functions performed by the placenta—respiration and nutrition. The baby relies on these functions for continued growth and development.

When a pregnancy is postdate, the placenta may fail to provide the respiratory function and essential nutrients the baby needs to grow, and an infant may begin to suffer nutritional deprivation. The baby is called *postmature*.

At birth, a postmature baby has dry, cracked, peeling, wrinkled skin, long fingernails and abundant hair. It also has less vernix covering its body. The baby appears almost malnourished, with decreased amounts of subcutaneous fat.

Because the postmature infant is in danger of losing nutritional support from the placenta, it's important to know the true dating of your pregnancy. This is one reason it's important to go to all of your prenatal visits.

At Jill's office visit, she wearily asked me, "How much longer?" She was 39 weeks pregnant, so I explained to her that most doctors agree that once a woman reaches 42 weeks of pregnancy, the baby should be delivered if the cervix is beginning to dilate and to thin, and the baby is in the proper presentation, with the head down.

She was disappointed that her baby wasn't coming yet. But when I explained that it's best for the baby to wait until it is ready to deliver, she agreed it was worth the wait for a healthy baby.

∿ Inducing Labor

If your doctor must induce labor, you will receive oxytocin (Pitocin) intravenously. Medication is gradually increased until

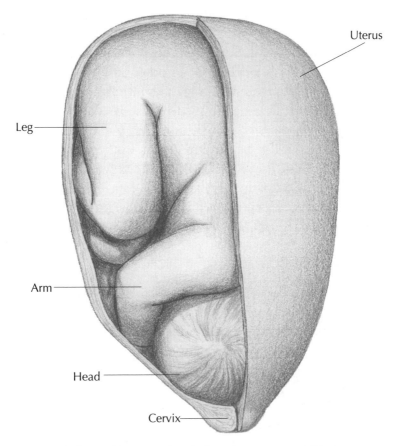

A full-term baby in the uterus has little room to move. This is one reason fetal movements may slow down in the last few weeks of pregnancy.

contractions begin. The amount of oxytocin you receive is controlled by a pump, so you can't receive too much of it. While you receive oxytocin, you are monitored for the baby's reaction to your labor.

✒ *Ripening the Cervix for Induction*

It is estimated that obstetricians in the United States induce labor in about 450,000 women a year. Prepidil Gel® (dinoprostone cervical gel 0.5mg) is a drug used to ripen the cervix and induce labor. "Ripening the cervix" means softening, thinning and dilating the cervix.

Prepidil Gel is most often used to ripen a cervix in a pregnant woman at or near term with a medical or obstetric need for labor induction. These conditions include postmaturity (overdue baby), hypertension, pre-eclampsia or other problems.

Cervidil™ (dinoprostone 10mg) is another preparation that ripens the cervix. It uses a controlled-release system.

In most cases, doctors use Prepidil Gel and Cervidil to prepare the cervix the day before induction. Both preparations are placed in the top of the vagina, behind the cervix. Medication is released directly onto the cervix, which causes it to ripen for induction of labor. Doctors do this procedure in the labor-and-delivery area of the hospital, so the baby can be monitored.

How Your Actions Affect Your Baby's Development

The delivery of your baby is the event you've been planning for! If this is your first baby, you may be very excited and a little apprehensive. Delivery of your baby is something you'll remember for a very long time.

You need to decide who you want with you during delivery. In some cases, family members assume they're invited to the delivery.

Some couples choose to bring young children into the delivery room to see the birth of a new brother or sister. Discuss this with your doctor ahead of time, and get his or her opinion. The delivery of the baby might be very exciting and special to you and your partner, but it may be frightening to a young child.

Many places offer special classes for brothers- and sisters-to-be to help prepare them for the new baby. This is a good way to help older children feel they are part of the birth experience.

You Should also Know

⌐ **What Happens When You Arrive at the Hospital?**

Don't be embarrassed if you have to go to the hospital to be checked for labor. This isn't a nuisance to hospital personnel or your doctor—that's why they're there! If you're concerned you might be in labor and you aren't sure, talk with your doctor or the nurses at labor and delivery. They'll tell you if you should come in to be evaluated.

When you go to the hospital, you'll be evaluated. A copy of your office record is kept in the labor and delivery area. Those seeing you in the hospital should know about any problems or complications that have occurred during your pregnancy and any other information that is important.

——— **Check-in at the Hospital** ———

You will probably be asked many questions when you arrive at the hospital to check in. They may include the following.

- Have your membranes ruptured? At what time?
- Are you bleeding?
- Are you having contractions? How often do they occur? How long do they last?
- When did you last eat and what did you eat?

Other important information for you to share includes medical problems you have and any medications you take or have taken during pregnancy. If you've had complications, such as placenta previa, tell them when you first come to labor and delivery.

If you think you're in labor, don't eat. Even something light in your stomach can cause nausea. You may have to ask for an antacid for relief of stomach upset.

After you check in, you will be put in a labor room or an evaluation room to determine if you're actually in labor. It's important to know whether you're having contractions, how often they occur, how long they last and how strong they are. This is normally done with an external fetal monitor (discussed in Week 38). The monitor is placed on your abdomen; it shows the frequency and duration of contractions.

It's very important to know whether your membranes have ruptured (your water has broken). Ruptured membranes can be confirmed in any of several ways:

- by your description of what happened, such as a large gush of fluid
- with the nitrazine paper test
- with a ferning test

You will also be checked to see if you are dilated. It's helpful to know if you were dilated (and how much) when last checked by your doctor. A nurse or doctor performs this exam.

You will be asked to give a brief history of your pregnancy. Mention any other medical problems you have. If you've had any complications during pregnancy, such as bleeding, or if you know your baby is breech, tell them. Don't assume they know. They note your vital signs, including your blood pressure, pulse and temperature.

Evaluation and determination of whether you're in labor is usually not a 5-minute experience. It takes time to check everything out.

If you are in labor and remain at the hospital, other things will happen. Your partner may have to admit you to the hospital if you haven't filled out preadmittance papers. You may be asked to sign a release form or a permission slip from the hospital, your doctor or the anesthesiologist. This is done to ensure you are informed and aware of the procedures that will be done for you and any risks that are involved.

After you have been admitted, you may receive an enema or an I.V. may be started. Your doctor may want to discuss pain relief, or you may have an epidural put in place.

Blood will probably be drawn to be tested for hematocrit and complete blood count (CBC). Other things that are done at the hospital vary depending on where you go, your doctor's preferences and arrangements you have made ahead of time.

◈ *Your Labor Coach*

In most instances, your partner is your labor coach. However, this isn't an absolute requirement. A close friend or relative, such as your mother or sister, can also serve as your labor coach. Ask someone ahead of time; don't wait until the last minute. Give the person time to prepare for the experience and to make sure he or she will be able to be there with you.

Not everyone feels comfortable watching the entire labor and delivery. This may include your partner. Don't force your partner or labor coach to watch the delivery if he or she doesn't want to. It's not unusual for a labor coach to get lightheaded, dizzy or pass out during labor and delivery. On more than one occasion, I've had a coach or partner faint or become extremely lightheaded when we just *talked* about plans for labor and delivery or a C-section!

Preparing ahead of time, as with prenatal classes, helps avoid some problems. In the past, you would have been alone with the nurses and doctor while your partner paced in the waiting room. Things have changed!

The most important thing about the labor coach is the support he or she gives you during pregnancy, labor, delivery and recovery following the birth of the baby. Choose this person carefully.

◈ *What Can a Partner or Labor Coach Do?*

Your partner or labor coach may be one of the most valuable assets you have during labor and delivery. He (or she) can help you prepare for labor and delivery in many ways. He can be there to support you as you go through the experience of labor together. He can share with you the joy of the delivery of your baby.

An important role of the labor coach is to make sure you get to the hospital! Work out a plan during the last 4 to 6 weeks of pregnancy so you know how to reach your coach. It's helpful to have an alternate driver, such as a neighbor or friend, who is available in case you are unable to reach your labor coach immediately and need to be taken to the hospital. Before going to the hospital, your labor coach can time your contractions so you are aware of the progress of your labor.

Once you arrive at the hospital, both of you are going to be nervous. Your coach can do things to help you both relax. Some of these include:

- talking to you while you're in labor to distract you and to help you relax
- encouraging and reassuring you during labor and when it comes time for you to push
- keeping a watch on the door and your privacy
- helping relieve tension during labor
- touching each other, hugging and kissing (If you don't want to be touched during labor, tell your coach.)
- reassuring you it's OK for you to deal vocally with your pain
- wiping your face or your mouth with a washcloth, rubbing your abdomen or your back, supporting your back while you're pushing
- helping create a mood in the labor room, including music and lighting (Discuss it ahead of time; bring things with you that you would like to have available during labor.)
- taking pictures (many couples find still pictures taken of the baby after the delivery help them best remember these wonderful moments of joy)

It's all right for your labor coach to rest or to take a break during labor. This is especially true if labor lasts a long time. It's better if your coach eats in the lounge or hospital cafeteria.

Many couples do different things to distract themselves and to help pass time during labor. These include picking names for the baby, playing games, watching TV or listening to music. A labor coach shouldn't bring work to the labor room. Talking on the phone to clients or doing work is inappropriate and shows little support for the laboring woman.

Talk to your doctor about your coach's participation in the delivery, such as cutting the umbilical cord or bathing the baby after birth. Things like this that can be done vary from one place to another. Understand the responsibility of your doctor is the well-being of you and your baby—don't make requests or demands that could cause complications for you or your baby.

Talk about who needs to be called ahead of time. Bring a list of names and phone numbers with you. There are some people you may want to call yourself. In most places, a telephone is available in labor and delivery rooms.

Talk to your labor coach about showing the baby to those who are waiting. If you want to be with your partner when friends or relatives first see the baby, make it clear. Don't allow your baby to be taken out of the room unless that's what you want. In most instances, you need some cleaning up. Take 10 or 15 minutes for yourselves. After that you can show the baby to friends and relatives and share the joy with them.

✎ *What Happens to You after the Birth?*

What happens to you after the birth of your baby depends on the hospital or birthing-center facilities where you have your baby. Hospitals vary in the arrangements and accommodations they have available.

With LDRP (labor, delivery, recovery and postpartum), the room you are admitted to at the beginning of your labor is the room you labor in, deliver in, recover in and remain in for your entire hospital stay. This isn't available everywhere, but these facilities are becoming more popular.

The concept of LDRP has evolved because many women don't want to be moved from the labor area to recovery to another part of the hospital after delivery. The nursery is usually close to labor and delivery and the recovery area. This enables you to see your baby as often as you like and to have your baby in your room for longer periods.

In many places, you will labor in the labor-and-delivery suite, then be moved to a delivery room at the time of delivery. Following this, you may go to a postpartum floor, which is an area in the hospital where you will spend the remainder of your hospital stay.

Most hospitals allow you to have your baby in your room as much as you want. This is called *rooming in* or *boarding in*. Some hospitals also have a cot, couch or chair that makes into a bed in your room so your partner can stay with you after delivery. Check the availability of various facilities in the hospitals in your area.

Another concept is the birthing room; this generally refers to delivering your baby in the same room you labor in. You don't have to be moved from the room you're laboring in to another place to have the baby. Even if you use a birthing room, you may have to move to another area of the hospital for recovery.

Whatever you choose, the most important thing is the health of your baby and the welfare of you both. When you decide where to have your baby, be sure you have answered the following questions, if you can.

- What facilities and staff do you have available?
- What is the availability of anesthesia? Is an anesthesiologist available 24 hours a day?
- How long does it take them to respond to and perform a Cesarean delivery, if necessary? (This should be 30 minutes or less.)
- Is a pediatrician available 24 hours a day for an emergency or problems?
- Is the nursery staffed at all times?
- In the event of an emergency or a premature baby that needs to be transported to a high-risk nursery, how is it done? By ambulance? By helicopter? How close is the nearest high-risk nursery, if not at this hospital?

These may seem like a lot of questions to ask, but the answers can help put your mind at ease. When it's your baby and your health, it's nice to know emergency measures can be employed in an efficient, timely manner when necessary.

✌ *What Happens to Your Baby after It's Born?*

When your baby is delivered, the doctor clamps and cuts the umbilical cord, then the baby's mouth and throat are suctioned out. The baby may be placed on your abdomen in clean blankets. Or the baby may be passed to a nurse or pediatrician for initial evaluation and attention. The Apgar scores (see Week 36) are recorded at 1- and 5-minute intervals. An identification band is placed on the baby so there's no mix-up in the nursery!

It's important to keep the baby warm immediately after birth. To do this, the nurse will dry the baby and wrap it in warm blankets. This is done whether the baby is on your chest or attended to by a nurse or doctor.

If your labor is complicated, the baby may need to be evaluated more thoroughly in the nursery. The baby's well-being and health are of primary concern. You'll be able to hold and to nurse the baby, but if your child is having trouble breathing or needs special attention, such as monitors, immediate evaluation is the most appropriate procedure at this time.

Your baby will be taken to the nursery by a nurse and your partner or labor coach. In the nursery, the baby is weighed, measured and footprinted (in some places). Drops to prevent infection are placed in the baby's eyes. A vitamin-K shot is given to help with the baby's blood-clotting factors. Your baby may receive the hepatitis vaccine if you request it. Then the baby is put in a heated bassinet for 30 minutes to 2 hours. The time period varies, depending on how stable the baby is.

Your pediatrician is notified immediately if there are problems or concerns. Otherwise, he or she will be notified soon after birth, and a physical exam will be performed within 24 hours.

✦ Keep Your Options Open during Labor and Delivery

An important consideration in planning for your labor and delivery is the method(s) you may use to get through labor and delivery. Will you have epidural anesthesia? Are you going to attempt a drug-free delivery? Will you need an episiotomy?

Every woman is different, and every labor is different. It's difficult to anticipate what will happen and what you will need during labor and delivery for pain relief. It's impossible to know how long labor will last—3 hours or 20 hours. It's best to adopt a flexible plan. Understand what's available and what options you can choose during labor.

During the last 2 months of your pregnancy, discuss these concerns with your doctor and become familiar with his or her philosophy about labor. Know what can be provided for you at the hospital you're going to. Some medications may not be available in some areas.

✄ **What Is Natural Childbirth?**

Some women decide before the birth of their baby that they are going to labor and deliver with "natural childbirth." What does this mean? The description or definition of natural childbirth varies from one couple to another.

Many people equate natural childbirth with "drug-free" labor and delivery. Others equate natural childbirth with the use of mild pain medications or local pain medications, such as numbing medications in the area of the vagina for delivery, or for an episiotomy and repair of episiotomy. Most agree that natural childbirth is birth with as few artificial procedures as possible. A woman who chooses natural childbirth usually needs some advance instruction to prepare for it.

Natural childbirth isn't for every woman. If you arrive at the hospital dilated 1cm, with strong contractions and in pain, natural childbirth may be very hard for you. In this situation, an epidural might be appropriate.

On the other hand, if you arrive at the hospital dilated 4 or 5cm and contractions are OK, natural childbirth might be a reasonable choice. It's impossible to know what will happen ahead of time, but it helps to be aware of, and ready for, everything.

There are three major philosophies of natural childbirth. *Lamaze* is the oldest technique of childbirth preparation. It conditions mothers, through training, to replace unproductive laboring efforts with fruitful ones and emphasizes relaxation and breathing as ways to relax during labor and delivery. *Bradley* classes teach the Bradley method of relaxation and inward focus; many types of relaxation are used. Strong emphasis is put on relaxation and deep abdominal breathing to make labor more comfortable. Classes begin when pregnancy is confirmed and continue until after the birth. *Grantly Dick-Read* is a method that attempts to break the fear-tension-pain cycle of labor and delivery. These classes were the first to include fathers in the birth experience.

It's important to keep an open mind during the unpredictable process of labor and delivery. Don't feel guilty or disappointed if you can't do all the things you planned before labor. You may need an epidural. Or the birth may not be accomplished without an episiotomy. Don't let anyone make you feel guilty or make you feel as though you've accomplished less if you end up needing a C-section, an epidural or an episiotomy.

Beware of instruction that tells you labor is free of pain, no one really needs a C-section, I.V.s are unnecessary or an episiotomy is foolish. This can create unrealistic expectations for you. If you do need any of the above procedures, you may feel as though you failed during your labor.

The goal in labor and delivery is a healthy baby. If this means you end up with a C-section, you haven't failed. Be grateful a Cesarean delivery can be performed safely. Babies that would not have survived birth in the past can be delivered safely. This is a wonderful accomplishment!

Tip for Week 40

If you want to use a different labor position, massage, relaxation techniques or hypnotherapy to relieve labor pain, discuss it with your doctor at one of your prenatal visits.

Glossary

abruptio placenta. See *placental abruption.*

acquired immune deficiency syndrome (AIDS). Debilitating and frequently fatal illness that affects the body's ability to respond to infection. Caused by the human immune deficiency virus (HIV).

aerobic exercise. Exercise that increases your heart rate and causes you to consume oxygen.

afterbirth. See *placenta.*

alpha-fetoprotein (AFP). Substance produced by the unborn baby as it grows inside the uterus. Large amounts of AFP are found in the amniotic fluid. Larger-than-normal amounts are found in the maternal bloodstream if neural-tube defects are present in the fetus.

alveoli. Ends of the ducts of the lung.

amino acids. Substances that act as building blocks in the developing embryo and fetus.

amniocentesis. Removal of amniotic fluid from the amniotic sac. Fluid is tested for some genetic defects.

amnion. Membrane around the fetus. It surrounds the amniotic cavity.

amniotic fluid. Liquid surrounding the baby inside the amniotic sac.

amniotic sac. Sac that surrounds baby inside the uterus. It contains the baby, the placenta and the amniotic fluid.

ampulla. Dilated opening of a tube or duct.

anemia. Any condition in which the number of red blood cells is less than normal. Term usually applies to the concentration of the oxygen-transporting material in the blood, which is the red blood cell.

anencephaly. Defective development of the brain combined with the absence of the bones normally surrounding the brain.

angioma. Tumor, usually benign, or swelling composed of lymph and blood vessels.

anovulatory. Lack of or cessation of ovulation.

anti-inflammatory medications. Drugs to relieve pain or inflammation.

areola. Pigmented or colored ring surrounding the nipple of the breast.

arrhythmia. Irregular or missed heartbeat.

aspiration. Swallowing or sucking a foreign body or fluid, such as vomit, into an airway.

asthma. Disease marked by recurrent attacks of shortness of breath and difficulty breathing. Often caused by an allergic reaction.

atonic uterus. Flaccid; relaxed; lack of tone.

autoantibodies. Antibodies that attack parts of your body or your own tissues.

back labor. Pain of labor felt in lower back.

beta-adrenergics. Substances that interfere with transmission of stimuli. They affect the autonomic nervous system.

bilirubin. Breakdown product of pigment formed in the liver from hemoglobin during the destruction of red blood cells.

biophysical profile. Method of evaluating a fetus before birth.

biopsy. Removal of a small piece of tissue for microscopic study.

birthing center. Facility in which a woman labors, delivers and recovers in the same room. It may be part of a hospital or a freestanding unit.

blastomere. One of the cells the egg divides into after it has been fertilized.

bloody show. Small amount of vaginal bleeding late in pregnancy; often precedes labor.

board certification. Doctor has had additional training and testing in a particular specialty. In the area of obstetrics, the American College of Obstetricians and Gynecologists offers this training. Certification requires expertise in care of a pregnant woman.

Braxton-Hicks contractions. Irregular, painless tightening of uterus during pregnancy.

breech presentation. Abnormal position of the fetus. Buttocks or legs come into the birth canal ahead of the head.

cataract, congenital. Cloudiness of the eye lens present at birth.

cell antibodies. See *autoantibodies.*

Cesarean section (delivery). Delivery of a baby through an abdominal incision rather than through the vagina.

Chadwick's sign. Dark-blue or purple discoloration of the mucosa of the vagina and cervix during pregnancy.

chemotherapy. Treatment of disease by chemical substances or drugs.

chlamydia. Sexually transmitted venereal infection.

chloasma. Extensive brown patches of irregular shape and size on the face or other parts of the body.

chorion. Outermost fetal membrane found around the amnion.

chorionic villus sampling. Diagnostic test done early in pregnancy. A biopsy of tissue is taken from inside the uterus through the cervical opening to determine abnormalities of pregnancy.

cleft palate. Defect in the palate, the part of the upper jaw or mouth.

colostrum. Thin, yellow fluid, which is the first milk to come from the breast. Most often seen toward the end of pregnancy. It is different in content from milk produced later during nursing.

condyloma acuminatum. Skin tags or warts that are sexually transmitted. Also called *venereal warts.*

congenital problem. Problem present at birth.

conization of the cervix. Surgical procedure performed on premalignant and malignant conditions of the cervix. A large biopsy of the cervix is taken in the shape of a cone.

conjoined twins. Twins connected at the body; they may share vital organs. Also called *Siamese twins.*

constipation. Bowel movements are infrequent or incomplete.

contraction stress test. Response of fetus to uterine contractions to evaluate fetal well-being.

corpus luteum. Area in the ovary where the egg is released at ovulation. A cyst may form in this area after ovulation. Called a *corpus luteum cyst.*

crown-to-rump length. Measurement from the top of the baby's head (crown) to the buttocks of the baby (rump).

cystitis. Inflammation of the bladder.

cytomegalovirus (CMV) infection. Group of viruses from the herpes virus family.

D&C (dilatation and curettage). Surgical procedure in which the cervix is dilated and the lining of the uterus is scraped.

developmental delay. Condition in which the development of the baby or child is slower than normal.

diastasis recti. Separation of abdominal muscles.

diethylstilbestrol (DES). Non-steroidal synthetic estrogen. Used in the past to try to prevent miscarriage.

dizygotic twins. Twins derived from two different eggs. Often called *fraternal twins.*

dysuria. Difficulty or pain urinating.

EDC (estimated date of confinement). Anticipated due date for delivery of the baby. Calculated from the first day of the last period counting forward 280 days.

eclampsia. Convulsions and coma in a woman with pre-eclampsia. Not related to epilepsy.

ectodermal germ layer. Layer in the developing embryo that gives rise to developing structures in the fetus. These include skin, teeth and glands of the mouth, the nervous system and the pituitary gland.

ectopic pregnancy. Pregnancy that occurs outside the uterine cavity.

effacement. Thinning of cervix.

electroencephalogram. Recording of the electrical activity of the brain.

embryo. Organism in the early stages of development.

embryonic period. First 10 weeks of gestation.

endodermal germ layer. Area of tissue in early development of the embryo that gives rise to other structures. These include the digestive tract, respiratory organs, vagina, bladder and urethra. Also called *endoderm* or *entoderm.*

endometrial cycle. Regular development of the mucous membrane lining the inside of the uterus. It begins with the preparation for acceptance of a pregnancy and ends with the shedding of the lining during a menstrual period.

endometrium. Mucous membrane that lines inside of the uterine wall.

enema. Fluid injected into the rectum for the purpose of clearing out the bowel.

engorgement. Congested; filled with fluid.

enzyme. Protein made by cells. It acts as a catalyst to improve or cause chemical changes in other substances.

epidural block. Type of anesthesia. Medication is injected around the spinal cord during labor or other types of surgery.

episiotomy. Surgical incision of the vulva (area behind the vagina, above the rectum). Used during delivery to avoid tearing or laceration of the vaginal opening and rectum.

estimated date of confinement. See *EDC.*

exotoxin. Poison or toxin from a source outside the body.

face presentation. Baby comes into the birth canal face first.

Fallopian tube. Tube that leads from the cavity of the uterus to the area of the ovary. Also called *uterine tube.*

false labor. Tightening of uterus without dilatation of the cervix.

fasting blood sugar. Blood test to evaluate the amount of sugar in the blood following a time period of fasting.

ferrous gluconate. Iron supplement.

ferrous sulfate. Iron supplement.

fertilization. Joining of the sperm and egg.

fertilization age. Dating a pregnancy from the time of fertilization. 2 weeks shorter than the gestational age.

fetal anomaly. Fetal malformation or abnormal development.

fetal arrhythmia. See *arrhythmia.*

fetal goiter. Enlargement of the thyroid in the fetus.

fetal-growth retardation (IUGR). Inadequate growth of the fetus during the last stages of pregnancy.

fetal monitor. Device used before or during labor to listen to and record the fetal heartbeat. Can be *external* monitoring (through maternal abdomen) or *internal* monitoring (through maternal vagina) of the baby inside the uterus.

fetal period. Time period following the embryonic period (first 10 weeks of gestation) until birth.

fetus. Refers to the unborn baby after 10 weeks of gestation until birth.

fibrin. Elastic protein important in the coagulation of blood.

forceps. Instrument used to help remove baby from the birth canal during delivery.

frank breech. Baby presenting buttocks first. Legs are flexed and knees extended.

fraternal twins. See *dizygotic twins.*

genetic counseling. Consultation between a couple and a specialist about genetic defects and the possibility of genetic problems in a pregnancy.

genital herpes simplex. Herpes simplex infection involving the genital area. It can be significant during pregnancy because of the danger to a newborn fetus becoming infected with herpes simplex.

genitourinary problems. Defects or problems involving genital organs and the bladder or kidneys.

germ layers. Layers or areas of tissue important in the development of the baby.

gestational age. Dating a pregnancy from the first day of the last menstrual period; 2 weeks longer than fertilization age. See *fertilization age.*

gestational diabetes. Occurrence or worsening of diabetes during pregnancy (gestation).

gestational trophoblastic disease (GTN). Abnormal pregnancy with cystic growth of the placenta. Characterized by bleeding during early and middle pregnancy.

globulin. Family of proteins from plasma or serum of the blood.

glucose-tolerance test. Blood test done to evaluate the body's response to sugar. Blood is drawn at intervals following ingestion of a sugary substance.

glucosuria. Glucose in the urine.

gonorrhea. Contagious venereal infection, transmitted primarily by intercourse.

grand mal seizure. Loss of control of body functions. Seizure activity of a major form.

group-B streptococcal infection. Serious infection occurring in the mother's vagina and throat.

habitual abortion. Occurrence of three or more spontaneous miscarriages.

heartburn. Discomfort or pain that occurs in the chest. Often occurs after eating.

hematocrit. Determines the proportion of blood cells to plasma. Important in diagnosing anemia.

hemoglobin. Pigment in red blood cell that carries oxygen to body tissues.

hemolytic disease. Destruction of red blood cells. See *anemia.*

hemorrhoids. Dilated blood vessels in the rectum or rectal canal.

heparin. Medication used to thin the blood.

Homan's sign. Pain caused by flexing the toes when a person has a blood clot in the lower leg.

human chorionic gonadatropin. Hormone produced in early pregnancy. Measured in a pregnancy test.

human placental lactogen. Hormone of pregnancy produced by the placenta. Found in the bloodstream.

hyaline membrane disease. Respiratory disease of the newborn.

hydatidiform mole. See *gestational trophoblastic disease.*

hydramnios. Increased amniotic fluid.

hydrocephalus. Excessive accumulation of fluid around the brain of the baby. Sometimes called *water on the brain.*

hyperbilirubinemia. Extremely high level of bilirubin in the blood.

hyperemesis gravidarum. Severe nausea, dehydration and vomiting during pregnancy. Occurs most frequently during the first trimester.

hyperglycemia. Increased blood sugar.

hypertension, pregnancy-induced. High blood pressure that occurs during pregnancy. Defined by an increase in the diastolic and/or systolic blood pressure.

hyperthyroidism. Elevation of the thyroid hormone in the bloodstream.

hypoplasia. Defective or incomplete development or formation of tissue.

hypotension. Low blood pressure.

hypothyroidism. Low or inadequate levels of thyroid hormone in the bloodstream.

identical twins. See *monozygotic twins.*

immune globulin preparation. Substance used to protect against infection with certain diseases, such as hepatitis or measles.

in utero. Within the uterus.

incompetent cervix. Cervix that dilates painlessly, without contractions.

incomplete miscarriage. Miscarriage in which part, but not all, of the uterine contents are expelled.

inevitable miscarriage. Pregnancy complicated with bleeding and cramping. Usually results in miscarriage.

insulin. Peptide hormone made by the pancreas. It promotes the use of glucose.

intrauterine-growth retardation (IUGR). See *fetal-growth retardation.*

iodides. Medications made up of negative ion of iodine.

iron-deficiency anemia. Anemia produced by lack of iron in the diet. Often seen in pregnancy. See *anemia.*

isoimmunization. Development of specific antibody directed at the red blood cells of another individual, such as a baby in utero. Often occurs when an Rh-negative woman carries an Rh-positive baby or is given Rh-positive blood.

jaundice. Yellow staining of the skin, sclera (eyes) and deeper tissues of the body. Caused by excessive amounts of bilirubin. Treated with phototherapy.

ketones. Breakdown product of metabolism found in the blood, particularly in starvation or uncontrolled diabetes.

kidney stones. Small mass or lesion found in the kidney or urinary tract. Can block the flow of urine.

labor. Process of expelling a fetus from the uterus.

laparoscopy. Minor surgical procedure performed for tubal ligation, diagnosis of pelvic pain or diagnosis of ectopic pregnancy.

leukorrhea. Vaginal discharge characterized by a white or yellowish color. Primarily composed of mucus.

lightening. Change in the shape of the pregnant uterus a few weeks before labor. Often described as the baby "dropping."

linea nigra. Line of increased pigmentation running down the abdomen from the bellybutton to the pubic area during pregnancy.

malignant GTN. Cancerous change of gestational trophoblastic disease. See *gestational trophoblastic disease.*

mammogram. X-ray study of the breasts to identify normal and abnormal breast tissue.

mask of pregnancy. Increased pigmentation over the area of the face under each eye. Commonly has the appearance of a butterfly.

McDonald cerclage. Surgical procedure performed on an incompetent cervix. A drawstring-type suture holds the cervical opening closed during pregnancy. See *incompetent cervix.*

meconium. First intestinal discharge of the newborn; green or yellow in color. It consists of epithelial or surface cells, mucus and bile. Discharge may occur before or during labor or soon after birth.

melanoma. Pigmented mole or tumor. It may or may not be cancerous.

meningomyelocele. Congenital defect of the central nervous system of the baby. Membranes and the spinal cord protrude through an opening or defect in the vertebral column.

menstrual age. See *gestational age.*

menstruation. Regular or periodic discharge of a bloody fluid from the uterus.

mesodermal germ layer. Tissue of the embryo that forms connective tissue, muscles, kidneys, ureters and other organs.

metaplasia. Change in the structure of a tissue into another type that is not normal for that tissue.

microcephaly. Abnormally small development of the head in the developing fetus.

microphthalmia. Abnormally small eyeballs.

miscarriage. Termination or end of pregnancy. Giving birth to an embryo or fetus before it can live outside the womb, usually defined as before 20 weeks of gestation.

missed miscarriage. Failed pregnancy without bleeding or cramping. Often diagnosed by ultrasound weeks or months after a pregnancy fails.

mittelschmerz. Pain that coincides with release of an egg from the ovary.

molar pregnancy. See *gestational trophoblastic disease.*

monilial vulvovaginitis. Infection caused by yeast or monilia. Usually affects the vagina and vulva.

monozygotic twins. Twins conceived from one egg. Often called *identical twins.*

morning sickness. Nausea and vomiting, with ill health, found primarily during the first trimester of pregnancy. Also see *hyperemesis gravidarum.*

morula. Cells resulting from the early division of the fertilized egg at the beginning of pregnancy.

mucus plug. Secretions in cervix; often released just before labor.

mutations. Change in the character of a gene. Passed from one cell division to another.

neural-tube defects. Abnormalities in the development of the spinal cord and brain in a fetus. See *anencephaly; hydrocephalus; spina bifida.*

nurse-midwife. Nurse who has received extra training in the care of pregnant patients and the delivery of babies.

obstetrician. Physician who specializes in the care of pregnant women and the delivery of babies.

oligohydramnios. Lack or deficiency of amniotic fluid.

omphalocele. Presence of congenital outpouching of the umbilicus containing internal organs in the fetus or newborn infant.

opioids. Synthetic compounds with effects similar to those of opium.

organogenesis. Development of the organ systems in the embryo.

ossification. Bone formation.

ovarian cycle. Regular production of hormones from the ovary in response to hormonal messages from the brain. The ovarian cycle governs the endometrial cycle.

ovulation. Cyclic production of an egg from the ovary.

ovulatory age. See *fertilization age.*

oxytocin. Medication that causes uterine contractions.

palmar erythema. Redness of palms of the hands.

Pap smear. Routine screening test that evaluates presence of premalignant or cancerous conditions of the cervix.

paracervical block. Local anesthetic for cervical dilatation.

pediatrician. Physician who specializes in the care of babies and children.

pelvimetry. Evaluation of the size of the birth canal or pelvis. Performed by X-ray.

perinatologist. Physician who specializes in the care of high-risk pregnancies.

petit mal seizure. Attack of a brief nature with possible short impairment of consciousness. Often associated with blinking or flickering of the eyelids and a mild twitching of the mouth.

phosphatidyl glycerol. Lipoprotein present when fetal lungs are mature.

phospholipids. Fat-containing phosphorous. The most important are lecithins and sphingomyelin, which are important in the maturation of fetal lungs before birth.

phototherapy. Treatment for jaundice in a newborn infant. See *jaundice.*

physiologic anemia of pregnancy. Anemia during pregnancy caused by an increase in the amount of plasma (fluid) in the blood compared to the number of cells in the blood. See *anemia.*

placenta. Organ inside the uterus that is attached to the baby by the umbilical cord. Essential during pregnancy for growth and development of the embryo and fetus. Also called *afterbirth.*

placenta previa. Low attachment of the placenta, covering or very close to the cervix.

placental abruption. Premature separation of the placenta from the uterus.

placentamegaly. Abnormally large growth of the placenta during pregnancy.

pneumonitis. Inflammation of the lungs.

polyhydramnios. See *hydramnios.*

postmature baby. Pregnancy of 42+ weeks gestation.

postpartum blues. Mild depression after delivery.

postpartum distress. A range of symptoms including baby blues, postpartum depression and postpartum psychosis.

postpartum hemorrhage. Bleeding greater than 15 ounces (450ml) at time of delivery.

pre-eclampsia. Combination of symptoms significant to pregnancy, including high blood pressure, edema, swelling and changes in reflexes.

pregnancy diabetes. See *gestational diabetes*.

premature delivery. Delivery before 38 weeks gestation.

presentation. Describes which part of the baby comes into the birth canal first.

propylthiouracil. Medication used to treat thyroid disease.

proteinuria. Protein in urine.

pruritis gravidarum. Itching during pregnancy.

pubic symphysis. Bony prominence in the pelvic bone found in the midline. Landmark from which the doctor often measures during pregnancy to follow growth of the uterus.

pudendal block. Local anesthesia during labor.

pulmonary embolism. Blood clot from another part of the body that travels to the lungs. Can cause closed passages in the lungs and decrease oxygen exchange.

pyelonephritis. Serious kidney infection.

quickening. Feeling the baby move inside the uterus.

radiation therapy. Method of treatment for various cancers.

radioactive scan. Diagnostic test in which radioactive material is injected into the body and scanned to find a problem within a particular part of the body.

Rh-negative. Absence of rhesus antibody in the blood.

RhoGAM®. Medication given during pregnancy and following delivery to prevent isoimmunization. See *isoimmunization*.

Rh-sensitivity. See *isoimmunization*.

round-ligament pain. Pain caused by stretching ligament on the sides of the uterus during pregnancy.

rupture of membranes. Loss of fluid from the amniotic sac. Also called *breaking of waters*.

seizure. Sudden onset of a convulsion.

sexually transmitted disease (STD). Infection transmitted through sexual intercourse.

sickle-cell anemia. Anemia caused by abnormal red blood cells shaped like a sickle or a cylinder.

sickle-cell trait. Presence of the trait for sickle-cell anemia. Not sickle-cell disease itself.

sickle crisis. Painful episode caused by sickle-cell disease.

skin tag. Flap or extra buildup of skin.

sodium. Element found in many foods, particularly salt. Ingestion of too much sodium may cause fluid retention.

spina bifida. Congenital abnormality characterized by a defect in the vertebral column. Membranes of the spinal cord and the spinal cord protrude outside the protective bony canal of the spine.

spinal anesthesia. Anesthesia given in the spinal canal.

spontaneous miscarriage. Loss of pregnancy during the first 20 weeks of gestation.

stasis. Decreased flow.

station. Estimation of the descent of the baby.

steroids. Group of medications of hormone origin. Often used to treat various diseases. Includes estrogen, testosterone, progesterone, prednisone.

stigma. Area on the ovary where the egg has been released at the time of ovulation.

stretch marks. Areas of the skin that are torn or stretched. Often found on the abdomen, breasts, buttocks and legs.

striae distensa. See *stretch marks.*

sulci. Groove or furrow on the surface of the brain.

surfactant. Phospholipid present in the lungs. Controls surface tension of lungs. Premature babies often lack sufficient amounts of surfactant to breathe without assistance.

syphilis. Sexually transmitted venereal infection caused by treponema pallidum.

systemic lupus erythematosus (SLE). Connective-tissue disorder common in women in the reproductive ages. Antibodies made by the person act against his or her own tissues.

Tay-Sachs disease. Inherited disease characterized by mental and physcial retardation, convulsions, enlargement of the head and eventually death. Trait is usually carried by Ashkenazi Jews.

telangiectasias. Dilatation or swelling of a small blood vessel. Sometimes called an *angioma.* During pregnancy, another common name is a *spider angioma.*

tertatogen. Anything that causes abnormal development in an embryo.

teratogenic. Causes abnormal development.

teratology. Branch of science that deals with substances that cause abnormal development.

thalassemia. Group of inherited disorders of hemoglobin metabolism, which results in a decrease in the amount of hemoglobin formed. Found most commonly in people of Mediterranean descent.

threatened miscarriage. Bleeding during the first trimester of pregnancy without cramping or contractions.

thrombosis. Formation of a blood clot (thrombus).

thrush. Monilial or yeast infection occurring in the mouth or mucous membranes of a newborn infant.

thyroid disease. Abnormality of the thyroid gland and its production of thyroid hormone. See *hyperthyroidism; hypothyroidism.*

thyroid hormone. Chemical made in the thyroid that affects the entire body.

thyroid panel. Series of blood tests done to evaluate the function of the thyroid gland.

thyroid stimulating hormone (TSH). Hormone made in the brain that stimulates the thyroid to produce thyroid hormone.

tocolysis. Stopping contractions during premature labor.

tocolytic agents. Medications to stop labor. See *beta-adrenergics.*

toxemia. See *pre-eclampsia.*

toxoid. Poison.

toxoplasmosis. Infection caused by toxoplasma gondii.

transverse lie. Fetus is turned sideways in uterus.

trichomonal vaginitis. Venereal infection caused by trichomonas.

trimester. Method of dividing pregnancy into three equal time periods of about 13 weeks each.

trophoblast. Cell layer important in early development of the embryo and fetus. It provides nourishment from the mother to the fetus and participates in the formation of the placenta.

umbilical cord. Cord that connects the placenta to the developing baby. It removes waste products and carbon dioxide from the baby and brings oxygenated blood and nutrients from the mother through the placenta to the baby.

umbilicus. Bellybutton.

ureters. Tubes from the kidneys to the bladder that drain urine.

urinary calculi. See *kidney stones.*

uterine atony. Lack of tone of uterus.

uterus. Organ an embryo/fetus grows in. Also called a *womb.*

vaccine. Mild infection given to cause production of antibodies to protect against subsequent infections.

vacuum extractor. Device used to provide traction on fetal head during delivery.

varicose veins. Blood vessels (veins) that are dilated or enlarged.

vascular spiders. See *telangiectasias.*

vena cava. Major vein in the body that empties into the right atrium of the heart. It returns unoxygenated blood to the heart for transport to the lungs.

venereal warts. See *condyloma acuminatum.*

vernix. Fatty substance made up of epithelial cells that covers fetal skin inside the uterus.

vertex. Head first.

villi. Projection from a mucous membrane. Most important within the placenta in the exchange of nutrients from maternal blood to the placenta and fetus.

womb. See *uterus.*

yeast infection. See *monilial vulvovaginitis; thrush.*

zygote. Cell that results from the union of a sperm and egg at fertilization.

Index

A

AIDS 31, 49, 335, 351
abdominal pain 164, 185
accident during pregnancy
    81, 165
Accutane® 79, 91, 220
acetaminophen 44, 148,
    155, 178, 189, 279, 331
Actinomycin D® 94
Advil® 148
aerobic exercise 40, 41, 42,
    157, 351
alcohol use 19, 20, 30, 34,
    80, 90, 256, 274, 330
alcoholism 74, 255
Aleve® 148
allergies 164
allergy medication 164
alpha-fetoprotein 139, 140,
    147, 351
alpha-fetoprotein testing
    131, 138
amino acids 72, 351
aminophylline 236
aminopterin 91
amitriptyline 318
amniocentesis 105, 136,
    138, 141, 188, 208, 351
amniotic fluid 110, 138,
    176, 202, 277, 351
amniotic sac 202, 351
Amoxipine® 318
Amphojel® 64, 148
ampulla 351
analgesics 35
androgens 90
anemia 9, 82, 89, 169,
    186,187, 188, 189, 256,
    267, 270, 271, 335, 351
    iron-deficiency 187
    sickle-cell 9, 188, 335
    thalassemia 9, 189
anencephaly 44, 139, 140,
    142, 351
anesthesia
    blocks 332
    cervical block 332
    epidural 300, 326, 347,
        348, 332
    general 107, 272, 332
    paracervical block 333
    pudendal block 332, 333
    spinal 300, 333
angel dust 32
angiomas 111, 351
antacids 64, 187, 148

antibiotics 11, 84, 107, 128,
    159, 171, 174, 200
anticoagulants 90
anticonvulsants 35
antidepressant medication
    35, 318
antihistamines 119
anti-inflammatory
    medications 213, 351
antithyroid medications 90
Apgar scores 305-306, 332,
    333, 346
appendicitis during
    pregnancy 56, 199-200
arcola 119, 352
arteriosclerosis 34
artificial sweeteners 59
Ashkenazi Jews 13, 134
aspartame 59
aspirin use 44, 147, 164,
    213
asthma
    before pregnancy 7
    during pregnancy
        235-236, 352
atherosclerosis 197
atonic uterus 334, 352

B

baby blues 319
baby's doctor, choosing 312
baby's heartbeat 62, 173
baby's sex 40, 59, 208
baby's weight 283
back labor 314, 352
back pain 189, 216, 276
back strain 158
backache 155, 185, 253
bag of waters 253
barbiturates 30, 32
bathing during pregnancy
    252
bed rest 122, 156, 242, 256,
    259, 268
before pregnancy
    alcohol use 20
    asthma 7
    cancer 250
    contraception 5
    dieting 4, 16
    eating habits 16
    epilepsy 10
    exercise 17
    health 2
    herb use 16
    high blood pressure 7

lifestyle of woman 1
    medical conditions 3
    mineral use 16
    mother's health 15
    nutrition 15
    smoking 20
    weight 4
benign exostosis 252
benzodiazepines 30, 32
beta-adrenergic agents 242,
    352
bicycling 41, 157
bilirubin 337, 352
biophysical profile
    282-283, 295, 352
biopsy 133, 352
birth defects 6, 14, 16, 20,
    31, 32, 52, 89
birth-control pills 5
birthing center 345, 352
birthing room 345
bladder cancer 34
bladder infections 8, 159
blastocyst 39
blastomere 39, 352
bleeding 19, 42, 43, 82, 94,
    122, 135, 164, 182,
    187, 252, 268, 275,
    292, 324, 342
bleeding after delivery 269,
    271
blood clots 177
blood clotting problems,
    after delivery 272
blood loss after delivery 271
blood pressure
    changes in 260
    control 73
blood pressure, high 7, 9,
    15, 135, 255, 258, 259,
    304
blood pressure, low 163,
    333
blood transfusions 270, 271
blood type 83, 313
blood volume increase 87
blood-flow problems in
    mother 255
blood-sugar test 6, 83
bloody show 287, 352
board certification of
    physician 29, 352
boarding in 345
body temperature of
    mother 142
bone, broken 211

bone tumors 251
bone-marrow transplants 334
bowling 158
Bradley classes 348
bras, maternity 297
bras, nursing 330
Braxton-Hicks contractions 287, 352
breaking of water 253, 277
breast changes 55, 119
breast engorgement 330, 354
breast implants 123
breast milk 123
breast pumps 330
breast shields 330
breast tenderness 24
breastfeeding 120, 328-331
breasts
  breast lump 224
  cancer 226, 251
  infected 331
  inverted nipples 330
  silicone breast disease 123
  tingling and soreness 99, 119
  tumors 250, 252
breech presentation 268, 269, 292, 300, 308, 321, 342, 352
broken bone during pregnancy 211
bronchitis 34

C
CBC, see *complete blood count*
CT scans 3, 125-127
caffeine consumption 30, 122, 147, 330
calcium supplementation 73, 179
caloric intake of mother 71
cancer
  benign exostosis 252
  bladder 34
  bone tumors 251
  breast 226, 251
  cervical 251
  endochromas 252
  gynecologic 250
  Hodgkin's disease 252
  in pregnancy 249-252
  leukemia 91, 250, 252, 334

lymphomas 250
melanomas 250, 252
pelvic 251
cancer before pregnancy 75, 250
carbohydrate intake 72
cardiovascular fitness 40
cataracts, congenital 92, 223, 352
cavities 127
cephalo-pelvic disproportion 299
cerebral palsy 51
cervical block 332
cervical cancer 251
cervical cultures 83
Cervidil™ 340
cervix, incompetent 19, 21, 204, 241
Cesarean delivery 4, 66, 135, 252, 258, 269, 292, 299-302, 315, 318, 321, 332, 333, 349, 352
  advantages of 301
  disadvantages of 301
  incisions 300-301
  recovery period 302
Chadwick's sign 171, 352
chemotherapy 226, 251, 252, 352
childbirth classes 228-229, 270, 343
childbirth, natural 348
children to office visits 107
chills 164
chlamydia infections 245-246, 352
chloasma 111, 352
chlordiazepoxide 32
cholesterol levels 72
chorionic villus sampling 98, 105, 188, 352
chromosomal abnormalities 14, 142, 256
chromosome analysis 83
chromosomes, number of 38
chronic illness 11
cigarette smoking 20, 30, 33, 80, 255, 256, 274
classes, prenatal 228-229, 270, 343
cleft lip 91, 352
cleft palate 91
Clomid® 267
clomiphene 267
cocaine use 20, 32, 52
codeine 31

colostrum 120, 329, 352,
colposcopy 33
complete blood count 9, 83, 342
complete breech presentation 321
computer terminal, working at 295
condyloma acuminatum 67, 353
cone biopsy 133
congenital abnormalities 31, 32; also see *birth defects*
congestive heart failure 188
conization of cervix 353
conjoined twins 264, 353
connective-tissue diseases 123
constipation 65, 188, 353
contraception 3, 5, 12
contracting, timing 288
contraction stress test 282, 317, 353
contraction of uterus after delivery 334
contractions 182, 185, 276
contractions, Braxton-Hicks 287, 352
contractions, labor 296
convulsions 217, 258
cord-blood banking 334
cordocentesis 169
corpus luteum of pregnancy 47, 353
costs of having a baby 149-151
cough and cold remedies 35, 61, 147
Coumadin® 179
crack cocaine 32, 52
cramping 82, 185
cramps, leg 216
cranial-nerve damage 91
Crohn's disease 74
crown-to-rump length 353
C-section, see *Cesarean delivery*
cystic fibrosis 13
cystinuria 142
cystitis 159, 353
cysts, ovarian 94
cytomegalovirus 92, 224, 256, 353

D
D&C 82, 94, 353
deafness 92

deep-vein thrombosis 178
delivery, see *labor and delivery*
Demerol® 31, 244, 332, 333
dental care 107
dental diagnostic tests 128
dental emergencies 127
Depo-provera® 5
depression during pregnancy 318
desipramine 318
developmental delay 218, 353
diabetes 6, 83, 193, 196-198, 214, 283, 304, 318, 335
diabetes, gestational 6, 197, 355
diarrhea 115, 205
diastasis recti 171, 353
diazepam 32
diet pills 16
dietary deficiencies during pregnancy 274
dietary habits during pregnancy 112
diethylstilbestrol 91, 353
dieting during pregnancy 4, 17, 61, 100
dieting before pregnancy 16
Dilantin® 91, 218
dilatation and curettage, see *D&C*
dinoprostone cervical gel 339, 340
diphtheria 97
disease exposure during pregnancy 98
diuretics 259
dizygotic twins 264, 353
dizziness 163, 218, 227
doppler listening device 109, 173
douching 171
Down syndrome 13, 14, 59, 99, 105, 134, 135, 136, 140, 142, 147, 155
drug use 30, 255, 256
drug-free labor and delivery 347, 348
due date of baby 24
dwarfism 13

E
eating during pregnancy 112
eating habits before pregnancy 16
eating out during pregnancy 204
eclampsia 258, 259, 353
ectoderm 47
ectodermal germ layer 47, 353
ectopic pregnancy 4, 56, 57, 58, 82, 105, 141, 353
  methotrexate to treat 58
  symptoms 57
  treatment 58
effacement 310, 353
electric blanket use 165
ELISA test 50
embolism, pulmonary 179
embryonic period 63, 95, 353
emotional changes 96, 97, 196, 293-294
emphysema 34
encephalocele 44
endocarditis 31
endochromas 252
endodermal germ layer 47, 353
endometrial cycle 354
enemas 262, 270, 279, 313, 342, 354
engorgement 330, 354
environmental pollutants 50
epidural anesthesia 300, 326, 332, 347, 348, 354
epilepsy 10, 13
episiotomy 262, 271, 278, 314, 347, 348, 349, 354
Equal® 59
erythroblastosis fetalis 142, 234
erythromycin 84, 246
estrogen 109, 111, 120, 131, 234
exercise 40, 41, 65,156, 157, 158, 180-182, 351
exercise, aerobic 40, 42, 156, 157, 351
exercise before pregnancy 17
exercise guidelines 18
exercise, target heart rates 41
exercise, weight-bearing 42
external fetal monitoring 283, 317, 342

F
FAS, see *fetal alcohol syndrome*
face presentation 322, 354
falling during pregnancy 226
false labor 287, 354
Family and Medical Leave Act 121
family practitioner 28
fasting-blood-sugar test 214, 354
fat intake 72
father's age at conception 13, 14
father's alcohol consumption 35
father's health 59
fatigue 24, 55, 89
feeling baby move 138, 219, 248
ferning test 277, 342
fertility medication 266
fertilization 38, 354
fertilization age 25, 354
fetal abnormalities 141
fetal alcohol syndrome 20, 34
fetal arrhythmia 354
fetal blood sampling 318
fetal death 33
fetal development, abnormal 89
fetal distress 269, 299, 317
fetal fibronectin test 185
fetal goiter 90, 354
fetal heart-rate monitoring 216, 283
fetal malformation 79, 83, 267
fetal monitoring 282, 296, 299, 304, 317, 354
fetal organ development 1, 11
fetal period 95, 354
fetal swallowing 176
fetoscopy 99
fetus
  Apgar score 305-306, 332, 333, 346
  nonstress test 244, 282, 295, 317
  "floating" 289
  heart arrhythmia 216
  infections in 256
  multiples 187, 229, 241, 255, 264-270, 304, 321
  presentation of 237, 268, 269, 314, 359
  stress on 282
  umbilical-cord knots 248
  weight 283

fever 164
fifth disease 113
fingernail changes 102
fitness activities 156
fitness, cardiovascular 40
flu 205
fluconazole 66
fluid intake during
    pregnancy 65, 156, 164,
    190, 206
fluoride supplementation 73
folic acid 33, 44, 45, 74,
    274
folic-acid deficiency 274
food additives 60
food cravings 65
footling breech
    presentation 322
forceps, use of 279, 315,
    354
formula, commercial 328
frank breech 321, 354
fraternal twins 264, 266,
    355
freebasing cocaine 52

G
Gelusil® 64, 148
general anesthesia 107, 332
genetic abnormalities 98
genetic counseling 12, 134,
    355
genital herpes simplex
    infection 66, 355
germ layers 47, 95, 355
German measles, see *rubella*
gestational age 25, 355
gestational diabetes 6, 197,
    355
gestational trophoblastic
    disease 94, 355
girdles, maternity 156
glucose-tolerance test 214,
    237, 355
glucosuria 214, 355
golf 158
gonorrhea 67, 355
grand mal seizures 218, 355
Grantly Dick-Read classes
    348
Graves' disease 8
group-B streptococcus
    infection 304-305, 355
growth retardation 20, 89,
    91
guidelines for exercise 18
gynecologic cancers 250

H
HCG levels 94
HIV 49
habitual miscarriage 355
hair changes 102
hallucinogens 31
hashish 32
headaches 11, 165, 190,
    216, 258
health of baby's father 59
heart arrhythmia 216
heart attack 197
heart defects 7, 155
heart disease, ischemic 34
heart failure, congestive 188
heart lesions 92
heart malformations 89
heartbeat, baby 62, 109, 173
heartburn 63, 112, 206,
    278, 355
hematocrit 186, 355
hemolytic disease 355
hemophilia 134, 142
hemorrhage, postpartum
    334
hemorrhoids 65, 191, 355
heparin therapy 178, 355
hepatitis 31, 35, 83
hepatitis vaccine after birth
    347
herbs 16
heroin 31
herpes 142
high-risk pregnancies 165,
    283
Hodgkin's disease 252
Homan's sign 178, 355
home uterine monitoring
    229
hormonal changes 102,
    156, 196, 320, 158
hospital check-in 341
hospital, choice of 28
hot tubs 142
Human Resources, Canada
    121
human chorionic
    gonadotropin 54, 131,
    147, 234, 355
human placental lactogen
    355
hyaline membrane disease
    308, 355
hydatidiform mole 94, 355
hydramnios 202, 241, 268,
    355
hydrocephalus 105, 161,
    321, 356

hydrocortisone 118, 236
hydroxurea 188
hyperactivity in children 33
hyperbilirubinemia 337,
    356
hyperemesis gravidarum 55,
    356
hyperglycemia 163, 356
hypertension 7, 15, 25, 73,
    229, 255, 258, 261,
    274, 340, 356
hypertension, pregnancy-
    induced 229, 261, 356
hyperthyroidism 8, 210,
    356
hypoglycemia 163
hypotension 163, 333, 356
hypotension, postural 163
hypotension, supine 163
hypothyroidism 8, 90, 210,
    356, 356

I
IUD 5, 56, 57, 105
IUGR, see *intrauterine-
    growth retardation*
ibuprofen 148
identical twins 264, 265
immune globulin 36
immunizations 97
incompetent cervix 19, 21,
    81, 204, 241
inducing labor 302, 338,
    339
    ripening of cervix 339
infant-restraint seats 114
infections 8, 9, 83, 92, 159,
    169, 188, 198, 205,
    224, 229, 245-246,
    256, 352, 353
    bladder 159
    chlamydia 245-246, 352
    fetal 256
    urinary-tract 8, 9, 159
    uterine 272
    viral 205
injuries from falling 226
injury during pregnancy
    165
insulin requirements 6
insurance coverage for
    pregnancy 21
insurance questions 149
intercourse during
    pregnancy 43, 75, 182,
    277
internal fetal monitoring
    317

intrauterine-growth
   retardation 7, 10, 19,
   31, 90, 167, 235, 241,
   255-258, 283
in-vitro fertilization 266
iodide 90, 211
iron intake 73, 74
iron stores, maternal 9
iron supplementation 268,
   270
iron-deficiency anemia 187
isoimmunization 140, 142
isotretinoin 79, 91, 220
itching 119

J
jaundice in a newborn 184,
   337
jaundice treatment 337
jogging 158
joint mobility, change in 155
junk food 100, 112, 205

K
kernicterus 337
ketones 72
ketoprofen 148
kidney disease 255
kidney problems 8
kidney stones 8, 189, 196
knots in umbilical cord 248

L
LDRP 345
L/S ratio 308
LSD 31
La Leche League 329
lab tests 83
labor and delivery 19, 31,
   270, 286-287, 296, 302,
   314, 321, 338, 341,
   343, 347, 348
   back labor 314
   coach 343
   contractions 296
   eating during 341
   false labor 287
   inducing 302, 338
   pain relief 347
   signs of 296
   stages of 286
labor-and-delivery suite 345
Lamaze classes 348
lanugo hair 131
laparoscopy 58, 200
laparotomy 58
laxatives 65
lead exposure 51, 91

leg cramps 216
leukemia 91, 250, 252, 334
leukorrhea 170
Librium® 32
lifestyle changes 3
lifestyle of woman, before
   pregnancy 1
lightening 289
limb defects 91
linea nigra 111
listeria 79
lithium 91
loss of urine 194
low-birth-weight baby 159,
   267
lung maturity in fetus 308
lupus 9, 83, 212-213, 216
Lyme disease 174
lymphomas 250

M
MRI 3, 125-127
Maalox® 64, 148
magnesium sulfate 244, 259
mammogram 3, 15, 225
maple-syrup-urine disease
   142
marijuana use 21, 32
mask of pregnancy 111
maternity bras 297
maternity girdles 156
maternity leave 21
measles 97
meconium 176
medical history 4, 13, 68
medication use 3, 4, 6, 11
medications
   Accutane® 79, 91, 220
   acetaminophen 44, 148,
      155, 178, 189, 279, 331
   Actinomycin D® 94
   Advil® 148
   Aleve® 148
   allergy medication 164
   aminophylline 236
   aminopterin 91
   amitriptyline 318
   Amoxipine® 318
   Amphojel® 64, 148
   analgesics 35
   androgens 90
   antacids 64, 148, 187
   antibiotics 11, 84, 107,
      128, 159, 171, 174, 200
   anticoagulants 90
   anticonvulsants 35
   antidepressants 35, 318
   antihistamines 119

   anti-inflammatory
      medications 213, 351
   antithyroid 90
   aspirin 44, 147, 164, 213
   barbiturates 30, 32
   benzodiazepines 30, 32
   beta-adrenergic agents
      242, 352
   Cervidil™ 340
   chlordiazepoxide 32
   Clomid® 267
   clomiphene 267
   codeine 31
   cough and cold remedies
      35, 61, 147
   Coumadin® 179
   Demerol® 31, 244, 332,
      333
   desipramine 318
   diazepam 32
   diet pills 16
   diethylstilbestrol 91, 353
   Dilantin® 91, 218
   dinoprostone cervical gel
      339, 340
   diuretics 259
   erythromycin 84, 246
   fertility 266
   fluconazole 66
   Gelusil® 64, 148
   heparin therapy 178,
      355
   hydrocortisone 118, 236
   hydroxurea 188
   ibuprofen 148
   iodide 90, 211
   iron 73, 74, 268, 270
   isotretinoin 79, 91, 220
   ketoprofen 148
   laxatives 65
   Librium® 32
   lithium 91
   Maalox® 64, 148
   magnesium sulfate 244,
      259
   meperidine 244, 332
   methimazole 90
   methotrexate 58, 91, 94
   methylprednisolone 236
   metronidazole 67
   milk of magnesia 64, 115,
      148
   morphine 31, 244
   Motrin® 148
   naloxone 333
   naprosyn 148
   Narcan® 333
   nasal spray 164

nystatin 66
Orudis® 148
over-the-counter
   147-149
oxytocin 269, 317, 334,
   338
pain medication 107,
   128, 147, 179, 212
phenacetin 147
Phenergen® 332
phenobarbital 11, 218
phenytoin 91
Pitocin® 269, 334, 338
prednisone 213
Prepidil Gel® 339
Promethazine 332
propylthiouracil 90, 211,
   359
Prozac® 318
pyrimethamine 84
Retin-A® 220
RhoGAM® 50, 82, 140,
   141, 142, 235, 359
ritodrine 242, 268
Robitussin® 148
Rufen® 148
seizure-control 218
Sinequan® 318
sleep medications 147
steroid creams and
   ointments 118, 221
steroids 10, 212, 236, 360
streptomycin 91
Sucrets® 148
Sudafed® 148
sulfadiazine 84
terbutaline 236, 244
tetracycline 91, 246
thalidomide 91
theophyline 236
tocolytic agents 242, 268
topicort 118
tretinoin 220
trimethadione 91
Tylenol® 148, 156, 178,
   189, 279, 331
Tylenol with Codeine®
   279
Valium® 30, 32
warfarin 90, 179
xylocaine 332
Yutopar® 242
melanomas 250, 252
meningomyelocele 161
menstrual age 25
menstruation 26
meperidine 244, 332
mercury exposure 51, 91

mescaline 31
mesoderm 47, 357
methimazole 90
methotrexate 58, 91, 94
methotrexate to treat
   ectopic pregnancy 58
methylprednisolone 236
metronidazole 67
microcephaly 51, 90, 91,
   92, 105, 218
microphthalmia 224
microwave oven use 200
midwife, certified nurse 28
migraine headaches 11
milk of magnesia 64, 115,
   148
minerals 16, 73
miscarriage 4, 6, 8, 9, 10,
   13, 19, 20, 25, 32, 33,
   43, 52, 56, 75, 79-83,
   84, 91, 99, 105, 140,
   157, 188, 267
   habitual 82
   incomplete 81
   inevitable 81
   missed 82
   threatened 81
mitral-valve prolapse 7
mittelschmerz 27
molar pregnancy 94
moles 125
monilial vulvovaginitis 66
monitoring, home uterine
   229
monozygotic twins 264
mood swings 97, 196,
   293-294
morning sickness 54, 70
morphine 31, 244
morula 39
mother's body temperature
   142
mother's health before
   pregnancy 15
mother's nutrition 70
motorcycles, riding 158
Motrin® 148
mucus plug 288
multiple births 135, 187,
   229, 241, 255, 264-270,
   272, 304, 321
multiple fetuses, problems
   during pregnancy 267
multivitamins 16, 74
mumps 97
muscle strength 41
muscular dystrophy 13, 134
myocardial infarction 197

N
nail changes 102
naloxone 333
naprosyn 148
Narcan® 333
narcotic analgesics 332
nasal problems 156
nasal sprays 164
natural childbirth 348
nausea 24, 54, 73, 94, 112,
   188
neural-tube defects 33, 44,
   45, 91
nipples, inverted 330
nipples, sore 331
nitrazine test 277, 342
nonstress test 244, 282,
   295, 317
Norplant® 5
nosebleeds 156
nurse midwife, certified 28
nursing bras 330
Nutrasweet® 59
nutrition before pregnancy
   15
nutrition during pregnancy
   70, 256
nystatin 66

O
obesity 40
obstetrician 27
older pregnant woman 13,
   135
oligohydramnios 202
omphalocele 117, 161
opioids 31
oral contraceptives and
   pregnancy 56
organ systems, fetus 1
Orudis® 148
osteogenesis imperfecta 142
ovarian cycle 26
overdue baby 338, 340
over-the-counter
   medications 147-149
over-the-counter
   pregnancy tests 36
ovulation 40
ovulatory age 25
oxytocin 269, 317, 334,
   338

P
PCB exposure 51
PCP 32
PID, see *pelvic
   inflammatory disease*

PUBS, see *percutaneous blood-cord sampling*
pain, abdominal 164, 185
pain, lower-back 189, 216, 276
pain medication 107, 128, 147, 179, 212
pain relief during labor 331-334, 347
pain, under ribs 219
palmar erythema 111, 358
Pap smear 3, 68, 83, 131, 133, 358
paracervical block 333, 358
partner involvement in pregnancy 128-129
parvo virus B19 113
pediatrician 312, 358
pelvic cancers 251
pelvic exam 68, 83, 310-312
  in late pregnancy 310-312
pelvic inflammatory disease 22, 56, 245
pelvic pressure 185
peptic-ulcer disease 34
percutaneous blood-cord sampling 105, 169
perinatologist 28, 165, 358
pertussis vaccine 97
pesticide exposure 51
petit mal seizures 218, 358
peyote 31
phenacetin 147
phencyclidine 31
Phenergen® 332
phenobarbital 11, 218
phenylalanine 59, 60
phenylketonuria 59
phenytoin 91
phosphatidyl glycerol 308, 358
phototherapy for jaundice 337, 358
physical injury during pregnancy 106
picking a hospital 28
Pitocin® 269 334, 338
placenta 43, 47, 232-234, 256, 358
placenta abnormalities 256
placenta, delivery of 280
placenta previa 34, 241, 268, 292, 300, 358
placenta, retained 272
placental abruption 32, 34, 52, 135, 227, 241, 268, 269, 274-276, 300, 358
polio vaccine 98

pollutants, environmental 50
polyhydramnios 198, 202, 241, 268, 321
postdate birth 239, 338
postmature 338, 340, 358
postpartum depression 320, 359
postpartum distress 319-320, 359
postpartum hemorrhage 334, 359
postpartum psychosis 320
postural hypotension 163
prednisone 213
pre-eclampsia 15, 25, 31, 73, 121, 135, 244, 255, 258-259, 261, 267, 340, 359
pregnancy legislation 120-121
pregnancy pillow 143
pregnancy signs and symptoms 24
pregnancy tests 54
pregnancy weight distribution 87
pregnancy-induced hypertension 229, 261, 356
premature birth 8, 9, 10, 21, 31, 122, 208, 229, 239, 240-241, 242-244, 321, 359
  causes of 241
  treatment of 242-244
premature labor 19, 31, 43, 75, 159, 165, 252, 268, 276, 321
prenatal appointments 129, 260
prenatal care 55
prenatal classes 228-229, 270, 343
prenatal vitamins 16, 55,73, 74, 187, 271, 330
preparing for birth 296
Prepidil Gel® 339
preregister at hospital 313
presentation of fetus 237, 268, 269, 292, 300, 308, 314, 321, 322, 342, 352, 354, 359
  breech 268, 269, 292, 300, 308, 321, 342, 352
  complete breech 321
  face 322, 354
  footling breech 322
  frank breech 321, 354
  shoulder 322

transverse lie 268, 269, 322
  vertex 322
products of conception 81
progesterone 82, 109, 234
promethazine 332
propylthiouracil 90, 211, 359
protein in urine 258
protein intake 72
provincial laws and parental leave 121
Prozac® 318
pruritus gravidarum 119, 359
pudendal block 332, 333, 359
pulmonary embolism 179, 359
pyelonephritis 8, 159, 188, 189, 195, 359
pyrimethamine 84
pyrosis 63

Q
quadruplets 264
quad-screen test 147
quantitative HCG 57, 82
quickening 138, 248, 359
quintuplets 264

R
radiation 251, 252
radiation therapy 226, 359
reflexes, changes in 258
respiratory system maturation 308
respiratory-distress syndrome 308, 310
retained placenta 272, 280, 324
Retin-A® 220
rheumatic disease 123
Rh-factor 3, 83, 140, 313
Rh-incompatability 169
Rh-negative 82, 359
RhoGAM® 50, 82, 140, 141, 142, 235, 359
Rh-sensitivity 140, 234
ritodrine 242, 268
Robitussin® 148
rooming in 345
root canal 127
round ligaments 145
round-ligament pain 146, 359
rubella 83, 89, 92, 97, 142, 223, 256

Rufen® 148
rupture of membranes 253, 277, 288, 359

S

SIDS, see *sudden infant death syndrome*
SLE, see *lupus*
saccharin 59, 60
saunas 142
sciatic-nerve pain 78
seat-belt use during pregnancy 113, 189
seizure-control medication 218
seizures 91, 217, 258, 259, 359
sex of baby 40, 208
sexual intercourse during pregnancy 43, 75, 182, 277
sexually transmitted diseases 22, 66-67, 359
shoulder presentation 322
Siamese twins 264
sickle-cell anemia 9, 134, 188, 335, 359
sickle-cell trait 134, 359
signs of labor 296
signs and symptoms of pregnancy 24
silicone breast disease 123
Sinequan® 318
skiing, snow 158
skiing, water 158
skin changes 111
skin tags 125, 359
sleep medications 147
sleeping positions during pregnancy 143
smoking during pregnancy 20, 30, 33, 80, 255, 256, 274
snacks 112
snow skiing 158
snowmobiles, riding 158
sodium intake 198-199, 205, 359
sonogram 104
soreness, breasts 99, 119
spas 142
sperm separation 59
spermicides 56
spina bifida 44, 74, 134, 139, 140, 161, 165, 360
spinal anesthesia 300, 333, 360
stages of labor 286

standing during pregnancy 21, 122
stasis 177, 360
state laws and parental leave 121
station 310, 360
steroid creams and ointments 118, 221
steroids 10, 212, 236, 360
stillbirth 6, 10, 20, 189
stomach upset 188
stool softeners 191
streptomycin 91
stress 96
stretch marks 117, 360
striae distensae 117
stuffiness in nose 156
Sucrets® 148
Sudafed® 148
sudden infant death syndrome 20, 52
sugar in urine 214
sulfadiazine 84
supine hypotension 163
surfactant 310, 360
surgery, trauma 81
swelling 164, 258, 261
swimming 41, 43, 157
syphilis 67, 79, 83, 92, 234, 360
systemic lupus erythematosus, see *lupus*

T

tanning booths 142
target heart rates 41
Tay-Sachs disease 134
telangiectasias 111
tennis 158
teratogens 79
teratology 89
terbutaline 236, 244
tests
  abnormal Pap smear 133
  alpha-fetoprotein 131, 138
  amniocentesis 105, 136, 138, 141, 188, 208, 351
  Apgar scores 305-306, 332, 333, 346
  biophysical profile 282-283, 295, 352
  biopsy 133, 352
  blood-sugar 6, 83
  breast exam 3
  CT scans 3, 125-127
  chorionic villus sampling 98, 105, 188, 352
  colposcopy 33

complete blood count 9, 83, 342
contraction-stress test 282, 317
dental diagnostic tests 128
ELISA test 50
external fetal monitor 283, 317, 342
fasting blood sugar test 214, 354
ferning test 277, 342
fetal blood sampling 318
fetal fibronectin 185
fetal heart-rate monitor 216, 283
fetal monitor 282, 296, 299, 304, 317, 354
glucose-tolerance test 214, 237, 355
home uterine monitoring 229
imaging tests 3
internal fetal monitoring 317
L/S ratio 308
laboratory 68
MRI 3, 125-127
mammogram 3, 15, 225
nitrazine test 277, 342
nonstress test 244, 282, 295, 317
over-the-counter pregnancy 36
Pap smear 3, 68, 83, 131, 133, 358
pelvic exam 68, 83, 310-312
pelvic exam in late pregnancy 310-312
phosphatidyl glycerol 308
pregnancy tests 54
quad-screen test 147
quantitative HCG 57, 82
triple-screen test 131
ultrasound 58, 62, 82, 94, 99, 104-106, 141, 161, 167, 168, 169, 178, 180, 225, 227, 244, 256, 264, 267, 276, 283, 284, 292, 322
urinalysis 83, 195
urine culture 83
Western Blot test 50
X-rays 3, 4, 125-127, 227

tetanus 97
tetracycline 91, 246
thalassemia 9, 189
thalidomide 91
theophyline 236
thrombophlebitis 177
thrombosis 177-179
thrombosis, deep-vein 178
thrush 66
thyroid disease 210
thyroid problems 8
timing contractions 288
tingling, breasts 119
tobacco use during
   pregnancy 30, 255
tocolytic agents 242, 268
toenail changes 102
tooth abscess 128
tooth discoloration 91
tooth enamel hypoplasia 91
tooth extraction 127
topicort 118
toxemia of pregnancy, see
   pre-eclampsia
toxoplasmosis 79, 84, 92,
   224
transvaginal ultrasound 106
transverse lie presentation
   268, 269, 322
trauma during pregnancy
   106, 211, 274
trauma, to bones 211
traveling during
   pregnancy 103-104
tretinoin 220
trichomonal vaginitis 66
trimesters 25
trimethadione 91
triple-screen test 131
triplets 264, 266
tubal ligation after
   delivery 326
tubal pregnancy 56
twins 264
Tylenol 148, 156, 178, 189,
   279, 331
Tylenol with Codeine® 279

U
U.S. Pregnancy
   Discrimination Act 120
ultrasound 58, 62, 82, 94,
   99, 104-106, 141, 161,
   167, 168, 169, 178,
   180, 225, 227, 244,
   256, 264, 267, 276,
   283, 284, 292, 322
umbilical cord

compressed 299
cutting 344
knots 248
tangled 295
umbilical-cord
   abnormalities 256
umbilical-cord prolapse 269
umbilical-cord-blood
   banking 334
urinalysis 83, 195
urinary-tract infection 8, 9,
   159, 195
urination, frequent 24, 55,
   159
urination, painful 165
urine culture 83, 195
urine, loss of 194
uterine abnormalities 274,
   321
uterine infection 272
uterus, growth of 167

V
VBAC, see *vaginal birth
   after Cesarean*
vaccinations 12, 83, 97-98
vacuum extractor 279, 315
vaginal birth after Cesarean
   299, 301, 303-304
   advantages of 303
   disadvantages of 303
vaginal discharge 170
Valium® 30, 32
valproic acid 91
varicella 92
varicose veins 172-173
vascular disease 34
vascular spiders 111
vegetarian diet 17, 72
venereal warts 67
vernix 168
vertex presentation 269,
   322
viral infections 205
vision blurring 164
vision, changes in 258
visiting the doctor 260
vitamin A 16
vitamin B 33
vitamin B-9 74
vitamin C 33
vitamin K shot after birth
   347
vitamins, prenatal 16, 55,
   73, 74, 187, 271, 330
vomiting 24, 54, 73, 94,
   112, 164, 188

W
walking 41, 43, 157
warfarin 90, 179
warts, venereal 67
water breaking 253, 277
water on the brain 161
water retention 259, 260
water skiing 158
weight gain during
   pregnancy 17, 60-61,
   86-87, 100, 156, 255,
   259, 268, 278
weight management
   during pregnancy 17,
   100
weight-bearing exercise 42
Western Blot test 50
whooping cough vaccine 97
Women's Bureau
   Publications 121
work, at a computer
   terminal 295
work risks 122
working during pregnancy
   120-122

X
X-ray therapy 91
X-rays 3, 4, 6, 96,
   125-127, 211, 227
xylocaine 332

Y
yeast infections 66
Yutopar® 242

Z
zinc 73
zygote 39

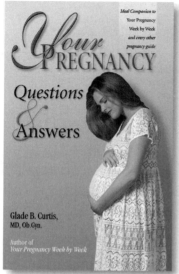

$12.95 pb • 1-55561-150-8
$17.95 Canada
6.125 x 9.25, 448 pgs, illus.

Your Pregnancy Questions & Answers

Glade B. Curtis, MD, Ob/Gyn

This bestseller is in an easy-to-read question-and-answer format. You'll find answers to over 1,200 questions pregnant women ask most often. They are thoughtfully answered in Dr. Curtis' warm style. Includes questions you worry about but may feel are "not important enough to bother my doctor," or too personal to discuss.

A detailed glossary explains all the terms your doctor and health professionals use, and helps you formulate questions to ask your own doctor.

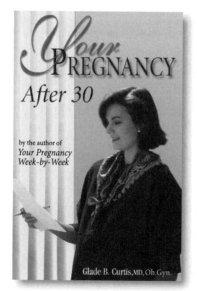

$12.95 pb • 1-55561-088-9
$17.95 Canada
6.125 x 9.25, 384 pgs, illustrated

Your Pregnancy After 30

Glade B. Curtis, MD, Ob/Gyn

The latest in this best-selling series—an important and timely resource for the rapidly growing number of women becoming pregnant after age 30.

Areas of greatest interest covered are:

- ❧ Achieving pregnancy after 30
- ❧ Multiple births
- ❧ Managing fatigue
- ❧ Tests for baby and mother
- ❧ Nutrition and weight management
- ❧ Workplace safety

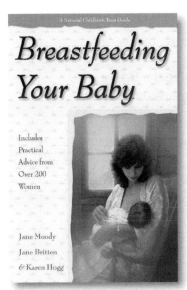

$12.95 pb • ISBN 1-55561-122-2
$17.95 Canada
6 x 9, 234 pgs

Breastfeeding Your Baby

Jane Moody, Jane Britten
and Karen Hogg

Reassuring, comprehensive advice on a subject of increasing interest to a new generation of mothers.

How does breastfeeding work? How do mothers breastfeed premature babies? What's special about breast milk? Can you breastfeed twins? Will I enjoy breastfeeding?

Over 200 mothers describe what helps and what hinders the breastfeeding experience. Written by three breastfeeding counselors, this up-to-date book answers the variety of questions parents have about breastfeeding, so they can decide what's right for *them.*

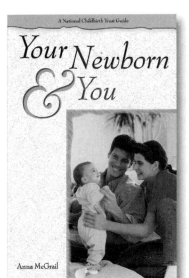

$12.95 pb • ISBN 1-55561-125-7
$17.95 Canada
6 x 9, 254 pages, b/w illustrations

Your Newborn and You

Anna McGrail

What will being a parent really be like? How will I cope with the basics, such as changing diapers? What's the best way to ensure a good night's sleep? How will we manage the change in our lives? Will sex ever be the same again?

Parenting is a hands-on skill—you learn as you go, but you can pick up most from the real experts: other parents. While there is often no right or wrong way to handle things, the suggestions and experiences of other mothers and fathers can help you decide what is right for you and your child.

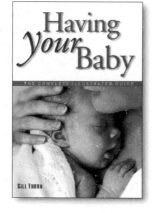

$15.95 pb • ISBN 1-55561-133-8
$22.95 Canada
6.25 x 9, 208 pgs; 93 color photographs;
34 color illustrations; index

Having Your Baby
The Complete Illustrated Guide

Gill Thorn

Packed with clear explanations, sound advice and color illustrations. Covers the questions and issues a pregnant woman and her partner need to know:

- pre-conception health and pregnancy planning
- how your growing baby develops month by month
- your relationship with your partner
- choices for prenatal care
- getting to know your newborn

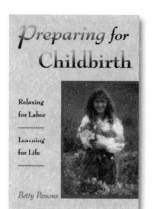

$9.95 pb • ISBN 1-55561-128-1
6 x 9, 144 pgs; b/w illustrations throughout

Preparing for Childbirth
Relaxing for Labor ~•~ Learning for Life

Betty Parsons

A voice pregnant women will listen to—encouraging, witty, understanding, calm. During her long career, Betty Parsons has coached more than 20,000 women through childbirth. Now even more women can take advantage of her unique insights. She takes the mystery out of labor, so readers know what to expect, what to do, and how to meet the challenge with confidence rather than fear. This is the book pregnant women will want for themselves, for their own well-being.

$9.95 pb • ISBN 1-55561-114-1
$13.95 Canada
7 x 10, 128 pgs, fully illustrated in two colors

Pregnancy & Childbirth
The Basic Illustrated Guide

Margaret Martin, M.P.H.

For pregnant women and their families, a conception-to-birth guide to pregnancy—written in clear, easy-to-understand terms, with informative two-color illustrations on almost every page. This unique book tells everything you need to know to enjoy a safer, more comfortable pregnancy and welcome a stronger, healthier baby.

With good care, a woman expecting a baby can avoid or significantly reduce many of the common complaints of pregnancy, from backache to nausea, and prevent or reduce health risks to herself and her baby as well. It emphasizes the basics of prenatal care. Simply written for quick, easy understanding—the best in its class!

Also available in Spanish—*Embarazo y Nacimiento*.

BUSINESS REPLY MAIL
FIRST-CLASS MAIL   PERMIT NO. 3499   TUCSON, AZ

POSTAGE WILL BE PAID BY ADDRESSEE

DEPT YPWW DRAWING
FISHER BOOKS
4239 W INA RD STE 101
TUCSON AZ 85775-4127

Fold Here

Fisher Books is engaged in publishing books
on pregnancy, childbirth and infancy. We also
publish related books on health, self-help and
other subjects. The organization has earned an
international reputation as a leading source of
books that are immediately useful to today's
mothers, parents, educators, caregivers and
healthcare providers.

FISHER BOOKS™

If you have enjoyed this book,
we'd like to here from you.

ENTER NOW!

Fill in the form below and return it to us to receive

our catalog featuring all Fisher Books titles

and enter the monthly drawing for

5 FISHER BOOKS Titles of

Your Choice

No stamp
required

Fold Here — Fold Here

**Return this form to enter the monthly drawing for free FISHER BOOKS titles.
We'll also send you our complete catalog.**

Name _____

Address _____

_____

_____

_____ Zip _____

e-mail address_____

How did you hear about this book?

Friend's Recommendation _____

Advertisement (name) _____

Book review (name) _____

Catalog _____

Other _____

Where did you buy this book?

Bookstore (name) _____

Department Store (name) _____

Maternity / Baby Store (name) _____

Mail Order / Internet _____

Other _____

What influenced you in the
purchase of this book?

❏ Cover Design
❏ Contents
❏ Other (please specify)

How do you rate the overall
contents of this book?

❏ Excellent
❏ Good
❏ Average
❏ poor

What did you find most useful about this book? _____

_____

_____

_____

What did you find least useful about this book? _____

_____

Please add any additional comments: _____

_____

_____

_____

_____